Library and Information Science

Consulting Editor: *Harold Borko*
Graduate School of Library and Information Science
University of California, Los Angeles

This list of books continues at the end of the volume.

Understanding Reference Transactions

Transforming an Art into a Science

Matthew L. Saxton

John V. Richardson Jr.

ACADEMIC PRESS

An imprint of Elsevier Science

Amsterdam   London   New York   Oxford   Paris   Tokyo   Boston   San Diego
San Francisco   Singapore   Sydney

This book is printed on acid-free paper.

Copyright © 2002, Elsevier Science (USA).

Academic Press
An imprint of Elsevier Science
525 B Street, Suite 1900, San Diego, California 92101-4495, USA
http://www.academicpress.com

Academic Press
Harcourt Place, 32 Jamestown Road, London NW1 7BY, UK
http://www.academicpress.com

Library of Congress Catalog Card Number: 2002102555

International Standard Book Number: 0-12-587780-3

Printed in the United States of America

02 03 04 05 06 MV 9 8 7 6 5 4 3 2 1

In memory of
Terence Crowley

"A librarian should be as unwilling to allow an inquirer to leave the library with his question unanswered as a shop-keeper is to have a customer go out of his store without making a purchase."

Samuel Swett Green, 1876

Contents

1

The Multilevel Nature of Reference Service   1

6

Conclusions and Implications   95

7

Systems Analysis of the Reference Process   102

Appendices   **117**

List of Tables and Figures

TABLES

FIGURES

Preface and Acknowledgments

This book is written for researchers and educators exploring a class of activities that can be labeled as "intermediation services," a term that encompasses a variety of interpersonal question-answering scenarios. In addition to researchers, the findings reported in this work will be of interest to administrators and practitioners in institutions that provide question-answering services to a user community, as well as students who are preparing to undertake such duties. The specific context for the research presented here is reference service in public libraries. We, the authors, believe that the factors found to influence the quality of service in this study can inform our understanding of many different information environments outside the public library.

Given the large number of variables that affect the dynamic, complex social interaction that occurs during the reference transaction, the concept of attempting to map and measure the reference process is daunting if not impossible. The subtitle of this work refers to the more conventional approach to understanding the reference transaction. Essentially, many practitioners comment that they learned little about the process of question answering in graduate school, and most of what they know about the reference work was acquired on the job. In short, we almost rely on an apprenticeship model to pass on the "craft" from one generation of professionals to the next. Without necessarily criticizing the importance and value of experiential learning in this area, which we do believe is essential to gaining mastery, this work is an attempt to advance understanding of the question-answering process, also known as intermediation, by describing a model of the reference transaction supported by empirical evidence that is capable of predicting service outcomes from a given set of conditions.

We would like to thank a large number of people who contributed to this work by participating in the research project, discussing our ideas, reviewing the text, and providing friendship.

To begin, we owe a debt of gratitude to Susan McGlamery who arranged speaking opportunities for recruiting libraries in the Metropolitan Cooperative

Library System and the Santiago Library System to participate in the research study presented here. We would also like to thank the reference staff of the 13 public libraries who participated in the research study: Anaheim Public Library, Azusa Public Library, Beverly Hills Public Library, El Segundo Public Library, Glendora Public Library, Orange County Public Library, Garden Grove Regional Branch, Orange County Public Library, Heritage Park Regional Branch, Orange County Public Library, San Juan Capistrano Regional Branch, Pomona Public Library, Santa Monica Public Library, South Pasadena Public Library, Torrance Public Library, and Yorba Linda Public Library. Without their interest and support, this project would not have been possible.

At UCLA, special thanks go to Yeow Meng Thum and Michael Seltzer for providing guidance and instruction on the research methodology. Likewise, special thanks go to Marcia Bates, Virginia Walter, Robert M. Hayes, and Pei-ling Wang for reviewing portions of the text and providing critical feedback to improve the work. At the University of Washington, we thank Misha Stone and Valerie Wonder for their help in proofreading and correcting various drafts.

In the earliest stages of this project, Kenny Crews and Maloy Moore worked as research assistants for John when he first began investigating the topics discussed in this work. In 1994, the initial phase of Matthew's research was funded through a grant awarded by the UCLA Academic Senate Committee on Research. Both authors are indebted to Matthew Schall, vice president, Research, Analysis, and Development at UNI Focus, for his insights on methodology as well as advice and encouragement.

For assistance in development of the chapter on systems analysis which originally appeared as "Modeling the Reference Process: A Systems Approach," *College & Research Libraries* 60 (May 1999): 211–222, we want to thank many individuals at the Online Computer Library Center (OCLC) for their support and encouragement: Terry R. Noreault, Director, Research and Special Projects; Keith E. Shafer, Senior Research Scientist; Ralph LeVan, Research Scientist II; Greg Feldman-Hill, Electronic Publications Division; Karen Nowak, Operations Division; Larry Olszewski, the OCLC Information Center; and Bradley Watson, OCLC Office of Research. James Robertson, principal of the Atlantic Systems Guild, helped clarify the section about the context of question answering and how to model it.

At Academic Press/Elsevier Science, we wish to acknowledge Mark Zadrozny, the senior acqusitions editor; Hal Borko, our LIS series editor; and especially Debbie Liehs, for shepherding the manuscript through the production process. And at UCLA, we thank Sally Diessner for her proofreading assistance.

We would also like to thank Sharon Saxton and Nancy Richardson for their loving support and patience while this project was being completed.

Introduction

This work evolved from two lines of research: Matthew Saxton's investigations in reference service evaluation and John Richardson's explorations into teaching reference work and the application of expert systems. Based on a meta-analysis of previous reference evaluation studies and an extensive literature review, Saxton identified the need for more sophisticated methods of analysis in order to assess service performance using multiple outcome variables. The study findings presented here were obtained during Saxton's doctoral work. Having previously identified a substantial number of factors that purportedly influence the outcomes of reference transaction, Richardson believed that an approach using multiple outcomes could result in the construction of a complex model of the reference transaction that would benefit both practice and teaching. This book summarizes their joint efforts in attempting to explain what occurs during the reference process.

Chapter 1 identifies unanswered questions in the area of reference service evaluation and the attendant problems these cause, justifies the need for research, presents definitions of reference service outcomes, and introduces the concept of hierarchical linear modeling.

Chapter 2 examines the history of reference service research and explores different visualizations of the intermediation process.

Chapter 3 identifies and evaluates the impact of the different approaches that have been applied to measuring both reference service performance and the variables that contribute to quality service.

Chapter 4 explicitly describes the methodology used in this study, specifically including issues pertaining to sampling, variables, data-gathering activities, and data screening.

Chapter 5 reports the study findings and describes four different models of the reference transaction based on different outcome models.

Chapter 6 presents interpretation of the findings and explains the implications for practice, research, and education.

Chapter 7 explores the application of systems analysis as a means of constructing alternatives to the predominant flowchart models or linear models such as the one discussed throughout this work.

1

The Multilevel Nature of Reference Service

1.1

What Is Good Reference Service?

Any experienced reference librarian knows that making the library user feel welcome, listening and probing to identify the user's exact question, and developing personal, in-depth knowledge of an extensive array of diverse reference resources all contribute toward success in the reference transaction. Although these observations are certainly logical, researchers in library and information science have failed to generate a cohesive body of evidence gathered through repeated studies to confirm or challenge these beliefs or to indicate to what extent these and other factors contribute to a successful outcome. Consequently, despite several decades of research, reference service evaluation remains in an embryonic stage. The question of what behaviors or resources have the greatest influence in contributing to reference service still remains unanswered.

When providing reference service, a librarian, or some other type of information professional, engages in a dialogue with a library user. The dialogue is initiated by the user's inquiry, or least by some form of contact in which the user applies for assistance regardless of whether or not that contact takes the form of a clearly defined inquiry. Frequently, the user requires assistance from a librarian to formulate the user's need into an explicit request for information, hereafter referred to as a reference query. Once a definition of the reference query has been formulated and agreed upon as a result of the initial part of the dialogue, the librarian will then respond with suggestions as to how find an answer to that query.[1] The librarian's response can take many forms which could include, but are not limited to, the librarian directing the user to specific information resources that contain the desired information, the librarian developing a strategy by which the user will be able to discover sources of information independently, or the librarian referring the user to another information professional who will presumably provide a better response to the query. Based on continuous feedback from the user, the librarian is then able to revise the response until the user determines that no further input from the librarian is necessary.

Accordingly, assessing the quality of the service which the user receives involves asking (1) how effectively does the librarian identify the user's need, and (2) how effectively does the librarian's response resolve or satisfy the user's need? The answer to the second question is related to the answer to the first. If it is possible to measure or assess the degree to which the librarian's response satisfies the user's need, then that measure is also an indirect assessment of the degree to which the librarian identified the user's need. If a library user indicates that he or she received a response that addressed his or her need, then an observer could infer that the librarian was successful in identifying the user's question (assuming that users will provide candid, critical responses when asked about the service they receive).

The research presented here in these chapters is an investigation of these two questions based on an analysis of indicators of the nature of the dialogue between the librarian and the library user, indicators of various factors affecting either the dialogue itself or the context in which that dialogue takes place, and indicators of the desirable outcomes of the reference process. The three desirable outcomes of the reference process that will be explored in the ensuing chapters are identified as utility, user satisfaction, and accuracy.

If reference service is to be of any benefit to the user, then the information which the user receives as the result of the process must be in a form that is understandable to the user and that can be readily applied to resolving the user's query. Utility is the degree to which the library user can employ the information received through the reference transaction. Utility is dependent on the librarian's effective recognition of the user's need and the user's abilities to comprehend the material necessary to answer that need.

User satisfaction pertains to the process of the transfer. The user must be satisfied that the librarian has provided good service and exhausted all necessary avenues to find an answer to the query. Regardless of how useful or accurate the information may be, if users believe they have been treated poorly then they are likely to doubt the value of the information. Alternatively, when an accurate and useful answer has not been found in response to an information need, a user who has been treated well is more likely to believe that the librarian has nevertheless performed well under the circumstances.

In addition to utility and satisfaction, the information being provided by the librarian must also be accurate. In other words, it must be factually correct and also complete in terms of addressing all the components of the query since a partial answer, though it may be accurate in itself, does not completely resolve the user's need. Thus, in short, the outcome of good reference service is a combination of high utility, high user satisfaction, and high accuracy.

1.2 ─────────────────────────────

Problems in Reference Research

At present, the body of research concerning reference service evaluation is characterized by numerous theoretical and methodological difficulties, which inhibit the discipline from advancing on this research front. These difficulties include:

1. A lack of agreement among researchers as to the definition of reference service, its role in society, and the goals of such service
2. Inconsistency in the operational definitions used from study to study for both independent and outcome variables
3. Bias introduced by a lack of random sampling when user samples are self-selected and no effort is made to assess whether or not a representative sample has been captured
4. The predominate use of simplistic statistical procedures that inadequately describe complex social interactions such as a reference interview where the researcher is interested in more than one outcome variable
5. Low sample sizes (a frequent criticism in social science research generally)
6. Little repetition of studies by subsequent investigators in order to confirm or dispute earlier findings
7. Inconsistent reporting of findings that inhibits research synthesis
8. A lack of attention given to theory

As a result, because of this weak theoretical underpinning and some gross deviations from conventional method, published findings are of little value in terms of explaining what factors influence the reference process. After 30 years of research beginning with the two initial studies conducted separately by Charles A. Bunge and Herbert Goldhor in the late 1960s,[2] the question of how to evaluate the quality of reference service remains unanswered. No widely accepted method for assessing reference service performance has been established.

Investigators have explored measuring the accuracy of information being provided to users, the customer satisfaction of users, the job satisfaction of librarians, the efficiency of the service, and various composites of all four. Contributing factors, which have been studied, include both quantitative and qualitative variables, ranging from counting the number of books in the library to asking librarians if they find their work rewarding. At present, this body of research has produced two conclusions: that questions are answered accurately about 55% of the time, which is doubted by many in the field, and that library users are highly satisfied and pleased with the service they receive, which is difficult to interpret when given the aforementioned accuracy rating.

The difficulty of interpreting confusing results is compounded by inadequate methodological techniques being employed in many cases. Sample sizes are far too small to defend the generalizability of the findings adequately. Random sampling, the most basic means of eliminating bias, is rarely utilized. Some researchers have used the "regression mill" approach, analyzing numerous quantitative variables without discussing the theory, which would indicate why these variables contribute to reference performance. In anticipating these criticisms, many researchers have described their works as "exploratory" studies or "pilot" studies, thereby cautioning the reader as to the limited value of the findings and providing an excuse for using small samples. The reader of this literature is left asking, "Where is the actual study? When will the full-scale research be performed?" In many cases, the formal research project never took place.

Of additional concern is that fact that the quality of the research can be questioned since it is likely that those primarily responsible for gathering the data, the reference librarians, did not share the enthusiasm of the investigator for obtaining the data. At best, conducting the study was probably viewed as one more task being added to an already overburdening workload. At worst, participants may have feared that performance ratings might be linked to raises and promotions (or lack thereof) and could be used as evidence to build a case for layoffs or other personnel decisions. Terry Weech and Herbert Goldhor observed that participants in such a study might feel "spied on."[3] Unless the investigator can convince the participants that the research project is nonthreatening to their position and that the resulting data will ultimately be of some use to them, most reference librarians are likely to view the intent of the study with some suspicion.

The lack of a reliable and valid means for empirically assessing the outcome of reference transactions represents a significant knowledge void within the discipline because it obstructs many branches of reference research. This void prevents any meaningful discussion of what methods of professional development and institutional policies are beneficial to the improvement of reference service. In addition, it prevents effective assessment of how well different reference procedures facilitate or hinder service. Furthermore, it impedes the development of sophisticated techniques for collection development evaluation.

The search for a reliable and valid means of measuring reference service is one of the most pressing research needs in library and information science. The significance of filling this knowledge void lies in the creation of a stable platform for many other branches of library science research. The benefits from this research include:

1. Improving curriculum for educating novice librarians
2. Improving staff training programs to enhance skills over the course of a career

3. Analyzing reference queries and user needs as an aid to collection development
4. Providing information to support decision-making in budget and staff planning

All four benefits will contribute to heightening the quality of reference service being provided to the service population of all libraries worldwide. The practical applications of this research will take the form of tested training programs for staff, computer software which could generate reports on the distribution of user queries and collection usage, and service policies based on anticipating actual user needs.

1.3

Multilevel Structure of Reference Service

Although earlier efforts have been made to investigate this problem, no studies have attempted to account for the danger of intraclass correlation caused by the multilevel nature of the data involved. For instance, most libraries have more than one reference librarian, and each librarian conducts numerous reference transactions over a given period of time. In any study of reference service, a portion of the variance in any outcome variable is likely to be caused in some part by characteristics unique to the librarian or library. This effect is constant for every transaction conducted by that particular librarian or taking place in that particular library. Consequently, the amount of unexplained variance at the reference transaction level is misleadingly small. The investigator is led to believe that the data indicate a relationship exists between dependent and independent variables when in fact hierarchical effects may obscure the true nature of the relationship. Obtaining a comprehensive understanding of reference transaction outcomes requires an analysis of the hierarchical effects that arise from the multilevel research design. Only in this manner can the investigator intelligently discuss the amount of variance that is explained by the predictors, the amount of variance that is explained by intraclass correlation, and the amount of variance that remains unexplained.

Therefore, a possible solution to the problem of reference service evaluation lies in the application of multilevel or hierarchical linear modeling (HLM) to describing reference transactions. This method enables the investigator to account for hierarchical effects when more than one observation is gathered from participating libraries and participating librarians.

Hierarchical linear modeling is not a true multivariate method because only one dependent value is used in the model.[4] This definition of what constitutes multivariate analysis is much narrower than the conventional usage

20 years ago where any analysis involving three or more outcome variables was considered multivariate.[5] According to the current, narrower definition, HLM is a univariate procedure.

As has been noted above, the outcome of reference service cannot be expressed in a single variable. Such a theory is reflected in the philosophy of the behavioral standards for reference librarians recently adopted by the Reference and User Services Association where the transfer of information is identified as only one facet of the reference process.[6] Logically, in order to measure the effects of independent variables on more than one outcome variable, it might be desirable to use a multivariate method, such as multivariate analysis of variance (MANOVA) or structural equation modeling (SEM). Although HLM may be considered a univariate method, it is possible to create a dependent variable based on multiple measures. Preferably, several outcome variables could be used to create a scale or could be combined into a single measure through the application of principal component analysis. Thus, the application of this method will bring a higher level of sophistication to the field in terms of describing multiple outcomes.

1.4
Research Objectives

In addressing the problem of reference service evaluation, this study described in the subsequent chapters focuses on reference service in public library settings. In this context, public library users who seek personal reference service are the primary group who will benefit from this project. In the past decade, this group has become increasingly composed of youth, senior citizens, and the economically disenfranchised, as the more affluent members of the community have a growing range of opportunities to access information through the Internet at home, information systems provided by their employers, or fee-based information services. This trend will continue as increasing amounts of government information is made available primarily through digital media. Thus, the immediate findings of this study will be applicable to reference service being provided to a more disenfranchised population.

The two goals of this study are to specify a model of reference service that can be used for the purpose of performance evaluation and to test that model at a higher level of methodological sophistication than has been previously recorded or described in the literature. To accomplish these goals, the following three objectives must be attained:

1. To assess the impact of many predictor variables on several outcome variables

2. To assess the magnitude of intraclass correlation which result from a multilevel research design
3. To interpret the apparent relationships between these variables in a manner which is meaningful for the purpose of evaluation

Each objective is necessary to avoid weaknesses found in earlier studies. The purpose of reference service cannot be captured in a single outcome variable. A hierarchical design is the only way to observe multiple events (i.e., reference transactions) that occur in the same environment (i.e., a library). In addition, while the findings of any study may have theoretical value, the results of this study must also have practical value in terms of service planning or decision making since the ultimate objective of this research is to provide a means for evaluation.

These objectives are original and innovative in that this study will move reference service evaluation beyond an "exploratory" phase of research by conducting a rigorous investigation in accordance with the rules of a recently elaborated statistical strategy. In fact, this study is the first to apply HLM to the evaluation of reference service.

1.5

Research Questions

In order to obtain all of the data necessary to achieve the objectives enumerated above, the design of this study will be guided by three research questions:

1. What are the factors that contribute to high levels of reference performance?
2. What are reliable indicators for both reference performance and the independent variables?
3. How well do the data support the proposed model?

The first question will be addressed in the hypothesis that is used to specify the model. The second question will be addressed through reliability testing of operational variables used in the study. The third question will be determined by devising a multiple regression equation that predicts a sizable proportion of the variance in the outcome variables (e.g., an equation that predicted 40% to 50% of the variance would be a notable contribution to the field). If the variables are judged reliable and the data supports a prediction equation, then a strong argument can be made that the proposed model comprises the right set of variables that contribute to high performance.

The first question has been asked repeatedly, yet it bears reexamination because of the advantages stemming from HLM methodology. The question pertaining to reliability has been asked rarely. Testing for reliability has only been applied rarely, most notably in the research conducted by Jo Bell Whitlatch.[7] Unlike construct validity that can only be determined from theoretical premises, reliability of measures can be tested statistically for a given data set. The justification for including this question is to obtain evidence to support using a particular variable in anticipation of challenges since no established measures currently exist.

1.6

Hypothesis

This study will test the hypothesis that reference service performance is determined by some combination of the joint effects of the difficulty of the query; the education of the library user and the user's familiarity with libraries and library services; the service behaviors exhibited by the librarian during the transaction; the experience, education, and job satisfaction of the librarian; and the size and policies of the library. The hypothesis reflects the multilevel nature of the research questions in that transactions are nested within librarians, which in turn are nested within libraries.

This hypothesis is expressed in a set of three prediction equations that, in total, account for any effects attributed to either the user and the individual transaction, the librarian, or the library. Anthony Bryk and Stephen Raudenbush provide an excellent explication of the standard three-level model.[8]

Level 1: Users and Transactions

$$Y_{ijk} = \pi_{0jk} + \sum_{p=1}^{P} \pi_{pjk} a_{pijk} + e_{ijk}$$

where

Y_{ijk} = the value of the outcome variable for the ith transaction conducted by the jth librarian in the kth library

π_{0jk} = the intercept for the jth librarian in the kth library

a_{pijk} = the value of the predictor variables for the ith transaction conducted by the jth librarian in the kth library

π_{pjk} = the coefficient associated with each predictor variable

e_{ijk} = the standard deviation for the ith transaction conducted by the jth librarian in the kth library

Level 2: Librarians

$$\pi_{pjk} = \beta_{p0k} + \sum_{q=1}^{Q_p} \beta_{pqk} X_{qjk} + r_{pjk}$$

where

β_{p0k} = the intercept for the kth library
X_{qjk} = the value of the librarian characteristic for the jth librarian in the kth library
β_{pqk} = the coefficient associated with each librarian characteristic
e_{ijk} = the standard deviation for the jth librarian in the kth library

Level 3: Libraries

$$\beta_{pqk} = \gamma_{pq0} + \sum_{s=1}^{S_{pq}} \gamma_{pqs} W_{sk} + u_{pqk}$$

where

γ_{pq0} = the intercept
W_{sk} = the predictor variable for the kth library
γ_{pqs} = the coefficient associated with each predictor variable
u_{pqk} = the standard deviation for the kth library

1.6.1 Reference Service Outcomes

The first element in this hypothesis, represented in the equation as Y_{ijk}, is the concept of reference service performance. As discussed earlier, the performance outcomes to be explored in this study are utility, user satisfaction, and accuracy. The actual value of Y_{ijk} in the equation may be that of a single variable, or instead it may equal some composite measure of multiple variables.

1.6.2 First–Level Predictors

The first-level predictors, represented in the equation as a_{pijk}, include variables that measure the difficulty of the query, the education of the library user, the user's familiarity with libraries, and the service behaviors exhibited by the librarian during the transaction. These variables will be fixed effects in the prediction equation.

The difficulty of the query refers to the complexity of the query and the currency of the information being sought. Logically, the more difficult a query is, the less likely it is that an accurate, satisfactory, and useful resolution will be discovered.

The education of the user refers the level of formal instruction that a user has received and the academic achievement of the user. The higher the education level, the more likely it becomes that the user is capable of comprehending a wider diversity of materials, in terms of both format and complexity.

The user's familiarity with libraries refers to that individual's frequency of use. A user who is familiar with library services and the manner in which reference transactions are conducted is likely to establish a better dialogue with the librarian than someone who is unfamiliar. Also, a familiar user may have developed preconceived expectations of service based on past experiences.

The service behaviors exhibited by the librarian during the transaction refer to the professional demeanor of the librarian during the transaction process, the librarian's ability to facilitate communication during the transaction process, and the librarian's ability to encourage the user to speak openly about his or her needs. Establishing open communication is essential to probing the needs of the user and seeking an answer that is useful. Users are also likely to be more satisfied with a librarian who expresses an active interest in speaking with them.

1.6.3 Second-Level Predictors

The second-level predictors, represented in the equation as X_{qjk}, include variables that measure the education, experience, and job satisfaction of the librarian. The education of the librarian refers to the academic achievement of the librarian. The values for these variables are constant for every transaction conducted by the same librarian.

The experience of the librarian refers to the amount of time the librarian has been performing reference work. The job satisfaction of the librarian refers to the extent to which the librarian is happy, interested, or challenged by his or her position. Logically, a librarian who has studied fundamental library principles, acquired years of experience in practice, and is pleased with the work environment is far more likely to offer a high caliber of service than a librarian who has received little instruction, is new to the field, and does not enjoy working with people.

1.6.4 Third-Level Predictors

The third-level predictors, represented in the equation as W_{sk}, include variables that measure the size and policies of the library. These variables describe characteristics of the reference environment where transactions take place. The values for these variables are constant for all transactions conducted within a given library participating in the study.

The size of the library refers to the volume of the collection. The service policies refer both to the level of service the institution provides to users and to the manner in which these policies are communicated to staff. Theoretically,

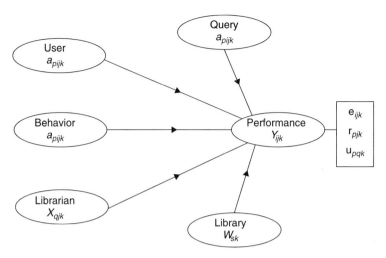

Figure 1.1
Reference service performance model.

libraries with larger collections are able to provide accurate information on a wider variety of topics a greater proportion of the time than libraries with smaller collections. Well-managed libraries where performance objectives are clearly communicated are also more likely to provide better service because of greater leadership on the part of supervisors and concern that performance objectives are achieved.

1.6.5 The Reference Service Performance Model

This study will collect data on 17 variables that have been discussed above and will be operationally defined as variables in the chapter on methodology. The hypothesis states the theoretical relationships between these variables. Each variable falls into one of six groups (one group of outcome variables and five groups of predictor variables) that are graphically described in a model of reference service performance (see Fig. 1.1).

1.7

Theoretical Framework

To demonstrate that the research questions create a perplexity in the knowledge state of the investigator and that the solution can actually be obtained by means of research (as opposed to deduction), it is necessary to frame the question from a theoretical perspective.[9] A simple means of establishing the theoretical framework is to define the question in terms of the known and unknown.[10] If the unknown component can be ascertained through observation, then the perplexity can be resolved empirically.

This study can be viewed in three dimensions: the known, the unknown, and the method for moving from the known to the unknown. The known dimension includes all the constructs used to described reference service outcomes as predictors of those outcomes as well as all the operational variables used to measure them. The unknown dimension includes the nature of the relationships between the predictors and the outcome variables. The method of multilevel level analysis will enable investigation of the unknown and result in the creation of new knowledge.

1.7.1 The Boundaries of the Study

In terms of what is already known, the definition of reference service establishes that high levels of utility, satisfaction, and accuracy are the desirable outcomes for good performance. In terms of the unknown, widely accepted measures for the performance characteristics described above have not been reliably established. In addition neither the factors that contribute to reference service performance nor measures for these factors have been reliably established.

The lack of acceptance or reliability is primarily the result of poor methodology, small sample size, and little repetition from study to study in the research literature. At least 38 variables, operationally defined in 162 different ways, have been examined as possible predictors of reference service performance.[11] Despite this variety, they can all be classified into five groups: variables concerning the reference environment, variables concerning the background and attitudes of the librarian, variables concerning the background and attitudes of the library user, variables concerning the communication between the librarian and the library user, and variables concerning the nature of the reference query. Because of the complex nature of reference transactions, the combined influence of numerous variables from each of the five groups is likely to produce the best model of reference service performance.

This study addresses the unknown through the formulation of a hypothesis as to which variables are the best predictors of reference performance. The hypothesis will be tested through the application of multilevel regression analysis in a hierarchical research design in order to determine how well a set of predictors explain the variance in an outcome variable. The advantage of this statistical technique is that it enables the researcher to measure the effects of multiple variables while accounting for the complex effects of intraclass correlation.

1.7.2 Means of Empirical Investigation

Multiple regression is a statistical method where the investigator can assess the ability of multiple independent variables to predict a dependent variable. Hierarchical linear modeling adds additional layers of complexity in adjusting for the nesting effects in multilevel data structures. In this study, hierarchical linear modeling was used in an effort to test the influence of 13 independent variables in a three-level hierarchical design on 4 dependent variables (making a total of 17 variables used in the study).

Because of the abstract nature of the concepts being examined in this study, all variables of interest will be measured on ordinal scales. On an ordinal scale, a greater value indicates a greater presence of the characteristic in question. For example, in the case of user satisfaction a score of "5" would indicate greater satisfaction than a score of "4." However, ordinal scales differ from interval scales in that the values do not represent proportional quantities of the given characteristic. In other words, a score of "6" would not indicate twice the amount of satisfaction as a score of "3." Ordinal scales are frequently used in social research for measuring human attitudes and opinions that defy physical measurement.[12]

1.7.3 The Unit of Analysis

Fortunately for researchers, reference service can be analyzed in discrete units known as reference transactions. The *ALA Glossary of Library and Information Science* defines a reference transaction as "an information contact which involves the use, recommendation, interpretation, or instruction in the use of one or more reference sources, or knowledge of such sources, by a reference staff member."[13] The information contact occurs between a librarian and a library user, although no mention of the user is made in the preceding quote. Each transaction begins with a user's query that precipitates an exchange of information between a librarian and a library user and ends when a resolution or a response to the query has been determined. All reference service occurs within the initiation and resolution of the transaction. Therefore, the reference transaction is the subject of this study and not the librarian, the user, or the library, although all three are involved in the transaction.

A useful way to describe a transaction is to classify it according to the type of query that initiates it. Samuel Rothstein reported that reference queries were frequently classified in the literature as one of four types: directional, ready-reference, search (or "research"), and reader's advisory queries. Directional queries involve informing the user about the location of a particular library facility, such as a photocopier or a restroom, or directing them to a specific title that the user requests. Ready-reference queries involve finding a brief fact for the user that is ascertainable from a standard reference source, such as an almanac or encyclopedia. Search queries involve advising the user which sources to consult and teaching the user how to use these sources in order to locate the desired information. Reader's advisory queries involve sharing opinions with the user regarding which books are most suitable for the user's expressed reading interests.[14]

In his popular reference textbook, William A. Katz proposed a different typology that also includes directional and ready-reference categories but specifies two levels of search queries: specific search queries and research queries. A specific search query involves finding a single document or section of a document that will answer the question, such as an encyclopedia article. Katz classified reader's advisory queries in this category. In contrast, a research query requires the user to consult multiple sources in order to develop an answer to the query.[15]

As evidenced by the preceding examples, the boundary between query types is indistinct. This study will identify queries, and thereby identify transactions, as either ready-reference or research. Any query that requires a short, factual answer from a published source is identified in this study as ready-reference. Research queries are those queries that often require the reader to collect a body of information, often from more than one source, and then evaluate and interpret the information to draw conclusions. The resolution to the query may include creating a search strategy for the reader to follow in addition to directing the reader to specific works.

Directional queries pertaining to library facilities or rules are not true reference queries in that they do not require any knowledge of library practice to answer, nor do they require consulting a source.[16] However, asking for a specific title, which Samuel Rothstein classified as directional, will be treated in this study as a ready-reference query since it may involve use of the catalog. Although the answers to reader's advisory queries are usually based more on professional opinion rather than fact, such queries will also be treated here as ready-reference queries since they generally require a brief answer from the librarian rather than a series of suggestions on how to locate the material.

1.7.4 Defining the Query

What is the reference query? Robert S. Taylor defined the query as an entity which undergoes a transformation through four stages, beginning with an undefined, unconscious information need felt by the library user and finally culminating in a formal request by the library user for information. This transformation frequently occurs as a result of the question negotiation process during the reference transaction.[17] Nicholas J. Belkin described the unconscious information need as an "anomalous state of knowledge" which discomfits an individual to the point where he or she is motivated to take action (e.g., driving over to the library) to resolve the anomaly.[18]

Where does the actual query exist along this continuum from unconscious anomaly to conscious inquiry? At what point in this "maturation" process does the query come into being? Does the query evolve into something new as it passes through each stage, or might one query be answered in many different ways?

For the purposes of this study, the reference query will be defined as the formal request for information negotiated between a library user and a librarian during the reference transaction. The evaluation of service performance will occur in the context of how well the negotiated query is answered. Evaluation in terms of accuracy can only be assessed on the observed query, and not the anomaly that exists in the mind of the library user. If the data which are gathered suggest that accuracy and satisfaction are uncorrelated, this may indicate that librarians are negotiating the query poorly; the user is unsatisfied because the actual query was not addressed, even though the formal query was answered accurately.

An important area for future study is the evaluation of the negotiation process itself. A study of this nature would record the initial statements expressed by the library user, note the manner in which the librarian probes the user to determine the actual information need, and compare the final formal request for information to the initial question. Herbert Goldhor and Paul Breed have already conducted pilot studies along these lines.[19]

1.7.5 Advantages and Disadvantages

The primary advantage that this theoretical structure has which previous studies do not is the recognition of the multilevel nature of the research environment. In addition, this structure is predicated upon the formulation of a hypothesis, which has not always been done in the past. Furthermore, the identification of the reference transaction, rather than the library or librarian, as the unit of study is a significant advantage in that the investigator can draw inferences as to the nature of service itself while controlling for the characteristics of the institution or individual, which may have a confounding effect on the results.

The main disadvantage, or limitation, of this structure is the reliance on quantitative methods that are unable to capture certain nuances of thought and opinion on the part of users and librarians which the investigator might be able to obtain through survey research. Open-ended responses, which might reveal much information about the reference process, are difficult to quantify and fall outside the boundaries of this study. This theoretical framework defines the research problem in the context of the current extent of knowledge within the discipline and identifies the knowledge void to be addressed by the study, thereby defining the perplexity being addressed by the investigator. This framework proposes a statistical model for moving from the known to the unknown, and establishes how abstract concepts can be quantified through the use of ordinal variables. This framework conceptually defines the subject of the study as the reference transaction. The query is defined for the purposes of this study. Accordingly, the problem is one that can be resolved through empirical analysis.

References

1. James I. Wyer, *Reference Work: A Textbook for Students of Library Work and Librarians* (Chicago: American Library Association, 1930), 4; Shiyali Ramamrita Ranganathan, *Reference Service* (London: Asia Publishing House, 1940), 53; Margaret Hutchins, *Introduction to Reference Work* (Chicago: American Library Association, 1944), 10–11; and Samuel Rothstein, "Reference Service: The New Dimension in Librarianship," *College & Research Libraries* 22 (January 1961): 12.

2. Charles A. Bunge, *Professional Education and Reference Efficiency* (Springfield, IL: Illinois State Library, 1967); and Herbert Goldhor, *A Plan for the Development of Public Library Service in the Minneapolis–Saint Paul Metropolitan Area* (Saint Paul, MN: State of Minnesota Department of Education, Library Division, 1967).

3. Terry Weech and Herbert Goldhor, "Obtrusive versus Unobtrusive Evaluation of Reference Service in Five Illinois Libraries," *Library Quarterly* 52 (October 1982): 305–324.

4. Ira Bernstein, *Applied Multivariate Analysis* (New York: Springer-Verlag, 1988), 4–5; and Laurence G. Grimm and Paul R. Yarnold, eds., *Reading and Understanding Multivariate Statistics* (Washington, D.C.: American Psychological Association, 1995), 4.

5. John P. Van de Geer, *Introduction to Multivariate Analysis for the Social Sciences* (San Francisco: W.H. Freeman, 1971), 85–86; and William W. Cooley and Paul R. Lohnes, *Multivariate Data Analysis* (New York: John Wiley & Sons, 1971), 3–5.

6. RASD Ad Hoc Committee on Behavioral Guidelines for Reference and Information Services, "Guidelines for Behavioral Performance of Reference and Information Services Professionals," *RQ* 36 (Winter 1996): 200–203.

7. Jo Bell Whitlatch, *The Role of the Academic Reference Librarian* (New York: Greenwood Press, 1990), 67.

8. Anthony S. Bryk and Stephen W. Raudenbush, *Hierarchical Linear Models: Applications and Data Analysis Methods* (Newbury Park, CA: Sage Publications, 1992), 178–180.

9. Fred N. Kerlinger, *Foundations of Behavioral Research: Psychological and Educational Inquiry* (New York: Holt, Rinehart, & Winston, 1964), 18–20.

10. John V. Richardson Jr. and Rex B. Reyes, "Government Information Expert Systems: A Quantitative Evaluation," *College & Research Libraries* 56 (May 1995): 238.

11. Matthew L. Saxton, "Reference Service Evaluation and Meta-analysis: Findings and Methodological Issues," *Library Quarterly* 67 (July 1997): 275–276.

12. Grimm and Yarnold, 5–8.

13. Hearstill Young, ed., *ALA Glossary of Library and Information Science* (Chicago: American Library Association, 1983), 189.

14. Samuel Rothstein, "The Measurement and Evaluation of Reference Service," *Library Trends* 12 (January 1964): 458.
15. William A. Katz, *Introduction to Reference Work: Basic Information Sources*, 4th ed. (New York: McGraw-Hill, 1982), 11–14.
16. Hutchins, 16.
17. Robert S. Taylor, "The Process of Asking Questions," *American Documentation* 13 (October 1962): 392.
18. Nicholas J. Belkin, Robert N. Oddy, and Helen M. Brooks, "ASK for Information Retrieval: Part I. Background and Theory." *Journal of Documentation* 38 (June 1982): 61.
19. Herbert Goldhor, "The Patrons' Side of Public Library Reference Questions," *Public Library Quarterly* 1 (Spring 1979): 35–49; and Paul F. Breed, "An Analysis of Reference Procedures in a Large University Library," Ph.D. dissertation, University of Chicago, 1955.

2

Defining and Modeling Reference Service

2.1

Defining Reference Service

In 1876, Samuel Swett Green suggested it was important for librarians to provide some assistance to readers in using the library. He believed it was desirable for the library to create an environment which would encourage "personal intercourse between librarian and readers."[1] The key element in Green's philosophy is the *personal* nature of reference service which represented a departure from the conventional belief that librarians can best serve readers indirectly and impersonally through the acquisition of materials and the creation of finding tools.

Despite initial resistance to Green's ideas at the time, the concept of assisting readers would become accepted as a core function of librarianship. In his *Library Primer*, published in numerous editions near the beginning of the 20th century, John Cotton Dana argued that conversation with readers was essential to determine their wants and make them feel welcome and comfortable in the library. He further wrote that it was necessary for librarians to help train people to use the library in order to stimulate the "inquiring spirit" which was necessary to promote and sustain self-education.[2] To accomplish these goals, Dana instructed librarians to greet persons who enter the library, to use tact and patience to "learn at once what the inquirer wishes to know"[3] (i.e., probe), and to show the reader how the information is found. Although Dana did not explicitly define reference service, he did establish the goals of such service and listed the three techniques just described to accomplish these goals.

In her pioneering *Guide to the Study and Use of Reference Books*, Alice Bertha Kroeger defined reference work as "the assistance given to readers in the use of the resources of the library."[4] However, this definition was obviously too narrow, as she then proceeded to describe in a later edition how a librarian must also search beyond the resources of the local collection as needed in order to address the needs of readers.

> Other institutions besides libraries are engaged in reference work and are important bureaus of information which the reference librarian should know and refer to when the resources of his library have been exhausted.[5]

She further reminds librarians to consider interlibrary loan when assisting "serious readers."[6] Thus, Kroeger expanded the evolving definition of reference service in two ways. First, the reference librarian's responsibility to readers is to guide them to information regardless of where it may be found, establishing referral as a basic principle of reference work. Second, reference service is an activity which is not limited to librarianship. From this latter concept it can be inferred that the practice of reference service must be governed by rules and principles which are applicable across many settings, including differing library settings.[7]

In 1924, William S. Learned wrote that the development of what he described as a specialized "intelligence service"[8] would be necessary to enable a public library to fulfill the mission of diffusing knowledge throughout a community in order to supply people with information in a form which can "best be utilized by the person in question."[9] Among the qualifications for a person providing such service, he listed "quick intellectual sympathies,"[10] which can be interpreted as the ability to grasp another person's thoughts and needs. Thus, the reason why reference service must be personal is because of individual differences among readers.

> The chief business of a community library is to produce a general diffusion of knowledge among small, ill-defined, and constantly shifting groups, where each need is peculiar to the individual himself, and must be dealt with separately.[11]

Learned believed that "wise personal attention"[12] was necessary to maximize the educational value of a well-ordered library.

In preparing his own textbook on reference service, James I. Wyer was heavily influenced by Learned and adopted the notion of sympathy in his own definition. He defined reference work as

> . . . sympathetic and informed personal aid in interpreting library collections for study and research. . . . Reference work exists because it is not possible to organize books so mechanically, so perfectly, as to dispense with personal service in their use. . . . It still is, and always will be, imperative to provide human beings as intermediaries between the reader and the right book.[13]

Wyer's main contribution is introducing the concepts of interpretation and mediation as the service being provided to the reader, in contrast to aid or direction. The librarian's role is clearly portrayed as something greater than merely pointing the reader to a source.

Wyer explicitly identifies the three of the five essential elements of the dominant paradigm[14]: ". . . the reference question completely and satisfactorily answered involves three factors: inquirer, reference librarian, sources or materials."[15] His presentation of the reference transaction suggests a straight-forward linear process without many complications. He noted that different institutions, as a matter of policy, would provide different levels of reference service, which he labeled as conservative, moderate, or liberal.[16]

In the late 1930s, both Isadore Gilbert Mudge and Louis Shores helped to expand the definition of reference service by using a functional approach. Mudge wrote that reference work encompassed *"everything* necessary to help the reader in his inquiry [emphasis added]." This definition goes far beyond the dimension of personal service to include most branches of library work. Mudge judged selection, arrangement, maintenance, and staff supervision to be just as much a part of reference work as instruction and the "constant work in answering individual questions."[17] Shores also took a functional approach by stating that the primary purpose of the reference department was to "interpret books to readers"[18] and enumerated five duties of reference staff: answering questions, locating material, performing research, providing instruction, and advising readers. While these five duties all involved personal contact with the reader, in the later *Basic Reference Sources*, Shores expanded his definition of reference work as "everything performed by the reference department."[19] Echoing Mudge, this broad definition included supervision and collection appraisal as reference functions.

Shiyali Ramamrita Ranganathan's theory of reference argued that the functional definition espoused by Mudge was too broad, although no evidence exists that he was necessarily familiar with her work. Ranganathan was familiar with Wyer's text, and the following definition is in accordance with the philosophy of Wyer and Learned.

> Reference service is the process of establishing contact between a reader and his documents in a personal way. ... It is not possible to do all this for a reader without an intimate understanding of his precise interest at the moment. To get this understanding, there must be an intimate communion between the librarian and the reader. ... Therefore, reference service is essentially personal service.[20]

Ranganathan envisioned reference work as a three-step process. He believed that the first step, classification of materials and maintenance of a collection, were preparatory tasks for the second step of reference service, which was initiated by the reader with an inquiry. The last step, which he labeled assimilation, dealt with the ongoing professional development of the librarian who used experiences with readers to prepare for future reference encounters. Service itself is only one phase of a larger process.[21]

In 1944, Margaret Hutchins attempted to draw many threads of reference theory into a coherent form. She stated that reference work encompassed both the personal, direct aid given to individual readers in interpreting library resources *and* the impersonal, indirect activities performed to make information more readily available to readers. She affirmed Kroeger's notions that the librarian should look beyond local resources when helping readers and also that the techniques for performing library service were the same in different institutional settings, regardless of the library's collection or intended service population. She also agreed with Wyer's observation that reference service could be provided at different levels according to the policies of the institution.[22]

In 1961, Samuel Rothstein sought to define the dichotomous nature of reference theory more precisely by using two different terms, although in so doing he reversed the conventional usage. Returning to the tradition of Kroeger and Wyer, he defined the personal assistance given to individual readers as *reference work*. This narrow concept is what Ranganathan had referred to as *reference service*. Rothstein then defined the responsibility and organization of a library to prepare for this work as *reference service*. This broad concept is what Mudge, Shores, and Hutchins had referred to as *reference work*.[23]

In 1966, Alan M. Rees also felt the need for greater specificity in describing reference theory. Whether intentionally or unintentionally, he ignored Rothstein's usage and reversed labels again. *Reference service* was the actual provision of assistance, and *reference work* was the library function performed by reference librarians in providing that service. Then he added the term *reference process* to describe the complex interaction between the reader and the librarian as well as the psychological, sociological, and environmental variables that affect them. He explained that the process begins with an inquiry and ends with an answer that is relevant to that inquiry.[24] These terms were later promoted by Frances Neel Cheney in her popular textbook *Fundamental Reference Sources*.[25]

This study is concerned with reference service as defined by Ranganathan, wherein the librarian is required to provide personal intermediation between the reader and the information being sought. The reference process, as defined by Rees, is the observable event in which reference service takes place. As such, the reference process, or reference transaction as it now commonly called, is the unit of study that will be examined to draw inferences about the nature of reference service. Reference service evaluation has almost exclusively been concerned with this aspect of reference work, although some efforts have gone into exploring the effects of unmediated reference work.[26]

The personal dimension of reference service has been seen as the central defining characteristic from Green up to the present. Why, then, did early researchers ignore the role of the user in designing studies of reference service? Why were reference questions treated as if they existed independently from the context in which they were asked? Beginning in the early years of this century, librarians have been instructed to seek information from external sources when necessary. Why, then, was the importance of evaluating the quality of referrals never discussed? And why were the institutional policies governing the limits of service never controlled as part of a research design?

The literature presents a fairly consistent thread of agreement as to what reference service is. The greatest controversy revolves upon where to draw the line between reference work and other library functions which support reference work. However, many researchers, in seeking to create measures of service performance, departed from conventional definitions and created numerous contradictory and incomplete alternatives which were more easily operationalized. This disagreement resulted in a confused understanding of the role of reference service in society. Information, instead of mediation, was often portrayed as the primary reference product.

2.2

Modeling Reference Transactions

Many scholars, especially Robert Taylor and Gerald Jahoda, have played an important part in advancing our understanding of the different steps in the question-answering process. Others such as Brenda Dervin and Nicholas Belkin have in some areas reinvented their work while also adding further complexity to these models. Conceptually, the literature on models of reference transactions can be characterized along several dimensions. For example, much of the research literature adopts, either implicitly or explicitly, a systems analysis approach or an input-process-output-feedback (IPOF) model. More recently, researchers have adopted the constructivist approach. The influence of the Shannon–Weaver communication model is also in evidence by 1962.

Graphically, these models are usually represented by line drawings and less often, but more recently, as a flowsheet or flowchart, a technique whereby detailed charting of the steps in the process takes place. Despite the fact that the flowcharting technique was developed between 1915 and 1920 to study manufacturing processes, it has found a more general applicability.[27] Nevertheless, it does involve some distortions of reality by treating the reference interview as a discrete process rather than the continuous process that it is. In that respect, a flowchart represents reality as crisp rather than fuzzy. This approach also assumes that the process is linearly progressive and composed of simple rather than complexly interdependent steps.

In 1936, Carter Alexander produced one of the earliest analytical statements about the reference process and at one time was one of the most frequently cited studies. He presented a detailed stepwise approach to searching for the answer to an inquirer's question that identifies six steps in the reference transaction:

    I. Find out precisely what the question really is.
    II. Decide which kind of library materials is most likely to have the answer to the inquiry.

   III. Decide which items in a given kind of library materials are most likely to have the answer, in order of likelihood.

   IV. Locate the chosen items.

   V. Search in the chosen items in order of likelihood until the answer is found or you are sure it cannot be found there.

   VI. If the answer is not found by the foregoing, go back over the previous steps and take next most likely sources.[28]

The first step consists of two general procedures: "find out what the inquirer intends to do with the answer to his question" and "examine the question to see what clues to its answer it carries."[29] It helps, he suggested, to classify the question into one of seven distinct types: (1) fact type including meaning type of fact, numerical or statistical type of fact, historical type of fact, exact wording type of fact, and proper name type of fact; (2) how to do type; (3) trends type; (4) supporting evidence type; (5) "all about" type; (6) evaluation of reference type; and (7) duplication of previous work type. The concept of classifying queries by type queries was used by several subsequent researchers and is discussed in the following chapter. By recommending analysis by type of reference format and then specific source within type (see Steps II and III), his technique foreshadows the shift to the proceduralist approach[30] articulated by Mudge and popularized by Hutchins.

As a proceduralist, Hutchins made an important distinction by differentiating between the clarification step (i.e., question negotiation) and the classification step (i.e., a mental analysis technique for identifying useful information resources) steps. Thus, she described the reference transaction as having two components. In the former, the reference librarian may need to clarify the inquirer's question further. For instance, "if the request seems peculiar a start may be made by restating it in a different way and asking if that is what is meant or would be satisfactory."[31] Note that she is recommending a closed-ended question (i.e., one that requires a yes or no response) at this point in the clarification step. This two-step model that Hutchins described is the dominant, basic framework used for analysis of reference transactions by subsequent researchers.

Just over 10 years later, Paul Breed elaborated on the two-step model. After identifying the discrete steps in the general reference process, Breed categorized the decision-making knowledge needed to accomplish each step according to a five-part scheme: (1) knowledge associated with a liberal arts education; (2) knowledge associated with library specialization (including experience); (3) personal knowledge; (4) knowledge gained in the search process; and (5) knowledge associated with subject specialization. Breed found that 81% of the decisions with his discrete steps required knowledge associated with library specialization.[32]

Originally circulated in mimeograph form during 1961, James W. Perry published the now-familiar four stages of query formulation that provided a theoretical structure for investigating the clarification step of the reference process. He identified the four stages as

> Q0 = some ideal "best" query to obtain information to deal with a given problem or situation
> Q1 = the mental conception developed by some person as to needed information
> Q2 = the statement of a query by a person without regard to a given information retrieval system
> Q3 = the statement of a query by a person with regard to a given information retrieval system.[33]

The motivation for querying an information retrieval system follows from his assumption that the information needed by the user is a combination of information the user already possesses with information acquired through using the retrieval system.

In popularizing the work of Perry, Taylor characterized question formation based on the inquirer's informational need as comprising four levels that move progressively from some form of Platonic ideal question, which is psychological, abstract, complex, diffuse, ill-defined, inchoate, and ambiguous; to a logical, more concrete, rigid, focused, and simplified state:

> Q1 = the actual, but unexpressed, need for information (the visceral need)
> Q2 = the conscious, within-brain description of the need (the conscious need)
> Q3 = the formal statement of the question (the formalized need)
> Q4 = the question as presented to the information system (the compromised need).[34]

He also discusses question input, answer output, and the role of interim feedback. Taylor also draws upon the concept of noise from Shannon's Theory of Information and points out that filtering system responses involves a relevance judgment on the part of the inquirer. He argues that the inquirer be included in the design of information retrieval systems.

In his later writing, Taylor presented a detailed analysis of the process of question negotiation based on the theoretical structure of four stages first introduced by Perry. Although this article, one of the most highly cited sources in the literature of reference service, includes an interesting chart of the prenegotiation decisions by the inquirer, Taylor's more significant contribution is in his description of the actual reference transaction itself. Based on personal interviews with 20 special librarians, he defined five "filters": (1) determination of subject; (2) objective and motivation; (3) personal characteristics of inquirer; (4) relationship of inquiry description to file organization; and (5) anticipated or acceptable answers. The second filter is the most important because it often reduces search time substantially and determines what constitutes an appropriate response.[35]

In an article originally presented as a conference paper for the American Documentation Institute in 1963, Alan Rees and Tefko Saracevic formulated a descriptive statement of the 10 "evolutionary steps" in question asking and answering. Despite the fact that it contains no explicit statement of methodology (except that analysis of reference questions is analogous to subject analysis of documents), this piece presents a comprehensive and detailed description of the reference process. Furthermore, the authors are the first to represent it graphically with boxes, dotted lines, and solid lines with arrows.[36]

The 10 steps are: (1) information problem and need; (2) initial formulation of question; (3) analysis by searcher; (4) negotiation between question analyst and questioner; (5) definition of question; (6) enumeration of concepts to be searched; (7) translation of search concepts into indexing language; (8) selection of search strategy; (9) conducting of search; and (10) formulation of alternate search strategies.

Acceptable answers or responses from the librarian will be based on:

1. What the questioner needs. . . .
2. What he thinks he wants. . . .
3. What he wants. . . .
4. What he is prepared to read. . . .
5. How much of what he gets he is prepared to read. . . .
6. How much time he is willing to devote to it all. . . .
7. In what sequence he would like to read what he gets. . . .
8. What value he will attach to what he gets. . . .[37]

In his investigation of using automation in the providing reference services, Jesse Shera appears to have read Taylor's 1962 article and heard Rees and Saracevic's 1963 conference paper, and based part of his work on theirs without explicitly identifying his sources. He describes the reference process as involving a complex series of linked events which he views as a communication flow. Echoing Taylor's work, one of his contributions is the explicit graphical recognition of the role of feedback in the process, or what he terms the "evaluation of pertinence" to the information need as well as the "evaluation of relevance" to the inquiry (i.e., its linguistic expression).[38] Shera applied decision theory in an attempt to outline the entire reference process, "from the problem that prompts the asking of a question to the evaluation of the response,"[39] and called for further research to achieve thorough understanding.

Accepting the four-stage model of query negotiation as expressed by Taylor, Norman Crum elaborated on the clarification process by observing that users present themselves at different "Q" stages and that the mediator's responsibility is to work back through these stages to the motivational information need or problem. In the process, there are: (1) physical, (2) personality, (3) psychological, (4) linguistic, and (5) contextual barriers. Although he does not provide an itemized list of each barrier, he indirectly suggests some; for instance, personality barriers might include coolness, indifference, and withdrawal, while informal contacts, direct assignment, and wise choice of locations would reduce other barriers. Finally, Crum recommends a second interview, a review process to check the results, as a kind of quality control assurance, just before the end of the transaction.[40]

Based on a study of 23 science and technical reference librarians, Jahoda presented the reference process as a simple six-step model: (1) message selection, (2) specificity, (3) selection of specific answer-providing sources, (4) selection of search headings, (5) answer selection, and (6) negotiation and renegotiation.[41] Jahoda argued that every query consisted of two parts: the "Given," information about the problem already known to the user, and the "Wanted," information about the problem desired by the user. The purpose of query negotiation, or the clarification step, is to enable the librarian to consciously identify these elements. One of Jahoda's important contributions was to describe eight situations where query negotiation is required:

- The real query may not be asked.
- Librarian is unfamiliar with the subject of the query.
- Ambiguity or incompleteness of query statement.
- Amount of information needed is not specified.
- Level of answer is not specified.
- The query takes more time than you can spend on it.
- Answer to query is not recorded in the literature.
- Language, time period, geography, or type of publication constraints need to be added to query statements.[42]

Echoing his earlier work on failure analysis in question answering, Jahoda, working with Judith Schiek Braunagel, developed a checklist for determining whether questions are truly answerable based on: (1) clarity, (2) specificity, and (3) freedom from overly restrictive constraints such as language, time period, and geography.[43]

2.3

Recent Development in Reference Theory

After a moderately extensive review of the literature, James Rettig lamented that the literature merely describes the process rather than presenting a theoretical or conceptual approach that would explain why things proceed the way they do during the reference transaction. Rettig, then, proposed the necessity of adding feedback and background noise into any model of the reference process, much like Taylor's drawing upon Shannon's theory.[44]

Rettig raises the question "how message-receiving ability relates to the ability to provide the level of service a patron wants" without answering it. He does, however, relate effectively how Wyer's three levels of service (conservative, moderate, and liberal, or Rothstein's minimum, middling, and maximum policy) should vary according to the inquirer's information need. He observes that the American Library Association Reference and Adult Services Division's "A Commitment to Information Services" affirms his view.[45]

In the early 1980s, the work of Nicholas Belkin called for a shift from a system-centered to a user-centered approach to thinking about queries. Whereas Jahoda focused on queries, Belkin wanted to examine the information needs underlying actual queries. Based on Taylor's four-stage model, he characterized the user's information need as an anomalous state of knowledge that constituted an information problem for the user. Belkin argued that it was too difficult for the user to articulate a query, and that many users were actually unable to do so. As an alternative, queries could possibly be better derived from the user's description of the problem.[46] The implication for reference service is that librarians should encourage users to share more about the context and nature of their information need rather than forcing the user to articulate a specific query. While Belkin's main interest was in the design of information retrieval systems that could derive queries from user input, his ideas influenced many researchers in the area of reference service evaluation.

In attempting to explain the cognitive processes that take place during the reference transaction, Marilyn White drew upon Minsky's concept of frames, data structures representing stereotyped situations, that he developed while working on artificial intelligence theory. She suggested that during the transaction, reference librarians are involved in a pattern-matching process and could use Minsky's concept of frames to classify reference questions.[47] White accepted Taylor's basic model, but postulated that interaction between Q1, Q2, Q3, and Q4 was more complex than a simple linear relationship.[48] In particular, White argues that the librarian's motivation to move back to Q1 from Q4 is based on a concern for possible errors that may have crept in, whereas Q2 and Q3 may be influenced by the inquirer's problem-solving skills and knowledge of information sources.[49]

Based on 13 years of empirical research, Brenda Dervin and Patricia Dewdney proposed that the inquirer's information need can be characterized as an attempt at "sense-making" that is "situationally bound."[50] Specifically, they propose a tripartite model of information need that is composed of a situation, a gap or stoppages, and uses. Interviews with 17 public librarians about troublesome reference interviews substantiate Taylor's second filter (i.e., motivation and use objective) as the most important one, although without explicitly saying so or referring to his work at this point.[51]

Although they identify the reference librarian's three options of closed, open, and neutral questions, they warn against the first because "all closed questions involve [a possibly premature] judgment already made by the librarian of what is relevant to the user."[52] Instead, they provide a set of illustrative neutral questions for use in negotiations and strongly recommend these as opposed to leading, but open questions, although they do not use the term "leading" in their article.

In her doctoral study of 24 reference librarians in three Ontario public libraries, Dewdney found that the inquirer's initial satisfaction was already high, and that satisfaction with those librarians trained in neutral questioning and microcounseling skills actually decreased over time. However, those librarians trained in neutral questioning were rated higher on premature diagnosis, use of open questions, and closure. Dervin's work is important to understanding the reference process because it revitalizes research interest in applying communication theory.[53]

Building upon Taylor and the later writings by Belkin and Dervin, Melissa Gross observed the dominant models of the reference process are predicated on the concept that visceral needs, cognitive anomalies, or the desire to resolve personal uncertainties prompts users to seek information, sometimes causing them to seek personal assistance from an intermediary. However, this assumption does not apply to situations where users are seeking information on behalf of others since no visceral need or cognitive anomaly exists. Since such situations are common (e.g., parents seeking for children, workers seeking for supervisors, gatekeepers seeking for community members), success or failure in the reference transaction might be affected by whether or not users are also query originators or are attempting to resolve needs imposed by others. The reference librarian attempting to serve someone with an imposed query is constrained both in the act of query negotiation to identify the information need and in verifying that the need has been resolved, since the actual owner of the need is not present. Gross' work suggests that any theory attempting to explain the reference process must also account for the presence of imposed queries and how they affect the motivation and responses of the user.[54]

In contrast to these explanations of reference transactions based on analysis of the user's behavior, thoughts, and emotions, John Richardson theorized that the reference transaction, specifically the searching component, was primarily guided by the decision-making process of the reference librarian.[55] Therefore, the activities and outcomes of reference transactions could be understood by examining the cognitive methods and strategies of reference librarians as well as exploring the patterns and structures of the tacit knowledge, also referred to as "expert" knowledge, of reference librarians.[56] This theoretical approach allows the possibility of creating expert systems that could emulate and support the work of reference librarians.

In an attempt to identify all the component parts of the process in order to create an optimal model, Richardson presented an extensive, evaluative review of more than 60 research studies on the reference process as well as examining the teaching and learning paradigm of reference service represented in the textbook literature.[57] Although his ultimate goal was to articulate the process in order to design expert systems, he also succeeded in constructing a testable, linear model of general reference work that allows researchers to make predictions about the effects of different variables in the process.[58] Richardson specified the inquirer, the librarian, and information resources as the primary entities engaged in the process, but does not investigate the elements of communication and interaction between the inquirer and librarian in any detail.

In addressing the interpersonal component of reference service, Marie Radford argued that studying the dynamics of face-to-face encounters is a critical element in understanding reference transactions. Drawing upon communication theory, Radford described the messages between inquirers and librarians as having a content dimension (the information being conveyed in the message) and a relational dimension (how the message is expressed). The relational elements establish the nature of the relationship between the inquirer and librarian (e.g., caring/indifferent, friendly/antisocial, equitable/authoritarian), thereby having a significant effect on the quality of communication during the reference transaction. Understanding the verbal and nonverbal behavior of librarians that sends relational signals to users may explain success or failure in reference transactions.[59]

After gathering data on 27 reference transactions conducted by nine academic reference librarians in three settings (community college, private university, and public college), she examined the paired perceptions of librarians and users toward the success or failure of the reference transaction, or "reference encounter." Her findings indicate that librarians and users can have different views towards the outcome of the encounter, with the majority (59%) of pairs exhibiting partial or total disagreement.[60] Radford's major findings are:

- Interpersonal relationships and communication are of great importance in librarian and user perceptions of reference interactions.
- Library users in academic settings place a high degree of significance on the attitude and personal qualities of the librarian giving reference assistance.
- Some users valued interpersonal aspects more than their receipt of information.
- Librarians were more likely than users to evaluate the reference encounter from content dimensions that involve the transfer of information.

Librarians also perceive relationship qualities to be important in the success of reference interactions (although to a lesser degree than users).[61]

Ultimately, despite the amount of information provided to the user, Radford suggests that success in the reference transaction might be explained better by focusing on the interpersonal skills of the librarian and user.

At present, many theories propose explanations of why librarians succeed or fail in their role as intermediator. As illustrated above, the earliest work attempted to articulate the steps in the reference process in order to understand factors that might affect various events during the reference transaction. These attempts were librarian-centered and ignored the role of the user other than as initiator and recipient. Later work identified the user's state of mind, in terms of motivation for information seeking, and the user's desire for mutual trust and respect during the reference process as critical elements determining success or failure in reference service. In summary, the literature reveals two complementary lines of inquiry. The first line pertains to understanding how intermediaries seek and locate accurate information in response to the expressed needs of users. The second line pertains to understanding how those needs are recognized and how the response is expressed. Ultimately, research in both areas could lead to the development of a broader theory of intermediation.

References

1. Samuel Swett Green, "Personal Relations Between Librarians and Readers," *American Library Journal* 1 (30 September 1876): 79.
2. John Cotton Dana, *A Library Primer*, 5th ed. (Chicago: Library Bureau, 1910), 130–132.
3. Ibid., 58.
4. Alice Bertha Kroeger, *Guide to the Study and Use of Reference Books* (Chicago: American Library Association, 1902), 3.
5. Alice Bertha Kroeger, *Guide to the Study and Use of Reference Books*, 2nd ed. (Chicago: American Library Association, 1908), x.
6. Ibid.
7. Ibid., ix–xii.
8. William S. Learned, *The American Public Library and the Diffusion of Knowledge* (New York: Harcourt, Brace, & Co., 1924), 13.
9. Ibid.
10. Ibid.
11. Ibid., 27.
12. Ibid., 38.
13. James I. Wyer, *Reference Work: A Textbook for Students of Library Work and Librarians* (Chicago: American Library Association, 1930), 4–5.
14. For a discussion and analysis of evolving models of curriculum for educating reference professionals, see John V. Richardson Jr., "Teaching General Reference Work: The Complete Paradigm and Competing Schools of Thought, 1890–1990," *Library Quarterly* 62 (January 1992): 55–89.
15. Wyer, 96.
16. Ibid., 12–13.
17. Isadore Gilbert Mudge, *Guide to Reference Books*, 6th ed. (Chicago: American Library Association, 1936), 1–2.
18. Louis Shores, *Basic Reference Books* (Chicago: American Library Association, 1937), 2–4.
19. Louis Shores, *Basic Reference Sources* (Chicago: American Library Association, 1954), 2.
20. S. R. Ranganathan, *Reference Service* (London: Asia Publishing House, 1940), 53.
21. Ibid., 213–214.
22. Margaret Hutchins, *Introduction to Reference Work* (Chicago: American Library Association, 1944), 10–13, 37–40.
23. Samuel Rothstein, "Reference Service: The New Dimension in Librarianship," *College & Research Libraries* 22 (January 1961): 12.

24. Alan M. Rees, "Broadening the Spectrum" in *The Present Status and Future Prospects of Reference/Information Service*, edited by Winifred B. Linderman (Chicago: American Library Association, 1967), 57–58.

25. Frances Neel Cheney, *Fundamental Reference Sources* (Chicago: American Library Association, 1971), 5.

26. Thomas Childers, "Using Public Library Reference Collections and Staff," *Library Quarterly* 67 (April 1997): 156–157.

27. For further discussion of the application of flowcharting techniques and the culmination of this approach, see John V. Richardson Jr., *Knowledge-Based Systems for General Reference Work: Applications, Problems, and Progress* (San Diego: Academic Press, 1995), 121–123.

28. Carter Alexander, "The Technique of Library Searching," *Special Libraries* 27 (September 1936): 230–238; reprinted, *How to Locate Educational Information and Data: A Text and Reference Book* (New York: Columbia University Teacher's College, 1941), Chapter 30.

29. Ibid, 231.

30. Richardson, "Teaching."

31. Hutchins, 25.

32. Paul F. Breed, "An Analysis of Reference Procedures in a Large University Library," Ph.D. dissertation, University of Chicago, 1955.

33. James W. Perry, "Defining the Query Spectrum — The Basis for Designing and Evaluating Retrieval Methods," Mimeograph, 1961, and id., "Defining the Query Spectrum — The Basis for Designing and Evaluating Retrieval Methods," *IEEE Transactions on Engineering Writing and Speech* 6 (September 1963): 20–27.

34. Robert S. Taylor, "The Process of Asking Questions, "*American Documentation* 13 (October 1962): 391–396.

35. Robert S. Taylor, *Question-Negotiation and Information Seeking in Libraries*, Studies in the Man-System Interface in Libraries, Report No. 3, Grant Number AF-AFOSR-724–66 (Bethlehem, PA: Lehigh University, July 1967), and id., "Question Negotiation and Information Seeking in Libraries," *College & Research Libraries* 29 (May 1968): 178–194.

36. Allan M. Rees and Tefko Saracevic, "Conceptual Analysis of Questions in Information Retrieval Systems," in *Automation and Scientific Communication, Topic 8: Information Storage and Retrieval; Annual Meeting of the American Documentation Institute, Part II* 1 (1963): 175–177.

37. Ibid., 175.

38. Jesse Shera, "Automation and the Reference Librarian," *RQ* 3 (July 1964): 3–7.

39. Ibid., 5.

40. Norman J. Crum, "The Librarian–Customer Relationship: Dynamics of Filling Requests for Information," *Special Libraries* 60 (May/June 1969): 269–277.

41. Gerald Jahoda, *The Process of Answering Reference Questions: A Test of a Descriptive Model*, Office of Education, Bureau of School Systems, Library Research and Demonstration Branch, Grant Number G007500619 (Tallahassee: Florida State University School of Library Science, January 1977); reprint ed. (Bethesda, MD: ERIC Document Reproduction Service, ED 136 769, 1977).

42. Ibid., 51–56.

43. Gerald Jahoda and Judith S. Braunagel, *The Librarian and Reference Queries: A Systematic Approach* (New York: Academic Press, 1980), 116–124.

44. James Rettig, "A Theoretical Model and Definition of the Reference Process," *RQ* 18 (Fall 1978): 19–29.

45. Ibid., 25.

46. Nicholas J. Belkin, Robert N. Oddy, and Helen M. Brooks, "ASK for Information Retrieval: Part I. Background and Theory," *Journal of Documentation* 38 (June 1982): 61–71; and id., "ASK for Information Retrieval: Part II. Result of a Design Study," *Journal of Documentation* 38 (September 1982): 145–164.

47. Marilyn D. White, "The Reference Encounter Model," *Drexel Library Quarterly* 19 (1983): 42.

48. Ibid., 45, Figure 1.

49. Ibid., 44.

50. Brenda Dervin and Patricia Dewdney, "Neutral Questioning: A New Approach to the Reference Interview," *RQ* 25 (Summer 1986): 507.

51. Ibid., 508.

52. Ibid.

53. Patricia Dewdney, "The Effects of Training Reference Libraries in Interview Skills: A Field Experiment," Ph.D. dissertation, University of Western Ontario, August 1986.

54. Melissa Gross, "The Imposed Query," *RQ* 35 (Winter 1995): 236–243; id., "The Imposed Query: Implications for Library Service Evaluation," *RQ* 37 (Spring 1998): 290–299; id., "Imposed Queries in the School Library Media Center: A Descriptive Study," *Library and Information Science Research* 21 (1999): 501–521; and id. and Matthew L. Saxton, "Who Wants to Know? Imposed Queries in the Public Library" *Public Libraries* 40 (May–June 2001): 170–175.

55. Richardson, *Knowledge-Based Systems*, 68–69.

56. Ibid., 151–153.

57. Ibid., 90–121.

58. Ibid., 124–138.

59. Marie L. Radford, "Communication Theory Applied to Reference Encounter: An Analysis of Critical Incidents," *Library Quarterly* 66 (April 1996): 123–137, and id., *The Reference Encounter: Interpersonal Communication in the Academic Library* (Chicago: American Library Association, 1999).

60. Id., *Reference Encounter*, 100.

61. Ibid., 104.

3

Evaluating and Measuring Reference Service

This review of reference service evaluation studies builds on earlier literature reviews by Rothstein, Powell, Crews, Richardson, and Saxton.[1] A portion of the analysis presented here is also based on Saxton's meta-analysis of reference service evaluation studies.[2] Following a number of studies examining types of reference questions conducted in the first half of the 20th century, two dominant methodologies have been applied to the study of reference service evaluation in the past three decades: the unobtrusive query-oriented approach primarily concerned with testing the accuracy of answers to reference questions, and the obtrusive user-oriented approach primarily concerned with testing for levels of user satisfaction with the service. While these lines of research have indicated a variety of factors that affect the quality of reference service, results have not been consistent or conclusive. In response, researchers are currently looking to formulate better operational definitions for service outcomes and develop more sophisticated methods for analyzing data. One important contribution that this area of study has made to our understanding of reference transactions is the identification of a number of causes for failure in the reference process.

3.1

Types of Reference Questions

The first investigations into evaluating reference service were descriptive rather than experimental in nature. This research was largely concerned with the nature of the types of questions being posed. Investigators attempted to identify the population of reference queries by determining what forms of questions were being asked, who was asking them, and how long was it taking to answer them.

In an early study, Mary De Jong categorized reference queries by the inquirer's characteristics. Based on 1 month's inquiries at the Appleton Public

Library (Wisconsin), she reported the amount of time spent on various groups as follows: study clubs (13 hours and 45 minutes to answer 20 questions); general public (13 hours and 30 minutes to answer 29 questions); students (2 hours and 25 minutes); teachers (2 hours); and all other persons (39 reference questions at the main desk and 12 questions over the telephone). In all, 31 hours were spent with questions that took more than 10 minutes to answer.[3]

Edith Guerrier described a project conducted in nine major metropolitan libraries (and their branches) where every question asked for a week and the source used to answer it was written down.[4] The answer itself was not noted. Based on analysis of 33 branch libraries participating in the study, Guerrier found that an average of 20% of librarians' time was being spent answering reference questions. Her other findings give insight into the relative utility of various reference formats and specific titles. Analyzing 1000 questions asked at these branches, Guerrier found that approximately 50% could be answered using: (1) encyclopedias, (2) dictionaries, (3) atlases, (4) *World Almanac*, (5) *Statesman's Yearbook*, (6) *Reader's Guide*, (7) *Who's Who in America*, (8) *Who's Who*, and (9) debate and quotation books. She found that a list of 80-plus reference titles answered another 33% of the questions, and the final 17% had to be answered with other titles. Anticipating later studies, she noted "the correct answering of a reference question at a public library is taken for granted."[5]

Participating as part of Guerrier's study, the Los Angeles Public Library and its then 48 branches collected 1 week's worth of questions. Faith Hyers reports that 50,000 reference questions were asked during that period, averaging 11 questions per minute per 12-hour day. Hyers concluded that individual differences exist among reference librarians in terms of the sources consulted to answer the same question, and that knowing a subject is different from knowing the literature (i.e., the reference formats and their relative importance) of that subject. She also implicitly questioned whether "the library should be able to answer any and every question."[6]

Several years after these initial efforts, Dorothy Cole collected 1026 questions from 14 public libraries in the Chicago area as well as in St. Louis and Billings, Montana.[7] She analyzed these questions in four ways: by Dewey subject areas, inquirer's characteristics, time period of query, and level of complexity. Cole found that the social sciences, useful arts, and history accounted for 72% of the questions asked.[8] Her occupational analysis indicated that students asked the most questions ($N = 356$, 35%), followed by unknown occupations ($N = 248$, 24%), professionals ($N = 210$, 21%), shopkeepers and salesmen ($N = 61$, 6%), and clerks and stenographers ($N = 59$, 6%).[9] As for time periods, most inquiries concerned the immediate year ($N = 196$, 19%), followed by the 20th century ($N = 539$, 53%), modern era ($N = 153$, 15%), Middle Ages ($N = 12$, 1%), ancient times ($N = 20$, 2%), no single period ($N = 99$, 10%), and future events ($N = 7$, 1%).[10] Cole's complexity analysis yielded the following results: (1) fact-type questions ($N = 565$, 55%); (2) general information about subjects ($N = 200$, 20%); (3) how-to information ($N = 105$, 10%); (4) supporting evidence ($N = 85$, 8%); (5) historical ($N = 35$, 3%); (6) trends ($N = 25$, 2%); and all others ($N = 11$, 1%).[11] She concludes her thesis with a list of actual sources used in answering the 1026 reference questions.

Florence Van Hoesen undertook an extensive survey of questions being asked at public libraries. Based on the type of information being sought, she created a query classification scheme with 11 categories: meaning type, numerical or statistical type, historical type, exact wording type, proper names, addresses of individuals or societies, books and publishing, biographical facts, geographical facts, book reviews, and illustrations.[12] This classification scheme was used by later researchers as a guide in creating sets of test questions.

All of these early studies focus on actual reference transactions from the field as the unit of study and attempt to describe various attributes of the query population. Curiously, as subsequent researchers began to develop more complex studies, they tended to ignore this body of work as a basis for research design with the one exception of noting that queries could be classified by type. Rather than fully developing this line of investigation, researchers turned their attention to examining the outcomes of reference service.

In the 1960s, researchers began with the simplistic model that service quality was equal to the accuracy of the information being provided in the reference transaction. Later, researchers began to express interest in user satisfaction. In addition to these two measures, the present study will add the concept of utility. Thus, instead of replacing accuracy, new variables have been added to explain additional dimensions of reference service outcomes.

Studies in reference service evaluation have historically measured performance according to one of two patterns. The first pattern involved administering reference test questions, both obtrusively and unobtrusively, to librarians and scoring the number of correct answers to obtain an estimate of accuracy. The second pattern consisted of surveying library users, either in person or through a questionnaire, in order to gauge the level of satisfaction with the service. While the first pattern employed proxy inquirers and queries, the second employed genuine inquirers and queries.

3.2

Tests of Accuracy

The 55% rule was "established" after a series of reference accuracy studies consistently indicated that just over half of the test questions were answered correctly. The domain of these tests only included ready-reference questions and not any other aspect of personal reference assistance such as directing readers to sources for resolving research queries and providing readers with bibliographic instruction. Although researchers frequently took efforts to ensure that proxy test questions were typical of actual reference queries, no study ever tried to ensure that the proportions of query types on the tests reflected the proportions of query types in practice. To use the findings of these studies to make any general predictions about the quality of reference service is nonsensical.

Of further cause for concern is that these studies are predicated on the belief that reference queries exist as entities outside the context of the inquirers who pose them. Reference service is examined as something performed by the librarian in relation to a question, and not to a reader. Such a concept is a clear contradiction to the reference philosophy of Wyer and Ranganathan.

Why, then, did these tests produce consistent findings if they suffered from the misapplication of theory? In actuality, the test queries in each study were often similar, and in some cases exactly the same queries were used. Logically, when similar tests are administered to samples from similar populations, the investigator should expect to see similar results.[13] The consistent findings suggest a high degree of reliability, but do not provide any degree of validity. Validity can only be argued in light of the theoretical basis of the study.

In 1967, Herbert Goldhor defined reference service as providing answers to fact-type questions and defined the quality of that service as the accuracy of the information being provided.[14] Looking at reference service as the product of an institution, he hypothesized that accuracy was dependent on the ability of the librarians at that library and the adequacy of the resources in the collection.[15] This conventional view was reflected in *Minimum Standards for Public Library Systems*, published by the Public Library Association the same year, which states that "quality library service depends upon adequate staff, collection, physical facilities, supplies, and equipment."[16] Although Goldhor never wrote it as such, this theory could be expressed as:

Performance = Accuracy = Staff Ability + Library Collection

Following up on an earlier study of a single public library,[17] Goldhor submitted in writing 10 test reference questions to "the person in charge" at 12 public libraries in the Minneapolis area. Despite the fact that librarians took about 20 minutes per question on average (based on five libraries reporting the total time taken), the accuracy rate was only 55% correct. This study was the first time the now-famous statistic on reference accuracy was reported in the literature. Goldhor made no attempt to correlate accuracy scores with any independent variables, and thus his theory remained untested until later researchers began to construct more elaborate measurement models.

During the same time that Goldhor was completing his investigation, Charles A. Bunge made the first attempt to link performance with staff ability by examining the effects of education and experience on reference service. He proposed efficiency, defined as the rate of accuracy over the time needed to answer a query, as a better measure of reference performance than accuracy by itself.[18] He hypothesized that professional training in reference work would enhance performance. His theory could be written as:

$$\text{Performance} = \text{Efficiency} = \frac{\text{Accuracy}}{\text{Time}}$$
$$= \text{Staff Ability} + \text{Library Collection Time}$$

Furthermore, he hypothesized that professionally trained reference librarians would outperform untrained staff members in terms of their ability to answer reference questions.[19] In other words, the librarian's skill in question-answering was the result of both the individual's education and experience in some proportion:

$$\text{Staff Ability} = \text{Education} + \text{Experience}$$

The relationship between efficiency and experience was actually expressed negatively. Bunge believed that the difference in performance between trained and untrained staff would decrease as the years of experience increased.[20] In other words, lack of education could be offset by experience. The underlying theory of accuracy is that for any given environment (e.g., library collection), accuracy over time is a function of the librarian's education and experience.

For his doctoral work, Bunge began to inquire into the relationship between professional education and performance on the reference desk. Studying nine pairs of participants with 1 to 20 years of experience in seven different libraries, he found that although trained reference librarians were not necessarily more accurate than untrained staff in answering questions, they were faster and more efficient than other staff.[21] Bunge used the Wilcoxon rank order coefficient, which was unable to test the cumulative effects of each of the independent variables, but did produce correlation values for individual variables. Among professional librarians, experience correlated with performance ($r^2 = 0.417$).[22] The data also indicates that in addition to the amount of time spent on the reference desk, the amount of time spent in selecting new books had a positive effect on efficiency.[23] Age alone and elapsed time from degree do not appear to be statistically significant predictors of success in the reference transaction.

Later, Bunge abstracted some information from his dissertation and made it more accessible by publishing his flowchart of "the major decisions and actions taken by the librarians in answering relatively simple 'fact' type questions."[24] Although efficiency was never widely adopted as an outcome measure, it was used by the Illinois State Library for several reference service research projects.[25]

During the year in which Bunge's research was published, Terence Crowley explicitly identified four of the five factors that are being used in the study detailed in the later chapters of this book. He described the reference transaction as a relationship between the inquirer, inquiry, and responder, and as a dialogue which utilizes a collection of resources prepared by an organization to resolve the inquiry.[26] Although Crowley identified these four factors, his study focused on only one independent variable, library expenditures. He hypothesized that those libraries which were able to spend more could build larger collections (resources) and hire and train more competent staff (responders). His theory could read as:

Performance = Accuracy = Library Collection + Staff Ability = Budget

Based on a study of 40 New Jersey public libraries where eight unobtrusive proxy users and Crowley himself posed 10 reference questions to each institution and recorded the number of accurate responses, the author found that accuracy is not a function of the library's budget as defined by expenditures per capita. Although the six "high budget" libraries answered more questions correctly (36 out of 60) than did six "low budget" libraries (29 out of 60), the difference was not determined to be statistically significant.[27] Although he admitted the possibility of intervening variables, Crowley did not analyze "experience, training, age, interests, imagination, and tenacity."[28]

These three studies score accuracy simplistically. Goldhor used a trivariate measure that labeled query resolutions as accurate ($y = 2$), partially accurate ($y = 1$), or inaccurate ($y = 0$). Both Bunge and Crowley both used a bivariate measure that identifies query resolutions as inaccurate ($y = 1$) or inaccurate ($y = 0$). When calculating an accuracy rate, Bunge measured it as a proportion of correct answers out of all queries attempted by the librarian, whereas Crowley calculated an accuracy rate as a proportion of correct answers out of all queries that were posed. Apparently dissatisfied with this rather simplistic measure, Thomas A. Childers introduced a more sophisticated measure that attempted to account for a broader range of outcomes. His system enumerated five different reference outcomes:

1. The answer given is wholly correct.
2. The answer given is wholly correct but uncertainty exists that this is so.
3. The answer given is partially correct.
4. The answer is wholly incorrect or no answer is given.
5. No attempt is made to answer the question.

This system allowed Childers flexibility in scoring. He could collapse categories in any combination and then assign numerical values in order to test different scales of scoring.[29] In order to maintain the objectivity of scoring, his study would only look at "requests for simple factual answers."[30]

In 1969, 2 years after Crowley's investigation, Childers performed the first analysis of reference service using multiple regression. This statistical method enabled him to analyze the cumulative effects of more than one independent variable on reference accuracy. For the first time, the theory espoused in Goldhor's research was tested using numerous independent variables to measure both staff ability and library collection. Unfortunately, Childers also examined some variables, such as hours of operation and circulation per capita, for which no theoretical relationship to reference service was advanced. Both of these variables were included in the final regression formula which explained 89.83% of the variance in the dependent variable.[31] However, regardless of the equation's high predictive power, the lack of theory prevented the ability to draw any causal inferences. Notwithstanding these criticisms, Childers did advance the level of statistical sophistication being used for analysis of reference service. Multiple regression would be used in five subsequent studies.[32]

Of these five studies, perhaps the most important was the first conducted in 1975 by Ronald Powell, who attempted to test the effects of reference collection size on reference performance. His review of the literature concluded that little statistical evidence existed to support the conventional theory that collection size has a significant effect on reference accuracy.[33] Powell, like Bunge, used the librarian rather than the library as the unit of study for his research. Consequently, Powell was able to test the cumulative effects of both librarian characteristics (e.g., education and experience) and library characteristics (e.g., collection size and budget) in his analysis. He determined that reference collection size had a curvilinear relationship to accuracy in that the size of the effect diminished as collection size exceeded 3500 volumes.[34] He further concluded that variables measuring librarian characteristics have a strong association with performance, specifically the attributes of having taken a number of reference and bibliography courses ($r = 0.25$) and being engaged in answering a substantive number of reference questions each week ($r = 0.52$).[35] The findings substantiate the theory that accuracy was dependent on the library collection and the ability of staff.

In another of these five studies, Hernon and McClure found extraordinarily low success rates in studying the reference service given in academic government document depository libraries in the northeast and southwest. Overall, only 37% of their unobtrusive questions were answered correctly, but that figure drops even lower when the day (3% on Saturday and Sunday) or time of day (15% in evening vs 42–43% during the morning or afternoon) is taken into consideration. Six factors including staff size, volumes held, depository items selected, and budget do not show any statistically significant relation to accuracy.[36]

Since the time of Childers's project in 1969, at least 25 studies of reference accuracy have been conducted that did not use multiple regression, including two in which Childers himself was an investigator. In one instance, a Pearson's product moment correlation was used.[37] In two instances, a chi-square test of significance was administered.[38] In all other instances, findings are reported as simple percentages of the number of questions answered correctly on a reference test.[39] Although many descriptive characteristics of libraries are discussed, none have been rigorously tested for association with reference performance. However, this body of research did serve to support, or perhaps "entrench," the 55% rule.

In the early 1980s, Nancy Van House conducted a study noteworthy for its methodological use of a panel of experienced reference librarians from outside the study area (i.e., California) to judge the quality of responses. The panel found that 79% were complete and correct, 15% were mostly correct, 1% were partially correct, 2% were incorrect, and 4% yielded no answer. Test questions were mostly fact-type or broad requests, such as requests for pictures or instructions. The average cost per reference question was $31, but this and other factors such as time spent were not correlated with accuracy. Her study is also one of the earliest to attempt to calculate a cost for the reference transaction.[40]

3.3

Tests of Satisfaction

As an alternative to accuracy, another measure of reference service which has been explored is user satisfaction. This vein of research tends to examine the effect of variables over which librarians have more direct control, such as behavior and communication abilities, rather than variables which are largely imposed on the librarian as part of the reference environment, such as collection size. Consequently, the results of these studies might have more immediate benefit to practitioners in the field. However, because of the greater complexity of the measures which are involved, significant findings have been harder to obtain. Notwithstanding this difficulty, research into user satisfaction has certainly contributed to heightening awareness within the profession regarding the theoretical variables that contribute to increased reference performance.

The earliest investigation evident in the literature pertaining to user satisfaction with reference service was performed in 1968 by the Enoch Pratt Public Library through a telephone survey of a random sample of readers who had asked questions at the reference desk. The findings indicate that readers were generally satisfied with the service, with only two out of 37 readers indicating that service quality was poor. The accuracy of information being provided to the reader was never examined. The purpose of this study was not to determine any statistically valid measure of satisfaction, or to test an instrument for gauging satisfaction, but merely to acquire some evidence regarding whether or not users were pleased with the service.[41]

In the early 1970s, Helen Gothberg conducted an experiment to determine the effect of verbal and nonverbal communication on user satisfaction with the reference process. Specifically, she examined the role of immediacy, the quality of liking or closeness in an interpersonal relationship, on three different dimensions of satisfaction: the user's satisfaction with the reference interview, the user's satisfaction with his or her own performance in the interview, and the user's satisfaction with the transfer of information between the librarian and the user.[42] Her research, based on speech communication theory, explored how empathy, warmth, and genuineness (or congruence) facilitate helping relationships and discussed how such feelings are dependent on both verbal and nonverbal behavior.

Gothberg studied two reference librarians using a two-by-two factorial design where the librarians role-played immediacy and nonimmediacy (defined as directness and intensity measured by physical distance and body, especially head orientation and eye contact). Using analysis of variance on data gathered from the observation of real reference transactions and a survey of real inquirers, she concluded that librarians who exhibit immediate communication skills will increase the amount of user satisfaction.[43] Gothberg noted that the "user was more satisfied with the reference interview when the reference librarian displayed immediate communication as opposed to nonimmediate communication."[44] The actual information transferred has less effect on user satisfaction.[45] Her work is important because for the first time, a study defines satisfaction as a function of librarians' behavior.

Although Gothberg's study is firmly based on theory, and the method for comparing 2 conditions is appropriate, data were gathered on only 2 librarians who conducted 15 reference transactions each. The small sample decreases the amount of confidence in the findings and later raised doubts when similar studies based on larger samples found no significant differences. While it is unlikely that anyone would argue against the importance of effective nonverbal communication during the reference transaction, the effects have yet to be measured statistically with any degree of consistency.

At the same time as Gothberg was investigating immediacy behavior, Elaine Jennerich was investigating the desirable attributes and behavior of reference librarians. During her doctoral work, Jennerich developed a rating sheet that presented a 5-point Likert scale of poor-to-excellent for evaluating the reference librarian's nonverbal interviewing skills: (1) eye contact; (2) gestures; (3) relaxed posture; (4) facial expression as well as verbal skills; (5) remembering; (6) premature diagnosis; (7) reflect feelings verbally; (8) restate or paraphrase comments; (9) open questions; (10) encouragers; (11) closure; and (12) opinions, suggestions.[46]

In a later work coauthored by Elaine and her spouse Edward, the Jennerichs discussed the ideal characteristics of reference librarians, identifying 11 attributes: (1) sense of humor; (2) dedication or commitment; (3) genuine liking for people; (4) good memory; (5) imagination; (6) creativity; (7) patience; (8) persistence; (9) energy; (10) stamina; (11) ability to jump quickly from one subject to another.[47] Their work is important because it more fully develops the counseling approach to the reference transaction.

In 1983, Marilyn J. Markham, Keith H. Stirling, and Nathan M. Smith conducted a study based on Gothberg's method, although the focus of their effort was determining the effect of self-disclosure, rather than immediacy, on user satisfaction. Self-disclosure is the extent to which an individual shares feelings or beliefs with another, and thereby increases the likelihood that the other person will respond candidly. Although Markham, Stirling, and Smith increased the number of reference staff from 2 to 4 and the number of interviews from 15 to 16 each, the findings of their study were subject to the same limitations of sample size which affected Gothberg's investigation. Markham, Stirling, and Smith concluded that self-disclosure has no significant effect on the outcome measure, although some significant differences do appear when items on the instrument are examined individually.[48] This finding suggests that the instrument itself required further testing and revision before conclusive findings could be obtained.

That same year, George D'Elia and Sandra Walsh conducted an analysis of user satisfaction with different forms of library service. Although reference service was not explicitly examined, variables concerning the openness and helpfulness of library staff were included. Their study utilized a sample of 523 library users, which was the largest sample taken for service evaluation up to that time. The goal of this investigation was to test a variable for measuring user satisfaction which had not been rigorously tested.[49] Multiple regression was used to measure the effects of numerous variables on the outcome variable. In reporting the findings, this study demonstrates a high methodological standard by discussing the content and construct validity of the measures and providing full descriptive statistics for each test. In conclusion, D'Elia and Walsh determined that the construct was not effective for describing relationships between user satisfaction and public library services.

> User behavior both in terms of evaluation and use of the library appears to be enigmatic. In the final analysis, this study demonstrates the complex nature of user behavior and our limited understanding of such behavior.[50]

This statement articulates the complexity of the reference transaction that argues the necessity for complex, multivariate methods of assessment.

In 1986, Joan Durrance introduced a new variable for measuring satisfaction when she asked users if they would return to a librarian for additional assistance in the future. Assuming that users of reference services are the best judges of quality service, Durrance and graduate students conducted 429 personal interviews with users of three Midwest academic libraries as they left the reference department during the morning, afternoon, evening, and weekend hours. Her objective was to examine factors affecting the client–librarian relationship. Her variables included the user's recognition of staff members and their different roles, the user's inclination to look for specific staff, and the user's inclination to return.[51] She found that only a tenth of those surveyed looked for particular staff, which she interpreted as a lack of true client–librarian relationship.[52] Most users expressed no criteria for selecting a librarian (including appearance, expertise, and personal knowledge). Reasons given for avoiding certain staff included "negative style of the staff member, based on past experience or perception."[53]

Also in 1986, Roma Harris and Gillian Michell reported the results of a more controlled investigation of user satisfaction that was not performed at the reference desk but in an experimental setting. A large sample of 320 public library users were asked to watch a video of a staged reference transaction and to answer questions about the behavior of the librarians. Using analysis of variance, the responses indicated that social variables such as gender, warmth of the librarian, and inclusion (i.e., the extent to which a librarian adopts a teaching role) have an effect on reference outcomes.[54] Although reference librarians may value attributes such as professional expertise and knowledge of the library's collection as indicators of competence, the users' judgment of the professionalism and competence of the reference librarian seems to depend more on communication skills.

In a follow-up study, Haris and Michell invited 64 librarians from different types of libraries to view a subset of the same videotapes. Comparisons were then drawn between the two groups (i.e., users and librarians). Overall, librarians were more critical than users in describing the competence of the librarians portrayed in the video. However, librarians and users agreed in perceiving the actors and actresses who exhibited more warmth as also being more competent. The investigators concluded that the "demeanor of the librarian toward the patron during the reference interview may be just as important as competently retrieving information."[55] Although these investigations did not serve to evaluate performance for any given institution, these studies did demonstrate a method for increasing the understanding of the reference process and for devising valid measures which can be used in later evaluation.

In 1987, Jo Bell Whitlatch conducted the most sophisticated study of user satisfaction with reference service that has been performed up to the present time. Proceeding from a strong theoretical base, Whitlatch tested a model of reference service that identifies three service outcomes: the librarian perception of service value, the user perception of service value, and the user's perception of success in locating needed materials.[56] Three stepwise multiple regressions were performed, one for each outcome variable, to identify strong predictor variables for performance. The findings indicate that a strong service orientation on the part of librarians and direct "feedback" from readers during the reference transaction contributed to higher levels of reference performance.[57]

The measures for independent variables Whitlatch used to predict service outcomes were originally developed for her study, but many were based on established measures from other disciplines (e.g., the Internal Work Motivation scale from the Michigan Organizational Assessment Questionnaire).[58] Her study employs 7-point Likert scales which were capable of registering a wide range of variation in the sample for any given variable. She also conducted a test of each measure for internal reliability prior to performing regression analysis. This strong concern with methodological issues exhibited by Whitlatch serves as an example to others and sets a high standard for subsequent researchers to follow. The study presented in the following chapters of this work emulates Whitlatch in many characteristics, but also goes beyond her efforts through the application of multilevel modeling.

In 1988, Marynelle DeVore-Chew, Brian Roberts, and Nathan M. Smith performed a study to examine the effects of nonverbal communication on user satisfaction. Although the method was similar to the earlier effort by Gothberg, the sample of 354 library users in this study was much larger. For the first time, multivariate analysis was used to examine reference service outcomes, although it was not effectively applied. No significant findings were observed. The investigators suggested that the sample was not large enough to account for differences in the population because of the high number of variables which were being examined, and thus the findings may be an example of Type II error in which an incorrect null hypothesis is accepted.[59]

In 1994, Patricia Dewdney and Catherine Sheldrick Ross described a study on the influence of librarian behavior on user satisfaction in public libraries ($N = 52$; 39 at main and 13 at branches) and academic libraries ($N = 24$; 19 main and 5 departmental). Seventy-seven MLIS students at the University of Western Ontario reported on their experiences in seeking help from a reference librarian. The students rated librarian behavior such as friendliness, pleasantness, understanding, and helpfulness on 7-point Likert scales. User satisfaction and Durrance's concept of the user's willingness to return were used as outcome measures. Their objective was to focus attention on sources of the user's dissatisfaction and to identify statistically significant relationships. The two highest relationships were overall satisfaction and helpfulness ($r = 0.81$) and friendliness ($r = 0.71$).[60]

3.4
Issues in Sampling and Observation

In terms of obtaining data that most closely resemble true field conditions, random sampling is the strongest defense against bias in any study design. While many studies in the area of reference service evaluation claim to utilize random sampling, it has rarely been executed. As mentioned earlier, the largest samples ever drawn for evaluation research suffer from self-selection bias. In addition, many studies take place within a single library system, or even within a single library. Although this may be appropriate for the goals and boundaries of the given investigation, the findings have little applicability to other institutions. Those studies that do gather data across multiple institutions fail to account for multilevel effects.

Of additional concern to the lack of random sampling is the prevalence of low sample sizes. Of 59 studies performed between 1967 and 1993, only 21 had more than 50 subjects, and 14 had 12 or fewer subjects.[61] Determining the preferred sample size for any study is affected by two concerns. First, as the number of variables being studied increases, the size of the sample should be increased. Second, as the magnitude of variance for a given variable within a population increases, the size of the sample should be increased. In the history of reference service evaluation, neither concern seems to have received a large amount of attention. Given the complexity of the subject, the number of variables being examined in most studies, and the lack of knowledge concerning the variance of variables, one would expect to see average sample sizes in the hundreds as a minimum.

The largest samples reported in the literature which have ever been drawn for the purposes of reference service evaluation all employ user satisfaction as the outcome measure (see Table 3.1).[62]

In these studies, after a reference transaction is completed, genuine inquirers are asked to fill out questionnaires regarding their satisfaction with the reference process. Whereas the Ohio–Wisconsin and California studies also attempt to measure accuracy, both studies employ the user's perception of accuracy (i.e., did you find the information you wanted?) as the outcome

Table 3.1
Largest Samples in Reference Service Evaluation Research

Study	Sample Size
Wisconsin–Ohio Reference Evaluation Program (1990)	4,800
California Reference Evaluation Program (1996)	13,000
D'Elia and Rodger (1996)	25,684

measure. This subjective measure is not comparable to the objective measures used in traditional accuracy studies.

The large samples in these studies produce high levels of statistical power, reducing the risk that the findings suffer from either Type I or Type II error. However, these studies suffer from threats to content validity in that the sample does not cover the total domain of library users. All three studies rely on users who are willing to fill out survey questionnaires. This practice results in self-selection bias since it is probable that those users who have good experiences are more willing to take the time to fill out the survey. Of additional concern is the fact that library staff are probably reticent to offer a survey to those users who are unpleasant or express dissatisfaction with service. Consequently, the subjects are not randomly selected. No attempt is made in any of these three studies to determine to what extent the sample is representative of the total population.

In addition to sampling practices, the method of observation can also affect the quality of data. Several researchers have suggested that unobtrusive observation of reference transactions will produce evidence that more closely resembles true field conditions than obtrusive observation.[63] Librarians who are aware they are being tested have greater motivation to perform well. Because of the logic and prevalence of this belief, more than half of the reference evaluation studies which test accuracy have been unobtrusive. Unfortunately, the practice of unobtrusive observation limits the investigator's capability to probe into the opinions and attitudes of librarians and users. Consequently, all of the studies which examine user satisfaction must employ obtrusive methods.

To what extent does obtrusive observation bias findings? Weech and Goldhor determined that reference departments evaluated using obtrusive methods answered 15% more questions correctly than those evaluated using unobtrusive methods, yet also determined that the statistical relationship between the method of evaluation and the results of evaluation was slight.[64] However, this finding is based on a sample of only five libraries. A larger sample might have resulted in a greater value for that relationship.

This evidence seems to indicate that obtrusive observation might bias findings toward describing higher levels of performance than would actually occur under field conditions. Nonetheless, the use of obtrusive observation is essential in order to gain personal information from human subjects. This personal data can be used to help investigators develop models of the reference process. Once this process is more clearly understood, sophisticated measures of service outcomes can then be devised which might enable unobtrusive observation of satisfaction and utility. Such measures could include recording the visible, nonverbal indicators of satisfaction and interest in the reference transaction, or surveying library users without the knowledge of the librarians.

3.5

Multivariate Analysis

Carol Kronus noted that much of the prior library user research is based on simple correlations and hence confounded because of the nonindependence of variables. In reviewing a study of public library use in Illinois, she found that the 14 variables identified in the study as having an influence on library use were partially correlated and went on to create a prediction model based on just three factors: education, family life cycle (marital status, family size, and employment status), and urban residence. Kronus argued the need for a more sophisticated approach to user analysis, such as multiple regression and factor analytic studies.[65]

Murfin and Gugelchuk were the first to utilize cluster analysis in comparing 35 variables related to the reference transaction.[66] Although this method cannot be considered a true multivariate method because it does not require that dependent variables be identified, cluster analysis is a precursor to other forms of multivariate analysis, such as factor analysis or canonical correlation. Murfin and Gugelchuk thus raised the level of statistical complexity being used in reference service evaluation beyond the sole reliance on univariate procedures such as multiple regression and analysis of variance (ANOVA).

As mentioned earlier, the first multivariate study in the area of reference service evaluation was performed by DeVore-Chew, Roberts, and Smith. They used the method of multivariate analysis of variance (MANOVA), although their sample was not large enough to use the method effectively.[67]

All other studies to the present have employed univariate statistical procedures to measure reference service. In cases where more then one dependent variable was examined, each variable was tested separately using a univariate method. Since the time of these initial investigations, advances in computer software have made it feasible for investigators to utilize multivariate methods.

3.6

Failure Analysis of Reference Service

While research presented in the literature clearly suffers from many methodological shortcomings, much anecdotal evidence has been acquired regarding what contributes to quality reference service. When the question is examined conversely, several reasons are suggested as causes for reference failure.

In their earliest work, Jahoda and Culnan studied 26 science and chemistry libraries for 1 month, but found only 47 unanswered questions. The reasons given for not answering these questions were categorized as: (1) no reference tool published to answer the question; (2) reference tool published but not in library; (3) existing reference tool not sufficiently up to date; (4) existing tool does not have adequate index; (5) existing tool does not have the information listed in a way to answer question; (6) answer probably in library — no time to answer; (7) question outside the scope of the library; (8) question not properly negotiated; and (9) other.[68]

Later research suggests that this failure to answer the questions was due to three general reasons: (1) 45% of the questions were unanswered because of reference tool limitations (i.e., categories 1, 3, 4, and 5); (2) 29% of the questions were unanswered because of library limitations (i.e., categories 2 and 7); and (3) 25% of the questions were unanswered because of personnel limitations (i.e., categories 6 and 8).[69]

Although Jahoda and Culnan identified poor query negotiation as one cause of failure, the remainder of their findings are collection-centered. Essentially, they argued that failure is frequently caused by a lack of adequate tools or resources. Other researchers paid more attention to deficiencies in the knowledge of librarians as a potential cause of failure. Investigators studying reference service in public libraries in New York cited both librarians' lack of familiarity with the library collection and lack of awareness of community resources as reasons for failure in answering queries.[70] Such explanations focus on inadequacies of the professional, rather than the inadequacy of information resources. In the literature, the behavior of the librarian is the most frequently discussed cause of failure.

In numerous studies the primary reason posited for not being able to answer a question was the librarian's failure to probe adequately.[71] Too often, librarians will take a question at face value without attempting to determine the actual information need. Wise noted that when librarians were asked for information about a given individual, two-thirds of those queried automatically assumed that the library user wanted short biographical information and began searching for an answer without any further question negotiation. Some studies have been specifically designed to study this phenomenon, using what are loosely termed "escalator questions."[72] These are questions which are initially presented to the librarian with missing or faulty information worded in such a way as to misrepresent the actual test question, requiring the librarian to probe in order to achieve success.

The failure to make referrals is another common cause attributed to reference failure. In some studies, librarians exhibited an apparent reluctance to make referrals to other agencies.[73] Such a finding is surprising when one considers that between Gale's *Encyclopedia of Associations* and the *United States Government Manual*, the librarian has more than 20,000 agencies and organizations from which to choose. Many librarians may find it difficult to accept the concept of others being able to resolve a question when they themselves have been unable to do so, or may equate the act of referral as personal failure. An alternative rationale is that librarians are unwilling to endorse the services of another agency that they know little about and have no control over. Regardless of the reason, this practice of failing to refer reduces accuracy rates because some studies did score higher points for making a referral than for giving no answer.

The failure to conclude the reference transaction with any kind of follow-up question to determine if the library user has received the answer they were after has a substantial impact on reference accuracy. In a study of public library reference service in Maryland, Ralph Gers and Lillie Serward found that librarians only used follow-up questions approximately 12% of the time even though, as they note, it "may be the single most important factor in the interview."[74] Librarians may be hesitant to risk uncovering more complex questions from a seemingly satisfied library user, particularly when the desk is busy or it is close to closing time. However, all librarians should conclude each reference transaction with the simple question, "Did you find what you wanted?" This practice would prevent the situation of having a user leave the library unsatisfied while the librarian is under the impression that the information need has been met. For this reason, Gers and Seward note that asking follow-up questions "may be the single most important factor in the interview."

Ross and Dewdney's analysis of negative closure is the most comprehensive, detailed examination of how unprofessional behavior on the part of the librarian leads to service failure, often as the result of the librarian consciously or subconsciously attempting to end the interview quickly rather than serve the needs of the user. Including those behaviors mentioned above, Ross and Dewdney presented a list of negative actions that will prevent a successful transaction: (1) providing an unmonitored referral, (2) immediately referring users elsewhere, (3) implying the user should have looked elsewhere first, (4) convincing the user to accept other information more easily found, (5) warning the user to expect defeat, (6) encouraging the user to give up the search, (7) signaling nonverbally that the transaction is over, (8) signaling verbally that the transaction is over, (9) claiming that the information is not in the library or doesn't exist, and (10) leaving to track down a document and not returning.[75] The authors also identified a set of counterstrategies they observed users employing to prevent a negative conclusion to the transaction. At root, all of these counterstrategies rely on the user's persistence and unwillingness to let a question go unanswered.[76] Ideally, all reference professionals should share this same zeal.

References

1. Samuel Rothstein, "The Measurement and Evaluation of Reference Service," *Library Trends* 12 (January 1964): 456–472; Ronald R. Powell, "Reference Effectiveness: A Review of the Research," *Library and Information Science Research* 6 (July–September 1984): 3–19; Kenneth D. Crews, "The Accuracy of Reference Service: Variables for Research and Implementation," *Library and Information Science Research* 10 (July 1988): 331–355; John V. Richardson Jr.,

Knowledge-Based Systems for General Reference Work: Applications, Problems, and Progress (San Diego: Academic Press, 1995); Matthew L. Saxton, "Evaluation of Reference Service in Public Libraries Using a Hierarchical Linear Model: Applying Multiple Regression Analysis to a Multi-level Research Design," Ph.D. dissertation, University of California, Los Angeles, June 2000.

2. Matthew L. Saxton, "Reference Service Evaluation and Meta-analysis: Findings and Methodological Issues," *Library Quarterly* 67 (July 1997): 267–289.

3. Mary DeJong, "Where Does the Reference Librarian's Time Go?" *Wisconsin Library Bulletin* 22 (January 1926): 7–8.

4. Edith Guerrier, "The Measurement of Reference Service in a Branch Library," *Bulletin of the American Library Association* 29 (September 1935): 632–637.

5. Ibid., p. 632.

6. Faith H. Hyers, "Librarians: Savants or Dilletantes?" *Pacific Bindery Talk* 8 (February 1936): 87–89.

7. Dorothy E. Cole, "An Analysis of Adult Reference Work in Libraries,"M.A. thesis, University of Chicago, September 1943.

8. Ibid., 28.

9. Ibid., 31.

10. Ibid., 35.

11. Ibid., 37.

12. Florence Van Hoesen, "An Analysis of Adult Reference Work in Public Libraries as an Approach to the Content of a Reference Course," Ph.D. dissertation, University of Chicago, December 1948, 64–67.

13. Ian Douglas, "Reducing Failures in Reference Service," *RQ* 28 (Fall 1988): 95–96.

14. Herbert Goldhor, *A Plan for the Development of Public Library Service in the Minneapolis–Saint Paul Metropolitan Area* (Minneapolis: Department of Education, Library Division, 1967), 29.

15. Ibid., 10.

16. Public Library Association, *Minimum Standards for Public Library Systems, 1966* (Chicago: American Library Association, 1967).

17. Herbert Goldhor, "Reference Service Analysis," *Illinois Libraries* 42 (May 1960): 319–322.

18. Charles A. Bunge, *Professional Education and Reference Efficiency*, Research Series No. 11 (Springfield, IL: Illinois State Library, 1967), 24–27.

19. Ibid., 20.

20. Ibid., 30.

21. Ibid., 56, 58–60.

22. Ibid., 72.

23. Ibid., 61–63.

24. Charles A. Bunge, "Charting the Reference Query," *RQ* 8 (Summer 1969): 245–260.

25. Danny P. Wallace, "An Index of Quality of Illinois Public Library Service," in *Illinois Library Statistical Report*, No. 10, 1983; id., An Index of Quality of Illinois Public Library Service," in *Illinois Library Statistical Report*, No. 10, 1984; Loriene Roy, "An Index of Quality of Illinois Public Library Service, 1984," in *Illinois Library Statistical Report*, No. 17, 1985; id., "An Index of Quality of Illinois Public Library Service, 1985," in *Illinois Library Statistical Report*, No. 17, 1985; and Jeanette Drone, "An Index of Quality of Illinois Public Library Service, 1986," in *Illinois Library Statistical Report*, No. 20, 1987.

26. Terence Crowley, "The Effectiveness of Information Service in Medium Size Public Libraries," in *Information Service in Public Libraries: Two Studies* (Metuchen, NJ: Scarecrow Press, 1971), 16–21.

27. Ibid., 52–53.

28. Ibid., 15.

29. Thomas A. Childers, "Telephone Information Service in Public Libraries: A Comparison of Performance and the Descriptive Statistics Collected by the States of New Jersey," in *Information Service in Public Libraries: Two Studies* (Metuchen, NJ: Scarecrow Press, 1971), 116–117.

30. Ibid., 81, 103.

31. Ibid., 157–159.

32. Peter Hernon and Charles R. McClure, "Testing the Quality of Reference Service Provided by Academic Depository Libraries: A Pilot Study," in *Communicating Public Access to Government Information*, edited by Peter Hernon (Westport, CT: Greenwood Press, 1983), 109–123; Marcia J. Myers, "Telephone Reference/Information Services in Academic Libraries in the Southeast," in *The Accuracy of Telephone Reference/Information Services in Academic Libraries: Two Studies* (Metuchen, NJ: Scarecrow Press, 1983); Jassim M. Jirjees, "Telephone Reference/Information Services in Selected Northeastern College Libraries," in *Telephone Reference/Information Services in Academic Libraries: Two Studies* (Metuchen, NJ: Scarecrow Press, 1983); Ronald R. Powell, "An Investigation of the Relationship between Reference Collection Size and Other Reference Service Factors and Success in Answering Reference Questions," in *Success in Answering Reference Questions: Two Studies* (Metuchen, NJ: Scarecrow Press, 1987); Frances Benham, "A Prediction Study of Reference Accuracy among Recently Graduated Working Reference Librarians (1975–1979)," in *Success in Answering Reference Questions: Two Studies* (Metuchen, NJ: Scarecrow Press, 1987).

33. Powell, "An Investigation," 166, 170.

34. Ibid., 238, 251–252, 257.

35. Ibid., 226–234, 258–259.

36. Hernon and McClure, "Testing the Quality."

37. Ralph A. Lowenthal, "Preliminary Indications of the Relationship between Reference Morale and Performance," *RQ* 29 (Spring 1990): 380–393.

38. Michael J. Ramsden, *Performance Measurement of Some Melbourne Public Libraries: A Report to the Library Council of Victoria* (Melbourne, Australia: Library Council of Victoria, 1978); Kathy A. Way, "Quality Reference Service in Law School Depository Libraries: A Cause for Action," *Government Publications Review* 14 (1987): 207–209.

39. Geraldine King and Rachel Berry, *Evaluation of the University of Minnesota Library Reference Department Telephone Information Service: A Pilot Study* (Minneapolis: University of Minnesota, 1973); David E. House, "Reference Efficiency or Reference Deficiency," *Library Association Record* 76 (November 1974): 222–223; Peat, Marwick, Mitchell & Co., *California Public Library Systems: A Comprehensive Review with Guidelines for the Next Decade* (Los Angeles: Peat, Marwick, Mitchell & Co., 1975; Washington, D.C.: ERIC Document Reproduction Service ED 105 906, 1975); Thomas Childers, "The Test of Reference," *Library Journal* 105 (15 April 1980): 924–928; Janine Schmidt, "Reference Performance in College Libraries," *Australian Academic and Research Libraries* 11 (June 1980): 87–95; Nancy Van House DeWath, *California Statewide Reference Referral Service: Analysis and Recommendations* (Rockville, MD: King Research Inc., 1981; Washington, D.C.: ERIC Document Reproduction Service ED 206 311, 1981); Terry Weech and Herbert Goldhor, "Obtrusive versus Unobtrusive Evaluation of Reference Service in Five Illinois Libraries," *Library Quarterly* 52 (October 1982): 305–324; Peter Wise, *The Unobtrusive Testing Survey*, Research and Development Report no. 6 (Kent, United Kingdom: Kent County Library, 1982); Lynn Yellot and Robert Barrier, "Evaluation of a Public Library's Health Information Service," *Medical Reference Services Quarterly* 2 (Summer 1983): 31–49; Beverly Rubinstein, "Maryland Reference Survey Concludes Our Service Is Worse Than We Thought," *The Crab* 14 (September 1984): 7–8; Nancy Van House and Thomas Childers, "Unobtrusive Evaluation of a Reference Referral Network: The California Experience," *Library and Information Science Research* 6 (July–September 1984): 305–319; Ralph Gers and Lillie J. Seward, "Improving Reference Performance: Results of a Statewide Survey," *Library Journal* 110 (November 1985): 32–35; Patsy J. Hansel,

"Unobtrusive Evaluation for Improvement: The CCPL&IC Experience," *North Carolina Libraries* 44 (Summer 1986): 69–75; Peter Hernon and Charles R. McClure, "The Quality of Academic and Public Library Reference Service Provided for NTIS Products and Services: Unobtrusive Test Results," *Government Information Quarterly* 3 (May 1986): 117–132; id., "Unobtrusive Reference Testing: The 55 Percent Rule," *Library Journal* 111 (15 April 1986): 37–41; Eleanor Jo Rodger and Jane Goodwin, "To See Ourselves as Others See Us: A Cooperative Do-It-Yourself Reference Accuracy Study," *Reference Librarian* 18 (Summer 1987): 135–147; Vaughan P. Birbeck and Kenneth A. Whittaker, "Room for Improvement: An Unobtrusive Testing of British Public Library Reference Service," *Public Library Journal* 2 (July–August 1987): 55–60; Roy Williams, "Reference Services in Public Libraries," *Library Association Record* 89 (September 1987): 469; Peter Lea and Lotta Jackson, "The Exception or the Rule? The Quality of the Reference Service in Public Libraries," *Library Association Record* 90 (October 1988): 582, 585; John O. Christensen, Larry D. Benson, H. Julene Butler, Blaine H. Hall, and Don H. Howard, "An Evaluation of Reference Desk Service," *College & Research Libraries* 50 (July 1989): 468–483; Prince George's County Memorial Library System [Maryland], "Branches' Unobtrusive Survey Results Up from Last Year," *PGCMLS Staff Newsletter* 18 (9 May 1990): 1, 5; Michael C. Head and Rita Marcella, "A Testing Question: The Quality of Reference Services in Scottish Public Libraries," *Library Review* 42 (1993): 7–13.

40. Van House DeWath, *California Statewide*.

41. Enoch Pratt Public Library, *Telephone Reference Service Evaluation* [Memorandum] (1968), 1–3.

42. Helen M Gothberg, "User Satisfaction with a Librarian's Immediate and Nonimmediate Verbal-Nonverbal Communication," "Ph.D. dissertation, University of Denver, August 1974, and id., "Immediacy: A Study of Communication Effect on the Reference Process," *Journal of Academic Librarianship* 2 (July 1976): 126–129.

43. Gothberg, "Immediacy," 129.

44. Gothberg, "User Satisfaction," 70–71

45. Ibid., 72.

46. Elaine Z. Jennerich and Edward J. Jennerich, "Teaching the Reference Interview," *Journal of Education for Librarianship* 17 (Fall 1976): 108.

47. Id., *The Reference Interview as a Creative Art* (Littleton, CO: Libraries Unlimited, 1987).

48. Marilyn J. Markham, Keith H. Stirling, and Nathan M. Smith, "Librarian Self-disclosure and Patron Satisfaction in the Reference Interview," *RQ* 22 (Summer 1983): 371.

49. George D'Elia and Sandra Walsh, "User Satisfaction with Library Service—A Measure of Public Library Performance?" *Library Quarterly* 53 (April 1983): 115.

50. Ibid., 132.

51. Joan C. Durrance, "The Influence of Reference Practices on the Client–Librarian Relationship," *College & Research Libraries* 47 (January 1986): 57–67.

52. Ibid., 64.

53. Ibid., 65.

54. Roma M. Harris and B. Gillian Michell, "The Social Context of Reference Work: Assessing the Effects of Gender and Communication Skills on Observers' Judgement of Competence," *Library and Information Science Research* 8 (January–March 1986): 94–99.

55. Id., "Evaluating the Reference Interview: Some Factors Influencing Patrons and Professionals," *RQ* 27 (Fall 1987): 99–100.

56. Jo Bell Whitlatch, "Client/Service Provider Perceptions of Reference Service Outcomes in Academic Libraries: Effects of Feedback and Uncertainty," Ph.D. dissertation, University of California, Berkeley, 1987, and id., *The Role of the Academic Reference Librarian* (New York: Greenwood Press, 1990), 23.

57. Ibid., 26–29.

58. Ibid., 72.

59. Marynelle DeVore-Chew, Brian Roberts, and Nathan M. Smith, "The Effects of Reference Librarians Nonverbal Communications on the Patrons' Perceptions of the Library, Librarians, and Themselves," *Library and Information Science Research* 10 (October–December 1988): 397–398.

60. Patricia Dewdney and Catherine Sheldrick Ross, "Flying a Light Aircraft: Reference Service Evaluation from a User's Viewpoint," *RQ* 34 (Winter 1994): 217–230.

61. Saxton, "Reference Service Evaluation," 283–288.

62. Charles A. Bunge, "Factors Related to Output Measures for Reference Services in Public Libraries: Data from Thirty-six Libraries," *Public Libraries* 29 (January–February 1990): 42; Thomas Childers, personal communication (Tallahassee, Fla., 2 November 1996); George D'Elia and Eleanor Jo Rodger, "Customer Satisfaction with Public Libraries," *Public Libraries* 35 (September–October 1996): 292.

63. Childers, 'Telephone Information Service," 120; Crowley, 25; and Myers, 15.

64. Weech and Goldhor, 316–319.

65. Carol L. Kronus, "Patterns of Adult Library Use: A Regression Path Analysis," *Adult Education* 23 (Winter 1973): 115–131.

66. Marjorie E. Murfin and Gary M. Gugelchuck, "Development and Testing of a Reference Prediction Assessment Instrument," *College & Research Libraries* 48 (July 1987): 324–325.

67. DeVore-Chew, Roberts, and Smith.

68. Gerald Jahoda and Mary Culnan, "Unanswered Science and Technology Questions," *American Documentation* 19 (January 1968): 100.

69. Charles A. Bunge quoting Elin Christianson in his Research in Reference column entitled "The Reference Query," *RQ* 8 (Spring 1969): 210.

70. *Emerging Library Systems: The 1963–1966 Evaluation of the New York State Public Library Systems* (Albany, NY: The University of the State of New York, State Education Department, Division of Evaluation, 1967), 39–42.

71. Egill Halldorsson and Marjorie E. Murfin, "The Performance of Professionals and Nonprofessionals in the Reference Interview," *College & Research Libraries* 38 (September 1977): 394; Childers, "The Test," 926; Wise, 27; Gers and Seward, 33; Rodger and Goodwin, 141–142; Lea and Jackson, 582; and Christensen *et al.*, 470.

72. Halldorsson and Murfin, 387; Childers, "The Test," 925–926.

73. Wise, 27; Myers, 109; Hernon and McClure, "Unobtrusive," 40–41; and Christensen *et al.*, 472.

74. Gers and Seward, 34.

75. Catherine Sheldrick Ross and Patricia Dewdney, "Negative Closure: Strategies and Counter-Strategies in the Reference Transaction," *Reference and User Services Quarterly* 38 (Winter 1998): 154–157.

76. Ibid., 157–160.

4

Multilevel Modeling and Reference Service Evaluation

This chapter begins with a discussion of the assumptions that must be met in conducting hierarchical linear modeling and how this study addresses the common threats to validity. Next, the target population will be identified, followed by an explanation of the sampling methods that will be used. Afterwards, a technical description of each variable will meticulously explain how each variable is to be measured. The chapter concludes with an organizational plan outlining the steps involved in conducting the experiment.

4.1

Assumptions and Threats to Validity

Hierarchical linear modeling requires that the following assumptions be met[1]:

1. All relevant variables have been included in the model.
2. All independent variables are fixed and measured without error.
3. The dependent and independent variables have a linear relationship.
4. The error term for each observation is independent and normally distributed with a mean of 0 and constant variance for every transaction (i.e., the first-level unit) performed by each librarian (i.e., the second-level unit) within each library (i.e., the third-level unit).
5. The error term is not correlated with the independent variables.
6. The vectors of random errors at the second and third levels exhibit multivariate normality.
7. The set of second-level independent variables is independent of the second-level error.
8. The set of third-level independent variables is independent of the third-level error.
9. The errors at first, second, and third levels are independent.

In addition to addressing the assumptions listed above, all data will be screened before analysis is performed. Each outcome variable has been examined for normality to determine whether these assumptions have been violated. Outliers, which are defined in this study as any value greater than two standardized residuals beyond the mean,[2] have been deleted from the sample. For cases with missing data, the conventional method of replacing missing data with the mean for that particular variable has been utilized. No systematic bias in variables with missing data was identified.

The literature review identified many threats to validity in previous research. To neutralize these threats, five elements have been included in the design of this study:

1. Obtaining data on a large sample ($N \geq 5000$)
2. Using random sampling of sites to minimize bias
3. Minimizing the distrust of participating librarians to reduce bias by guaranteeing confidentiality and inviting them to help design portions of the instrument unique to their institution
4. Achieving high participation among librarians to minimize selection bias by engaging enthusiasm for successful completion of the project and promising valuable results
5. Achieving high participation among library users to minimize selection bias by designing a survey instrument that can be completed easily and quickly

These efforts should minimize the effects of bias and help strengthen arguments against potential criticism regarding the validity of the study findings.

4.2

The Population, Sampling, and Sample Size

The target population of this study is all reference transactions that occur in public libraries. According to the National Center for Education Statistics, this population totaled approximately 242.7 million transactions in fiscal year 1993.[3]

All 76 public library jurisdictions in the California counties of Los Angeles and Orange were invited to participate in the study. The sampling of reference transactions occurred during a 3-week period. Data collection occurred for 1 hour at a time. Sampling took place twice a day on each day the library was open 6 or more hours, and once a day on each day the library was open less than 6 hours. The total amount of hours sampled at each library over the 3-week study period varied from approximately 30 to 36 hours depending on the service hours of the institution. Each hour-long timeslot was randomly staggered throughout the 3-week test period. All reference queries asked during each hour-long timeslot were recorded.

Reference transactions were recorded by having each librarian write down the negotiated query, the answer that was given, and the source. Although the task seems labor intensive, similar techniques have also been used successfully in past studies.[4] Writing down the question and answer arguably takes less time than answering a 15-item questionnaire about the reference transaction. If the volume of traffic at the reference desk grew so busy that it became unfeasible to record every query, librarians were asked to record as many as they could and tally the remainder of queries they did not record. In this fashion, the investigator was able to determine what proportion of queries during the sampling period were captured and how many queries were unrecorded.

The librarian receiving the query determined whether or not the query was a ready-reference or a research query. Although the boundary between the two query types is not clearly demarcated, Hutchins proposed a general distinction. She wrote that a ready-reference query requires locating information in a published source that has already addressed the question, whereas a research query requires the reader to collect and analyze information in order to draw his or her own interpretations. She specifically criticized using the measure of time it takes to answer the question as a means of distinguishing the two.[5] Bereft of any mechanical means for labeling queries, this study relied on the judgment of participants. These random individual judgments spread over a large number of transactions should have prevented any systematic error from skewing the data.

To facilitate the recording effort, some ready-reference questions were identified as frequently asked questions (FAQs). A FAQ is a question that is asked so frequently that the query resolution has become routine. Each library has its own unique set of FAQs which arise from the most common needs of the service population and the special strengths of the library collection. Reference librarians at each site were surveyed to determine the top five most frequently asked questions for their library. Once these queries were identified, they were enumerated on the transaction instrument and librarians recorded them by simply "checking off" the category. FAQs were tabulated to determine what proportion they represent of the total sample.

During the sampling period, directional queries were simply tallied. By categorizing not only reference queries but also any interaction with the public in this manner, reference staff stayed focused on the goal of recording each and every transaction. Ideally, this practice also prevented librarians from initially dismissing queries posed by the homeless or other disenfranchised persons if these interactions developed into genuine reference transactions.

4.3

Variables

As discussed in the first chapter, all the variables in this study were measured on an ordinal 7-point Likert scale. The seven degrees on the scale limit the influence of range restriction by allowing a wide variety of response. Using a 7-point scale for each variable also facilitated the interpretation of standardized scores. In accordance with standard practice in the behavioral sciences, such variables can be treated as approximating an interval scaled variable.

4.3.1 Dependent Variables

This study assessed reference service performance in terms of three desirable outcomes: utility, satisfaction, and accuracy. Past research supports the idea that accuracy and satisfaction are unrelated, but this situation might be the result of range restriction in the case of measuring accuracy as a bivariate variable (i.e., accurate = 1, inaccurate = 0). Logically, better service should result in better communication that would increase the degree of accuracy of the information being given to the user, as well as increasing the probable utility of that information. Allowing additional degrees of response in the measurement of accuracy could reflect a relationship that has been heretofore hidden.

These three outcomes will be measured by four variables. Two variables will measure utility. One variable will measure satisfaction. One variable will measure accuracy. These variables are labeled, coded, and scaled as follows:

COMPLETENESS (Code: COMPLETE)

Users will select a value on a scale of 1 to 7 to indicate their degree of agreement with the statement, "I found everything I needed."

USEFULNESS (Code: USEFUL)

Users will select a value on a scale of 1 to 7 to indicate their degree of agreement with the statement, "I found useful information today."

These two constructs only measure the immediate utility that users perceive from brief inspection of the materials or information provided to them by the librarian. This trait might be more descriptively named "short-term utility." Ideally, measuring utility would occur at some later point after users had enough time to work with the information they received. However, measuring "long-term utility" would require gaining the consent of users to be contacted and obtaining addresses, telephone numbers, or e-mail addresses. At present, short-term utility may be the only quality that can be feasibly measured. One hopes that this variable would have a high correlation with a variable measuring long-term utility. In the future, a study whose object is to correlate short-term and long-term utility would indicate how well the first measure could predict the second.

Whitlatch measured some facets of utility when she asked users whether they had received enough information and also asked them to evaluate the degree of relevance the materials had to the query.[6] Relevance is an imprecise term that may confuse many public library users (not to mention confusing librarians). In this study, the question of usefulness is asked directly and simply.

SATISFACTION (Code: SATISFY)

Users will select a value on a scale of 1 to 7 to indicate their degree of agreement with the statement, "I am satisfied with the service I received."

This measure is a variation of the type used by Whitlatch. In order to encourage more users to fill out the survey, the question asked here has been rephrased to appear less clinical than her version, "Indicate how satisfied you are on the following scale."[7]

ACCURACY (Code: ACCURATE)

Each transaction response will be awarded a value on a scale of 1 to 7. Each value is defined as follows:

7 — Wholly accurate: A complete answer, and all information is correct.
6 — Partially accurate: An incomplete answer, but the information provided is correct.
5 — Accurate referral: User is referred to an agency that can supply the correct answer.
4 — No answer.
3 — Partially inaccurate: User is given both accurate and inaccurate information.
2 — Inaccurate referral: User is referred to an agency that cannot supply the correct answer.
1 — Inaccurate answer: No correct information is given.

The rank order indicates increasing degrees of accuracy and information being provided. On this scale, a complete answer is scored higher than a referral because more information is being provided to the user. A "No answer" is scored higher than an inaccurate answer because less inaccurate information is being provided to the user. An inaccurate referral is scored higher than an inaccurate answer because the user receiving an inaccurate referral might ultimately be directed to an appropriate agency and obtain the accurate answer, whereas providing a wrong answer does not leave the user with any other option to pursue.

This scale is a modification of Childers's design for assessing the accuracy of telephone queries.[8] According to the Childers scale, distinction is made between a librarian refusing to answer a question and a librarian searching for an answer but finding none and making no reply. In this scale, both outcomes are categorized together as a nonanswer because the response to the user is the same. Also, because it was only intended for ready-reference queries, Childers' scale did not account for the role played by referrals in answering queries.

Unlike previous attempts to measure rates of accuracy, this study will examine real queries drawn from the field rather than a set of test queries. Furthermore, this study will not be limited to ready-reference queries as has been practiced in the past. Consequently, the resolution of many queries in this study will not require a discrete, factual response, but will involve multiple sources and multiple search strategies to satisfy the needs of the user. Sometimes, the response will require the librarian to provide instruction to the user. In order to assess accuracy according to the foregoing scale in a consistent manner for all queries, each query response was examined to determine whether the best source was used, an effective strategy was implemented, or an appropriate referral was given. Thus, this study investigates accuracy in terms of the librarian's recommendations to the user, rather than the specific data obtained by the user.

4.3.2 First-Level Independent Variables

The study examines nine different variables as first level predictors of reference performance. These variables describe either characteristics of the query, characteristics of the service behavior exhibited by the librarian during the transaction, or characteristics of the user. The following descriptions explain how each variable is operationalized.

Characteristics of the query are described using two variables, query difficulty and query currency.

QUERY DIFFICULTY (Code: DIFFICULT)

Each query will be scored on a scale of 1 to 7 as to its level of difficulty with a value 7 indicating great difficulty and a value of 1 indicating low difficulty.

What makes one question more difficult than another? Is the degree of difficulty merely a situational condition dependent on the librarian's own knowledge state? Or does a question contain identifiable elements that make it more difficult to answer? In reviewing the literature, Childers, Lopata, and Stafford concluded that no standard definitions of query difficulty exist.[9] Who is the best judge of difficulty? Often, a reference transaction is a difficult process not because of the query but because of the personality of the inquirer or the library user's lack of research skills. A librarian's assessment of the query is likely to be biased by the difficulty experienced in working with the user. To separate user traits from query traits, difficulty was assessed by outside observers. A panel of judges rated the queries for difficulty.

QUERY CURRENCY (Code: CURRENT)

Each query will be awarded a value on a scale of 1 to 7 defined as follows:

7 — The required information was produced within this week.
6 — The required information was produced within 2 weeks.
5 — The required information was produced within this month.
4 — The required information was produced within 3 months.
3 — The required information was produced within 6 months.
2 — The required information was produced within this year.
1 — The required information was produced more than 1 year ago.

Current awareness has long been recognized as a significant problem leading to reference failure.[10] This scale represents currency as a property that decreases exponentially as time passes. In other words, a query regarding something that occurred 6 years ago has about the same degree of currency as something that occurred 8 years ago. However, something that occurred this past week has a far greater degree of currency than something that occurred last month.

Characteristics of the service behavior exhibited by the librarian are described using four variables: readiness, interest, understanding, and verification. In 1996, the Reference and User Services Association (RUSA) published a set of standards outlining behavior, which is generally accepted as contributing to improved performance.[11] These behaviors are concerned with optimizing the quality of communication between the librarian and library user. These standards have been operationalized here in four questions that will be addressed to library users. This study is the first attempt to test these standards empirically. These variables are measured as follows:

READINESS (Code: READINESS)

Users will select a value on a scale of 1 to 7 to indicate their degree of agreement with the statement, "The librarian was ready to help me."

INTEREST (Code: INTEREST)

Users will select a value on a scale of 1 to 7 to indicate their degree of agreement with the statement, "The librarian was interested in my question."

UNDERSTANDING (Code: UNDERSTAND)

Users will select a value on a scale of 1 to 7 to indicate their degree of agreement with the statement, "The librarian understood my question."

VERIFICATION (Code: VERIFY)

Users will select a value on a scale of 1 to 7 to indicate their degree of agreement with the statement, "The librarian made sure I found what I wanted."

Characteristics of the user are described using three variables: library usage, reference service usage, and user's education level.

In the reference process, the library user assists in discovering the resolution to the query.[12] The inquirer works with the librarian to determine the exact query. The inquirer provides feedback to the librarian regarding whether they can comprehend a particular source. Clearly, the user is in part responsible for a successful outcome. Logically, user characteristics that indicate the ability to interact with the librarian and to use a greater proportion of the library collection are likely to influence service performance.

Users who visit the library frequently are more likely to feel at ease and more open to expressing their questions to the staff who work there. They are more likely to view the institution as a place to seek help, and are also more likely to have had good experiences at the library. Likewise, people who use reference service frequently are more likely to feel at ease with librarians, are more likely to be familiar with the reference process, and are more likely to have a greater degree of trust in working with librarians based on good experiences in the past. This familiarity contributes to better service performance because the experience of the library user reduces potential anxiety and encourages openness. In this study, familiarity is measured in two ways as follows:

LIBRARY USAGE (Code: LIB-USE)

Users will select the appropriate answer on a scale of 1 to 7 in response to the question, "How often do you use the library?" Possible values are defined as

7 — Two to three times each week.
6 — Once a week.
5 — Twice a month.
4 — Once a month.
3 — Two to three times each year.
2 — Once a year.
1 — First time.

REFERENCE SERVICE USAGE (Code: REF-USE)

Users will select the appropriate answer on a scale of 1 to 7 in response to the question, "How often do you ask questions at the reference desk?" Possible values are defined as

7 — Two to three times each week.
6 — Once a week.
5 — Twice a month.

4 — Once a month.
3 — Two to three times each year.
2 — Once a year.
1 — First time.

The first variable is taken from the study performed by Whitlatch.[13] The second measure specifically measures familiarity with reference service and the response values are identical to those in the first measure.

Logically, persons with greater educational attainment are more likely to be able to comprehend a wider variety of library materials, in terms of both breadth of format and depth of knowledge. Educational attainment of users is measured in this study as:

USER'S EDUCATION LEVEL (Code: UEDU)

Users will select the appropriate answer in response to the question, "How much formal education have you received?"

7 — Graduate degree.
6 — Some graduate school.
5 — Bachelor's degree.
4 — Associate degree.
3 — Some college.
2 — High school graduate.
1 — Some high school.

This measure is derived from the United States Census. However, whereas the census specifically delineates between the attainment of a master's degree or a doctorate, this study will not because persons with such a high level of education are a small proportion of the service population for public libraries. Assigning a value for each graduate level would needlessly skew the distribution of scores and constrain the amount of variation within the population that could be assessed by the measure.

4.3.3 Second-Level Independent Variables

The characteristics of individual librarians comprise the second level in the hierarchical design of this study. To what extent does the preparation, training, and experience affect reference performance? Measures of education and job experience have often been used to operationalize ability. In recent studies, job satisfaction has also been used. This study examined the effects of all three concepts.

The librarian's experience is a characteristic that has been examined in seven previous studies, yet quantification has always proved problematic.

Frequently the number of years an individual has worked in libraries does not accurately reflect the amount of time that person has spent in reference work, nor does it distinguish between full-time and part-time employees. Arguably, many other professional tasks, such as collection development and cataloguing, all contribute toward better performance at the reference desk, yet probably not as effectively as actual reference service experience. Likewise, experience in other service professions will also contribute to one's performance. If a researcher attempts to quantify total library work experience, or total work experience regardless of setting, extra weight should be given to reference experience over other types.

For this study, experience was limited to reference desk experience measured as an estimate of total hours the librarian has spent on desk. Each librarian received a score from 1 to 7 based on the following scale:

LIBRARIAN'S EXPERIENCE (Code: EXP)

7 — 24,001 or more hours	(approximately 26+ years)
6 — 20,001–24,000 hours	(approximately 22 years)
5 — 16,001–20,000 hours	(approximately 18 years)
4 — 12,001–16,000 hours	(approximately 14 years)
3 — 8001–12,000 hours	(approximately 10 years)
2 — 4001–8000 hours	(approximately 6 years)
1 — 1–4000 hours	(approximately 2 years)

The approximate years of experience are based on a librarian who worked an average of 20 hours on the reference desk per week each year.

Historically, research on the effects of a librarian's education has followed two lines: comparisons between librarians with and without a Master of Library and Information Science (MLIS) degree or its equivalent (e.g., Master of Library Science, Master of Science in Information Science) and comparison between librarians with and without expertise in a second discipline as evidenced by multiple graduate degrees. The former comparison is less viable today since a majority of librarians do possess a graduate degree in library science. The second comparison is perhaps of increasing importance as information becomes more specialized. The following measure accounts for these concerns:

LIBRARIAN'S EDUCATION LEVEL (Code: LEDU)

7 — MLIS and second graduate degree.
6 — MLIS and some other graduate work.
5 — MLIS.
4 — Other graduate degree, some LIS education.
3 — Other graduate degree.
2 — Some graduate work.
1 — No graduate work.

This measure has been originally devised for this study. This variable does not take into account the effect of continuing education programs beyond on MLIS graduate degree that many librarians pursue, whether they be workshops, night courses, professional association events, or simply professional reading.

To determine levels of job satisfaction, Whitlatch asked librarians to indicate the extent to which they agreed or disagreed with six statements on a scale from 1 to 7.[14] The six statements are as follows:

I frequently think of quitting this job.
I am generally satisfied with the kind of work I do on this job.
Generally speaking, I am very satisfied with this job.
I get a feeling of personal satisfaction from doing my job well.
I feel bad when I do a poor job.
Doing my job well gives me a good feeling.

In Whitlatch's study, factor analysis determined that values for the six responses loaded on two factors. She identified one factor as relating to good feelings about performing good work and the other pertaining to bad feelings about performing poorly. In this study, factor analysis was used to create two factors that are used as predictor variables. These variables are labeled LIBRARIAN'S MOTIVATION (Code: MOTIVE) and LIBRARIAN'S DISTRESS (Code: DISTRESS), respectively.

4.3.4 Third-Level Independent Variables

The characteristics of individual libraries comprise the third level in the hierarchical design of this study. In reference service evaluation, collection size has been the most frequently used measure of the library environment. In addition to collection size, this study examines the effects of service level and the formal articulation of service policy.

Perhaps the relationship that has been most frequently tested in reference service evaluation is the association between performance and the size of the library collection. Theoretically, larger collections are more likely to provide greater coverage than smaller collections for any given subject.

In past studies, size has frequently been operationalized as number of volumes, which is an interval measure since each interval of one indicates an equal quantity (i.e., one book). However, this measure is a poor indicator because volumes are not proportionate in the amount of information they contain, nor is the concept of coverage well defined on an interval scale. For example, a library of 100,000 titles has a greater breadth of coverage than a library of 20,000 titles, yet a library of 500,000 titles and a library of 580,000 titles have approximately the same amount of coverage. In each case the difference in number of titles is the same, yet in the former example one library is perceived as being much larger than the other, while in the latter comparison the two libraries are perceived as being approximately the same size. The number of titles required to achieve greater depths of knowledge for any given subject grows exponentially.[15] Consequently, this study operationalizes the concept of collection size on a geometric scale:

COLLECTION SIZE (Code: SIZE)

7 — More than 1,280,000 titles.
6 — 1,280,000 titles or fewer.
5 — 640,000 titles or fewer.
4 — 320,000 titles or fewer.
3 — 160,000 titles or fewer.
2 — 80,000 titles or fewer.
1 — 40,000 titles or fewer.

This measure is originally developed for this study. These levels cover the range of library collection sizes in the target population.[16] The investigator sorted California public libraries by size and then looked for increases of 5% or more. The levels in this measure loosely describe the natural tiers within the population where these large size increases occur.

The level of service provided by the librarian is likely to influence the satisfaction of the inquirer and perhaps increase the utility of the information that the inquirer discovers. Wyer described levels of reference service on a scale with three categories: conservative, moderate, and liberal. This scale indicated the amount of effort that would be expended by reference staff in assisting readers. To Wyer, the terms conservative and liberal denote either a thrifty or munificent character of the service.[17]

In this study, the terms basic, moderate, and extensive are used to preserve the sense of Wyer's descriptors and remove any political connotations associated with the terms liberal and conservative. However, this range of values is unlikely to show a wide variation within a population of one library type. Generally, the level of reference service provided increases as one compares academic to public to special libraries. Consequently, the measure used in this study expands the range of values for moderate service to reveal more variation within the sample. The variable uses the following scale:

SERVICE LEVEL (Code: SERVICE)

7 — Extensive	Librarian actively performs research and packages information for users.	
6 — Extensive	Librarian performs limited research, regularly searches indices (print and online) to locate materials, locates excerpts and passages for readers, packages some information.	

5 — Moderate   Locates excerpts and passage in sources for reader, guides
                 readers to the stack, recommends particular works,
                 answers ready-reference questions, consults sources,
                 provides instruction.
4 — Moderate   Guides readers to the stacks, recommends particular
                 works, answers ready-reference questions, consults
                 sources, and provides instruction.
3 — Moderate   Answers ready-reference questions, consults reference
                 sources, and provides instruction.
2 — Basic   Directs readers to the catalog, indices, and reference
                 sources and provides some instruction on how to use
                 them efficiently.
1 — Basic   Directs readers to the catalog, indices, and other
                 reference sources.

Librarians at each participating institution were asked to rate the typical level of
service provided at their library. Scores were tabulated and the most common
value was used. This method is preferred to averaging the scores since that
would almost preclude the possibility of achieving a score of either 1 or 7.

The relationship between the presence of a formally articulated reference
service policy from reference managers and reference performance has rarely
been examined, even though management has a direct effect on reference
staff in terms of working conditions, staffing patterns, training, and rewards.
Improving the quality of reference service is dependent on understanding this
relationship.[18]

This study will examine the aspect of management leadership in terms of
providing staff with a vision of reference service to be provided. This variable
is operationalized as follows:

SERVICE POLICY (Code: POLICY)

7 — The library has developed a comprehensive written reference policy that
     clearly establishes job expectations.
6 — The library provides has developed some written guidelines which provide
     a general sense of job expectations.
5 — Library supervisors frequently issue memos in response to problems as they
     arise.
4 — Library supervisors frequently make spoken announcements in response to
     problems as they arise.
3 — Traditions of service are passed word-of-mouth among staff members with
     a high degree of uniformity in understanding regarding policy.
2 — Traditions of service are passed word-of-mouth among staff members with
     a low degree of uniformity in understanding regarding policy.
1 — The library has no service policy of any kind.

This scale indicates the method of communication used to share vision with the staff. Increases in value indicate a greater likelihood that expectations are clearly and uniformly understood. The more management explains to staff what should be accomplished, the more leadership is being demonstrated. Birbeck and Whittaker noted in their study that libraries with written reference service policies did not outperform libraries without them, yet their findings are inconclusive because of a small sample size ($N = 10$) and an inadequate performance measure.[19]

4.3.5 Summary of Variables

The 4 dependent and 16 independent variables which have been described are summarized in Table 4.1.

Table 4.1
Summary of Dependent and Independent Variables

Dependent Variables	Code
COMPLETENESS	COMPLETE
USEFULNESS	USEFUL
SATISFACTION	SATISFY
ACCURACY	ACCURATE
Level-1 Independent Variables	
DIFFICULTY	DIFFICULT
CURRENCY	CURRENT
READINESS	READINESS
INTEREST	INTEREST
UNDERSTANDING	UNDERSTAND
VERIFICATION	VERIFY
LIBRARY USAGE	LIB-USE
REFERENCE SERVICE USAGE	REF-USE
USER'S EDUCATION LEVEL	UEDU
Level-2 Independent Variables	
LIBRARIAN'S EXPERIENCE	EXP
LIBRARIAN'S EDUCATION LEVEL	LEDU
LIBRARIAN'S MOTIVATION	MOTIVE
LIBRARIAN'S DISTRESS	DISTRESS
Level-3 Independent Variables	
COLLECTION SIZE	SIZE
SERVICE LEVEL	SERVICE
SERVICE POLICY	POLICY

4.4

Conduct of the Study

Because of the scale and complexity of this study, a pilot study was conducted within a single library to test the logistics of the operational plan and to uncover potential problems with instruments and measures. Discussion with librarians revealed areas of confusion in the instruments and instructions. Revisions to the instruments and operations were incorporated into the final design.

Letters of invitation to participate in the study were sent to the library directors in 41 public library jurisdictions in the Metropolitan Cooperative Library System (MCLS) and the Santiago Library System (SLS). The invitation included an example of the statistical report which could be produced from the data gathered during the course of the study in order to help these directors determine whether the results will be useful or beneficial to them. Thirteen libraries elected to participate in the study.

The invitation to participate was extended to central library facilities and regional branch locations only. Smaller branch libraries posed unique problems to the investigator because the collections are significantly smaller, the service population includes fewer business, professional, or municipal users, and the small staff would result in every query being answered by two or three librarians. Once the findings of this study provide a better understanding of the variables that contribute to reference performance, an area for future study is the difference in performance between central and branch libraries, both within a single jurisdiction and across jurisdictions.

After the library sites were determined, staff members from each site were invited to an orientation. The primary goal of the orientation was to gain the favorable disposition of the participants in regard to the study in order to achieve as high a degree of enthusiastic participation as possible. What is the benefit of having a library manager agree to hold a study when it is the librarians themselves who will be responsible for the quality of the data being collected? The orientation served as a "sales pitch" to minimize the amount of animus that staff might have toward the study and maximize the amount of enthusiasm participants would have to see the study successfully completed.

To engage the enthusiasm and interest of participating reference librarians, the investigator attempted to instill the librarians with a sense of ownership in the project. The process of generating enthusiasm was accomplished in three steps. First, librarians were asked to give authorization for the study to take place. No one could be forced to participate against their will. Second, librarians were allowed to choose the level of their involvement by electing whether or not to share, in confidence, detailed information about their professional background. Third, librarians at each site helped design the FAQ portion of the instrument that was unique to their library. The purpose of these actions was to demonstrate concern for participants' privacy, to show respect for the value of their work and knowledge, and to establish a degree of familiarity and trust in order to dismiss any suspicion of the study's intent. During the orientation session, lunch was provided as a token of appreciation for the effort the study required on the part of staff.

Another critical objective of the orientation was to gather data regarding the service policies at each institution, to record characteristics concerning participating librarians' experience, and to determine the FAQs for each site. The Library Environment Assessment Instrument, the Librarian Profile Instrument, and the FAQ Survey Instrument were utilized to obtain this information (see Appendix A for these instruments).

Once the results from the FAQ survey were obtained, the Reference Transaction Assessment Instruments for each site were prepared (see Appendix A for one example). These instruments took two formats. For libraries with computers at the reference desk, an online version of the instrument was available for the librarian to enter data. During the course of the study, the investigator periodically downloaded this information. For libraries without these technological resources, print instruments were used. Print instruments were also made available at all sites in the event of power failure or computer malfunction, or for the convenience of staff members who felt uncomfortable using completing a form online.

For 1 week prior to the beginning of the test period, staff were encouraged to practice using the survey instruments to record reference transactions. User data was not solicited during this time. This preparation was solely intended to allow librarians to gain confidence and efficiency in using the instruments.

During the test period, every query and the answer given were recorded on the Reference Transaction Assessment Instrument. For ready-reference and research queries, the User Response Instrument (see Appendix A) was employed to obtain data concerning user satisfaction and utility, although only a portion of these were returned. After the transaction was completed, the User Response Instrument was matched with the Reference Transaction Assessment Instrument. Recording all reference queries allowed the final number with complete information from both the librarian and the user tobe compared with the total number of queries to determine whether a representative sample had been obtained.

Reference accuracy was assessed by an examination of every reference query and resolution being asked at all sites during the test period by a panel of three judges using the Transaction Accuracy Assessment Instrument (see Appendix A). Each judge determined the extent to which a query had been answered correctly. Librarians with more than 10 years of experience in public library reference work and who were currently practicing were eligible to serve on the panel and were given an honorarium in recompense for their participation. A random set of queries drawn from the total sample was scored by all three judges to assess the degree of interjudge reliability.

In preparation for the hierarchical linear analysis, the data were further screened for normality, missing values, and the presence of outliers. Finally, the dataset was ready for model building and hypothesis testing. Statistical reports describing the service characteristics at each site were compiled and delivered to each respective agency. At this point, the interaction with the study participants was concluded.

4.5

Plan of Operation

The following is a detailed, stepwise plan of operation that was implemented in conducting the study.

1. Construct instruments.
2. Compose HTML instrument for computer-aided data gathering.
3. Prepare instructions for participants.
4. Prepare invitations to participate.
5. Conduct pilot study.
6. Revise instruments as necessary.
7. Invite participants.
8. Receive acceptances.
9. Schedule orientations.
10. Conduct orientations.
11. Gather data on libraries.
12. Gather data on librarians.
13. Gather data on FAQs.
14. Input data of reference environment and librarian background.
15. Customize reference transaction assessment instruments for each site.
16. Distribute instruments to each site.
17. Conduct 1-week trial period.
18. Conduct 3-week data-gathering period.
19. Gather data for Level-1 predictors.
20. Perform data entry.
21. Screen data for skewness, outliers, and input errors.
22. Prepare queries for panel of judges.
23. Conduct query analysis.
24. Gather data on accuracy.
25. Input data from judges on queries.

26. Screen data from judges on queries for skewness, outliers, and input errors.
27. Test data for reliability of constructs.
28. Prepare reports for participants on query distribution and collection development.
29. Perform hierarchical linear modeling analysis.
30. Summarize findings.

During the project implementation, the investigator made all necessary efforts to ensure that information on study participants was kept confidential and anonymous. Each participating librarian and the transactions he or she conducted were identified by a random number. No names were ever recorded. No reports on individual librarians were ever created. Participants were fully educated regarding the aims of the study, the intended use of the data, and the means that were employed to ensure anonymity and confidentiality. Participants were asked to sign a statement of informed consent before taking part in the project.

4.6
Limitations of the Methodology

Regardless of the efforts that were taken to overcome the limitations of earlier studies, this research study was also subject to certain constraints.

First, since the only the most enthusiastic and conscientious librarians were likely to record the most transactions, and since the more satisfied users were more likely to take the time to participate in the survey, performance scores are likely to be biased upward. Analysis of the distribution of performance variables will suggest whether or not this bias constitutes a serious problem.

Second, this study did not include any mechanism for determining how often the same user participates in the survey. This situation may bias the results since an influence attributed to the user characteristics measured here could be masking some other trait unique to one individual. The large sample should minimize the effect of this bias.

Third, since the query analysis was performed after the query had been recorded, it was not possible in this study to determine how well the negotiated query represented the actual query brought by the user. This is an important area for future research.

Fourth, this study did not determine the quality of service being provided at branch libraries in comparison to central libraries. This is also an important area for future research.

Fifth, data regarding satisfaction and utility for telephone inquiries were not captured. Fortunately, the queries were still recorded in order to determine to what extent they compare with the in-person inquiries for which more complete performance data were obtained. This enables the investigator to draw inferences about the probable satisfaction and utility rates for telephone inquiries.

Finally, this study only measured short-term perceptions of utility rather than long-term perceptions of utility. To conduct a study of long-term utility would require obtaining a serious commitment of time and effort from a large sample of library users. Extensive resources for offering incentives (e.g., cash or prizes) would be required.

References

1. Anthony S. Bryk and Stephen W. Raudenbush, *Hierarchical Linear Models: Applications and Data Analysis Methods* (Newbury Park, Calif.: Sage Publications, 1992), 200.
2. Elazar J. Pedhazur, *Multiple Regression in Behavioral Research: Explanation and Prediction* (Fort Worth, TX.: Harcourt Brace Jovanovich, 1982), 37–38.
3. National Center for Education Statistics, *Public Libraries in the United States: 1993* (Washington, D.C.: United States Department of Education, Office of Educational Research and Improvement, 1995), 30.
4. Edith Guerrier, "The Measurement of Reference Service," *Library Journal 61* (July 1936): 529–531. Florence Van Hoesen, "An Analysis of Adult Reference Work in Public Libraries as an Approach to the Content of a Reference Course," Ph.D. diss., University of Chicago, December 1948.
5. Margaret Hutchins, *Introduction to Reference Work* (Chicago: American Library Association, 1944), 16–17.
6. Jo Bell Whitlatch, *The Role of the Academic Reference Librarian* (New York: Greenwood Press, 1990), 58 and 67.
7. Ibid., 57 and 67.
8. Thomas Childers, "Telephone Information Service in Public Libraries," in *Information Service in Public Libraries: Two Studies* (Metuchen, NJ: Scarecrow Press, 1971), 115–117.
9. Id., Cynthia Lopata, and Brian Stafford, "Measuring the Difficulty of Reference Questions," *RQ 31*(Winter 1991): 238–239.
10. Terence Crowley, "The Effectiveness of Information Service in Medium Size Public Libraries," in *Information Service in Public Libraries: Two Studies* (Metuchen, NJ: Scarecrow Press, 1971), 54–56.
11. RASD Ad Hoc Committee on Behavioral Guidelines for Reference and Information Services, "Guidelines for Behavioral Performance of Reference and Information Services Professionals," *RQ 36* (Winter 1996): 200–203.
12. Jo Bell Whitlatch, "Reference Service Effectiveness," *RQ 30* (Winter 1990): 208–209. Janet Dagenais Brown, "Using Quality Concepts to Improve Reference Services," *College & Research Libraries 55* (May 1994): 213–214.
13. Whitlatch, *The Role*, 68.
14. Ibid., 72.
15. Howard D. White, *Brief Tests of Collection Strength: A Methodology for All Types of Libraries* (Glenview, IL: Greenwood Press, 1995), 42–45.
16. California State Library, *California Library Statistics 1997* (Sacramento, CA: California State Library, Library Development Services Bureau, 1997).

17. James I. Wyer, *Reference Work: A Textbook for Students of Library Work and Librarians* (Chicago: American Library Association, 1930), 6–10.
18. Rao Aluri, "Improving Reference Service: The Case for Using a Continuous Quality Improvement Method," *RQ 33* (Winter 1993): 224–225.
19. Vaughan P. Birbeck and Kenneth A. Whittaker, "Room for Improvement: An Unobtrusive Testing of British Public Library Reference Service," *Public Library Journal 2* (July–August 1987), 64.

5

Data Analysis and Findings

The Sample

This section discusses the sampling procedure and the nature of the sample. The investigator describes successful efforts in obtaining a random sample and presents arguments that the sample of transactions with complete information from both librarians and library users is representative of the total sample.

5.1.1 Size and General Characteristics

At 13 public libraries in southern California, reference transactions were recorded over a 3-week period from 5 to 25 October, 1998. At each site, sampling occurred anywhere from 10 to 13 hours per week depending on the library's operating hours and the number of days the library was open to serve the public. Approximately 1 hour was sampled at each site for every 6 hours the library was open. The exact hours to be sampled were randomly determined across a range of morning, afternoon, and evening shifts.

During this sampling period, 9274 persons inquired for assistance at the reference desk, either in person or by the telephone (see Table 5.1). Thirty-seven percent of these inquiries were directional queries. Ten percent of these inquiries were referred to other service points in the library. Thirty-eight percent of these inquiries were reference queries. Fifteen percent of these transactions went unrecorded by the librarian.

Since both directional queries and internal referrals were recorded by marking a single "tally" on the instrument, it is likely that the 15% unrecorded transactions were reference queries of one type or another that would require more effort to record. If this assumption is correct, then the transaction records captured 72% of the total number of reference queries transacted during the sampling period. If only half of the unrecorded transactions were reference queries, then the transaction records captured as much as 84% of the total number of reference queries transacted during the sampling period (see Table 5.2).

The reasons that a reference librarian might not complete a transaction record included heavy traffic at the desk or the need to leave the reference desk suddenly. However, if a librarian failed to record a transaction because of poor performance during the transaction, then self-selection bias on the part of the librarian could be introduced into the data set with the consequence of possibly inflating scores for items on the user survey. This danger was minimized by the high percentage (i.e., 72%–84%) of transactions that were recorded, although it is likely that some bias may have been introduced.

Reference queries can be classified as one of three types: frequently asked questions, ready-reference queries, and research reference queries. An analysis of the 3520 reference queries recorded in this study indicate that approximately

Table 5.1

Classification of 9274 Requests for Assistance

Type	Actual Number	Percent of Total
Directional queries: How do I get to the library? Where is the photocopier? How do I get a library card?	3473	37%
Internal referrals: Go to the children's room. Go to the circulation desk	887	10%
Reference queries: What is the current unemployment rate? What is the phone number for Cisco Systems?	3520	38%
Unrecorded approaches	1394	15%
Total	9274	100%

Table 5.2

Assumptions Regarding Unrecorded Transactions

	Total Reference Queries	Potential Reference Queries	Potential Total Reference Queries	% of Potential Total Queries Recorded
Assume all unrecorded transactions were reference queries	3520	1394	4914	71.6%
Assume half of all unrecorded transactions were reference queries	3520	697	4217	83.5%

Table 5.3
Classification of 3520 Reference Queries

	FAQ	Ready Reference	Research Reference	Total
Received in person	575	892	237	1704
				48.4%
Received via telephone	604	478	57	1139
				32.4%
Received from a minor	182	403	92	677
				19.2%
Total	1361	1773	386	3520
	38.7%	50.4%	10.9%	100.0%

one-half are ready reference queries, one-third are frequently asked questions, and one-tenth are research reference queries (see Table 5.3). Further analysis indicates that just under half the queries were received in person, just under a third were received via the telephone, and just over a sixth were received from a minor.

Although in this study only those who visited the library in person were asked to fill out a survey, the librarian also recorded telephone queries. These records make it possible to compare the set of queries received in person to the set of queries received via telephone in terms of two variables: ACCURATE and DIFFICULT. Likewise, although minors were not asked to participate in the study, their queries were also recorded to enable similar comparisons. In this way it can be determined if one set of queries is significantly different from the other in regard to these two variables.

5.1.2 Rate of Return

Only those who visited the library in person had an opportunity to complete a user survey. Of the 1704 users who were asked to participate, 1148 survey forms were collected, producing a high return ratio of 67.4% (see Table 5.4). One explanation for the high return ratio may be the brevity of

Table 5.4
Rate of Return

Library users invited to complete a survey	1704
Completed survey forms collected	1148
Return ratio	1148/1704 = 0.6737
	67.4%

the survey instrument and its ease of completion. The high return ratio of the random sample is a strong indication of low self-selection bias on the part of the participants.

Despite the high return ratio, one potential source of bias might be unwillingness on the part of users to complete a survey if they did not find an answer to their inquiry (e.g., "I can't waste any more time here — I've got to go find what I'm looking for!"). To assess the likelihood of this potential source, the investigator compared the scores for ACCURATE and DIFFICULT to determine if the transactions where the user failed to complete a survey were characterized by low rates of accuracy or high rates of difficulty.

5.1.3 Subdividing the Sample

Data from the user surveys and from the judges' review of the queries constitute the first-level data in the hierarchical linear model. Data at the second level describing the background characteristics and attitudes of participating librarians were obtained from the questionnaires completed by librarians prior to the beginning of the study. Data at the third level, regarding institutional characteristics, were drawn from the American Library Directory and the librarian questionnaires.

Third-level data are available for all transactions since it is evident where the transaction was recorded. However, not all librarians who recorded queries opted to complete a questionnaire. Consequently, second-level data are only available for a portion of those transactions where the librarians in that institution opted to complete a questionnaire as part of the study. Of the 13 libraries participating in the study, only 12 had librarians who opted to share information about themselves. Only these libraries are eligible for multilevel analysis. Of the 1148 queries for which the user completed a survey form, only 696 also have second-level data. Only these transactions with complete data for all three levels of the model can be used to conduct the multilevel analysis. Accordingly, the total sample can be divided into six different subsets:

1. All queries received via telephone
2. All queries received from a minor
3. All queries received in person
   - 3a. All queries received in person for which the user did not respond to the survey
   - 3b. All queries received in person for which a user responded to the survey but the librarian did not complete orientation question-naires
   - 3c. All queries received in person for which the user responded to the survey and the librarian completed orientation questionnaires

Table 5.5

Comparison of Six Subsets to the Total Query Sample in Terms of ACCURATE and DIFFICULT

	Number of Queries (without FAQs)	Variable	Mean	SD	t	p
Total number of queries	2159	ACCU.	6.38	1.09		
		DIFF.	1.46	0.97		
1. Telephone	535	ACCU.	6.26	1.28	2.85	$p > .05$
		DIFF.	1.46	0.95	—	$p > .05$
2. Minor	495	ACCU.	6.49	0.96	2.67	$p > .05$
		DIFF.	1.32	0.82	3.94	$p < .05$
3. In person	1129	ACCU.	6.40	1.04	0.64	$p > .05$
		DIFF.	1.53	1.04	2.33	$p > .05$
3a. In person—No user response	348	ACCU.	6.47	0.98	1.98	$p > .05$
		DIFF.	1.53	1.09	1.43	$p > .05$
3b. In person—User response and no librarian response	313	ACCU.	6.36	1.04	0.32	$p > .05$
		DIFF.	1.55	1.08	1.05	$p > .05$
3c. In person—Librarian and user responses	468	ACCU.	6.37	1.07	0.18	$p > .05$
		DIFF.	1.52	0.97	2.86	$p > .05$

Comparing these different subsets will indicate whether the set of transactions for which complete data is available are representative of the total sample.

All queries except FAQs were scored for accuracy and difficulty by the panel of judges. These are the only two variables available for comparing transactions without a user response to those with a user response. A simple t-test was used to determine if the subsets were significantly different. The sample size for each subset is equal to the total number of queries in the subset less the number of FAQs in the subset. When each subset was compared to the total sample, only one case was found where the two samples were significantly different. On average, queries posed by minors were less difficult than those in the total sample (see Table 5.5).

5.2

Data Screening

This section describes the methods used by the investigator to maintain the quality of the data set. This includes discussion of avoiding and correcting input error, treatment of missing observations, and assessing interrater reliability across members of the judges' panel.

5.2.1 Data Input

After being entered into a database, all observations were inspected for data entry errors to ensure that all values fell within the range of possible responses for a given variable. Observations across variables were also examined to ensure that values in one variable were appropriate given the values of another. For example, if user responses were recorded, then the case should not be marked as a "telephone" query since users who telephoned the library did not complete a survey. When an error was detected, the original source was checked to determine the accurate value for the observation. If more than one response was marked, the item was treated as a missing observation.

5.2.2 Missing Observations

For the subset of 696 transactions that were used in the multilevel analysis, 115 had missing observations (see Table 5.6). No missing observations were contained in the second-level and third-level cases.

Overall, a slightly higher percentage of missing cases are contained in the sample of 696 transactions that have complete data at all three levels than are contained in the total sample of 1148 transactions. This minor difference is unlikely to bias the results of the study. An analysis of missing values for each variable by library did not indicate any systematic trend for the missing values (see Table B.1 in Appendix B).

The mean imputation method was employed to account for missing data and all 696 cases were retained in the final analysis. As noted previously, FAQs

Table 5.6
Analysis of Missing Variables in Total Sample and Subsample

Variable	Total Sample of User Surveys ($n = 1148$)		Cases with Complete Level-3 Information $n = 686$	
	Number of Missing Observations	% of Sample	Number of Missing Observations	% of Sample
COMPLETE	32	2.79%	21	3.06%
USEFUL	25	2.18%	14	2.04%
SATISFY	9	0.78%	7	1.02%
READINESS	5	0.44%	1	0.15%
INTEREST	17	1.48%	11	1.60%
UNDERSTAND	15	1.31%	8	1.17%
VERIFY	28	2.44%	22	3.21%
LIB-USE	23	2.00%	11	1.60%
REF-USE	62	5.40%	36	5.25%
UEDU	64	5.57%	41	5.98%

were not scored for accuracy or difficulty. In the final set of 696 transactions, each FAQ was scored a "7" for accuracy and a "1" for difficulty based on the premise that routine questions that librarians were expecting to receive would be answered with an exceptional degree of accuracy and a minimum degree of difficulty.

5.2.3 Interrater Reliability

Scores for query accuracy (ACCURATE) and query difficulty (DIFFI-CULT) were determined by a panel of three judges. To assess the degree of interrater reliability, a random sample of 50 transactions was drawn from the total sample. Each judge was provided with a set of these 50 transactions and asked to score them. An interrater reliability coefficient was obtained by averaging the Spearman–Brown correlations between all pairs of judges.[1]

The evidence from comparing the results of each judge's score indicates that the judges exhibit a moderate degree of interrater reliability. For ACCURATE, the interrater reliability coefficient equaled 0.5444. For DIFFI-CULT, the interrater reliability coefficient equaled 0.5545. Two of the judges agreed more frequently than the third judge, with the single pair yielding interrater reliability coefficients of 0.6315 and 0.6952 for ACCURATE and DIFFICULT, respectively. Although a higher degree of interrater reliability would be desirable, the values indicated here do fall within the typical range for performance assessment.[2] Agreement between judges is sufficient to include both ACCURATE and DIFFICULT as variables for analysis.

5.3

Descriptive Statistics

The first-level data comprise 13 variables that are drawn from the user surveys and the judges' reports. Four of these are defined as outcome variables (COMPLETE, USEFUL, SATISFY, and ACCURATE) and nine are introduced as predictor variables (CURRENT, DIFFICULT, READINESS, INTEREST, UNDERSTAND, VERIFY, LIB-USE, REF-USE, UEDU). CURRENT was the only variable recorded for all 3520 cases. ACCURATE and DIFFICULT were recorded for all queries other than FAQs, totaling 2159. The other first-level variables were drawn from the user survey, allowing for a maximum of 1148 observations for each variable.

The second-level data comprise four variables drawn from surveys of participating librarians (EXP, LEDU, MOTIVE, and DISTRESS). All four of these variables are potential predictor variables.

The third-level data comprised three variables drawn from the librarian surveys and data reported in the *American Library Directory* (SIZE, SERVICE, and POLICY). All three of these variables are potential predictor variables.

5.3.1 First-Level Variables

An examination of the 13 first-level variables indicates that the data are highly skewed with most observations clustered closely around the mean (see Table 5.7; for full descriptive statistics for each variable, see Appendix B). Scores for measures of utility (COMPLETE and USEFUL) exhibit substantially less skewness than scores for measures of satisfaction, accuracy, or librarian behavior. Scores for measures describing the characteristics of library users exhibit a low degree of skewness.

Two variables used to measure characteristics of the query were CURRENT and DIFFICULT. The high degree of skewness exhibited by the variable CURRENT substantially reduces its value as a predictor. Theoretically, when the information being sought by a user is more current (e.g., a copy of a new bill signed by the governor or the unemployment rate for last week), it may be harder to locate than less current information. However, in the sample almost all queries (97.2%) required information from a source that was updated only annually or less frequently. Consequently, in this dataset CURRENT is not useful for explaining the variance in the outcome variables and is dropped from consideration for modeling. Consequently, DIFFICULT was the only variable used to describe the nature of the query.

Three variables were introduced to determine if the evidence supported the theory that the user's level of education (UEDU) or the user's familiarity with the library (LIB-USE, REF-USE) has an effect on the outcome of the transaction. Two of the variables, REF-USE and LIB-USE, are highly

Table 5.7
Descriptive Statistics for Level-1 Predictor Variables

Variable	N	Mean	Std. Dev.	Skewness
COMPLETE	696	5.14	1.97	−0.70
USEFUL	696	5.72	1.60	−1.17
SATISFY	696	6.35	1.20	−1.95
ACCURATE	696	6.57	0.93	−3.10
DIFFICULT	696	1.36	0.84	2.55
CURRENT	696	1.45	0.84	3.81
FAMILIAR	696	0.00	1.00	−0.11
UEDU	696	4.43	1.72	−0.01
BEHAVIOR	696	0.00	1.00	−2.02

correlated ($r = 0.82$; see Table C.3). To avoid problems of multicollinearity, a factor variable was created through principal components analysis of LIB-USE and REF-USE. FAMILIAR is the factor variable that was used in the analysis as a measure of how frequently the user visits the library, either to ask questions at the reference desk or to work independently.

The four variables measuring the impact of the behavioral guidelines on reference outcomes are highly correlated ($0.75 < r < 0.89$; see Table C.2). A principal components analysis indicated that all four variables load heavily on one factor. Thus, evidence suggests that all four are indicators of the same phenomenon, and each variable is measuring the same influence, or perhaps differing properties of the same influence. BEHAVIOR is the factor variable that was used in the analysis to measure the extent to which the librarian followed the principles outlined in the RUSA *Behavioral Guidelines for Information Professionals*.

5.3.2 Second-Level Variables

The four variables used to measure librarian characteristics include the librarian's experience at the reference desk (EXP), the librarian's level of education (LEDU), the librarian's job satisfaction derived from performing well (MOTIVE), and the librarian's anxiety regarding poor performance (DISTRESS). EXP is normally distributed. LEDU is moderately skewed. Both variables exhibit a large standard deviation that indicates a wide range of responses around the mean (see Table 5.8).

Both DISTRESS and MOTIVE are factor variables created through principal components analysis of six items on the librarian job satisfaction questionnaire (see Appendix A). The six variables loaded on two factors. This finding is consistent with findings reported by Whitlatch.[3] The first factor, MOTIVE, assesses the extent to which a librarian feels good for performing well. The second factor, DISTRESS, assesses the extent to which a librarian feels bad for performing poorly.

Table 5.8
Descriptive Statistics for Level-2 Predictor Variables

Variable	N	Mean	Std. Dev.	Skewness
EXP	52	4.38	1.89	0.05
LEDU	52	4.85	1.75	−1.03
MOTIVE	52	0.00	1.00	−1.70
DISTRESS	52	0.00	1.00	−2.50

Table 5.9
Descriptive Statistics for Level-3 Predictor Variables

Variable	N	Mean	Std. Dev.	Skewness
SIZE	12	3.50	0.67	0.64
SERVICE	12	4.75	0.62	0.64
POLICY	12	5.75	0.97	0.64

5.3.3 Third-Level Variables

SIZE, SERVICE, and POLICY are the three variables used to measure library characteristics. These attributes include collection size (SIZE), the library's level of reference service (SERVICE), and the extent to which the library has formally articulated a reference service policy (POLICY). Both SERVICE and POLICY exhibit a normal or near-normal distribution. SIZE exhibits a moderately skewed distribution. The range of responses for each variable lies close to the mean (see Table 5.9).

5.4

Model-Building

Hierarchical linear modeling is a univariate procedure in that each model can only predict the variance of a single outcome variable. In this study, four models will be constructed in an attempt to explain the variance of four outcome variables: the extent to which the user located all the information needed (COMPLETE), the extent to which the user located any of the information needed (USEFUL), the extent to which the user is satisfied with the service received (SATISFY), and the extent to which the query response is an accurate or appropriate response to the formalized query (ACCURATE).

The first step in developing a hierarchical linear model is to examine the extent to which the outcome variable varies at different levels of the model without accounting for the influence of any predictor variable. This type of model, labeled an unconditional model, establishes that amount of variance in an outcome measure that could potentially be explained at each level of the model.

The unconditional model is defined as

$$Y_{ij} = \gamma_{00} + u_{oj} + r_{ij} \tag{5.1}$$

where

$Y_{ij} = $ the value of the outcome variable for the ith librarian in the jth library
$\gamma_{00} = $ the intercept

u_{0j} = the random effect for jth library

r_{ij} = the error effect for the ith librarian in the jth library

In the case of the unconditional model, the intercept γ_{00} is equal to the grand mean. Thus, this formula estimates the predicted value of Y as being equal to the grand mean plus the unexplained deviation for each observation. In other words, because the model does not include any information about possible independent variables, the best prediction for the outcome would be the grand mean of the outcome variable.

Conditional models include the influence of variables (i.e., conditions) that are entered as predictors of the outcome variable. The proportion of variance predicted by the variables used in each conditional model may be determined by comparing the amount of unexplained variance in each conditional model to the amount of unexplained variance in the original unconditional model. Differences in the amount of variance between different conditional models also explain the amount of variance that can be attributed to specific variables. In building each level-1 model, variables describing the user and query characteristics were entered into the model alone prior to entering the variables describing librarian behavior during the transaction. Thus, it is possible to determine how much variance may be attributed to the librarian's behavior as opposed to query or user characteristics.

The level-1 model, in simple terms, indicates that the service performance outcome is determined by the behavior of the librarian during the transaction, the difficulty of the query, the background characteristics of the user, and the background characteristics of the librarian. The level-1 model can be crudely summarized as

Outcome = Query Difficulty + User Characteristics + Librarian

The level-2 and level-3 models then build upon this foundation by attempting to explain the effects that the librarian characteristics or library characteristics may have on the slopes for each level-1 predictor variable.

5.4.1 The COMPLETE Model

Almost all (i.e., −98%) of the variance in the unconditional model is explained at level 1 of the model (see Table 5.10). Differences between librarians were not determined to be significant. Differences between libraries were determined to be significant, although these differences account for a small amount of variance (i.e., 2%).

In building the level-1 model, three variables were used to control for elements pertaining to a characteristic of the query and characteristics of the user.

Table 5.10

Variance in COMPLETE at Different Levels of the Unconditional Model

COMPLETE	Value	Percent of Total Variance
Level-1 variance	3.7679	97.6%
Level-2 variance (not significant)	0.0011	0.0%
Level-3 variance	0.0926	2.4%

One variable measured the difficulty of the query (DIFFICULT), one query measured the user's level of education (UEDU), and one query measured the user's familiarity with using the library (FAMILIAR). DIFFICULT and UEDU did not exhibit a significant effect on the outcome variable COMPLETE and were dropped from the model. FAMILIAR exhibited a small but significant positive influence on the outcome. Less than 1% of the variance was explained by entering FAMILIAR as a predictor (see Table 5.11).

One variable (BEHAVIOR) was then entered in the model to account for the effect that the librarian's actions during the transaction may have had on the outcome. After entering BEHAVIOR along with FAMILIAR, the model explained almost a fifth of the level-1 variance (see Table 5.11).

Before any level-3 predictors were entered, the slopes for FAMILIAR and BEHAVIOR for each librarian were allowed to vary randomly between libraries in the model. This determined the amount of variance in the level-3 model that was attributable to differences in the FAMILIAR and BEHAVIOR slopes between libraries and the amount of level-3 variance that remained unexplained. After entering FAMILIAR and BEHAVIOR slopes as random in the model, the evidence indicated that the slopes for

Table 5.11

Variance in COMPLETE for Different Conditional Models

	FAMILIAR	FAMILIAR and BEHAVIOR
Level-1 variance		
Value	3.7381	3.0289
% explained	0.8%	19.6%
Level-2 variance (n.s.)		
Value	0.0001	0.0007
% explained	90.9%	36.4%
Level-3 variance		
Value	0.0938	0.0487
% explained	−1.3%	47.4%

each librarian did not vary widely between libraries. Furthermore, the random effects were not significant. Consequently, further analysis of the model was conducted with the FAMILIAR and BEHAVIOR slopes entered as nonrandom.

Three variables were used to measure the effects of the characteristics of the library on the outcome variable: the size of the library's collection (SIZE), the level of service provided to library users (SERVICE), and the extent to which the library has established a formal reference service policy (POLICY). Each variable was entered into the model individually. None of the variables exhibited a significant effect when entered as predictors of the level-1 intercept. SIZE exhibited a small but significant positive effect as a predictor of the FAMILIAR slopes. SERVICE exhibited a small but significant negative effect as a predictor of both the BEHAVIOR and FAMILIAR slopes. However, when SIZE and SERVICE were entered together as predictors of the FAMILIAR slopes, neither effect was significant. SERVICE was used in the final model because it explained a greater amount of the level-3 variance than SIZE.

Seven variables were tested as predictors of COMPLETE. In the final model, three variables (FAMILIAR, BEHAVIOR, and SERVICE) were determined to have a significant effect in predicting the extent to which a user located all the information they needed (see Table 5.12). The model explains one-fifth of the level-1 variance and just over half of the level-3 variance (see Table 5.13).

Table 5.12
FAMILIAR, BEHAVIOR, and SERVICE as Predictors of COMPLETE

$Y = $ COMPLETE Fixed Effects	Coefficient	Std. Error	p Value
Intercept	5.1336	0.1007	$p < .05$
For BEHAVIOR slope			
INTERCEPT	0.8580	0.0302	$p < .05$
SERVICE	−0.1038	0.0500	$p < .05$
For FAMILIAR slope			
INTERCEPT	0.1134	0.0407	$p < .05$
SERVICE	−0.1463	0.0670	$p < .05$
RANDOM EFFECTS	Stand. Dev.	Var. Comp.	p Value
Intercept 1/Intercept 2	0.2169	0.0470	$p < .05$
Intercept 1	0.0145	0.0002	$p > .05$
Level-1 R	1.7374	3.0185	

Table 5.13
Variance in COMPLETE for the Final
Conditional Model

	FAMILIAR, BEHAVIOR, and SERVICE
Level-1 variance	
Value	3.0185
% explained	19.9%
Level-2 variance (n.s.)	
Value	0.0002
% explained	81.8%
Level-3 variance	
Value	0.0470
% explained	49.2%

5.4.2 The USEFUL Model

Almost all (i.e., −96%) of the variance in the unconditional model is explained at level 1 of the model (see Table 5.14). Differences between librarians were not determined to be significant. Differences between libraries were determined to be significant, although these differences account for a small amount of variance (i.e., 2%).

As with the COMPLETE model, three variables (DIFFICULT, FAMILIAR, and UEDU) were entered into the model to test for the effects of user and query characteristics. DIFFICULT did not exhibit a significant effect on the outcome variable USEFUL and was dropped from the model. FAMILIAR and UEDU exhibited a small but significant positive influence on the outcome. Just over 1% of the level-1 variance was explained by adding these two variables as predictors (see Table 5.15).

One variable (BEHAVIOR) was then entered in the model to account for the effect that the librarian's actions during the transaction may have had on the outcome. After BEHAVIOR was entered along with FAMILIAR and UEDU, the model explained almost a third of the level-1 variance (see Table 5.15).

In the constrained, conditional model, the remaining variance at level 3 was determined to be not significant. In exploring the level-3 variance, the slopes for FAMILIAR, UEDU, and BEHAVIOR for each librarian were allowed to vary randomly between libraries in the model. This determined the amount of variance in the level-3 model that was attributable to differences in the FAMILIAR, UEDU, and BEHAVIOR slopes between libraries and the amount of level-3 variance that remained unexplained. After FAMILIAR, UEDU, and BEHAVIOR slopes were entered as random in the model, the

Table 5.14
Variance in USEFUL at Different Levels of the Unconditional Model

	Value	Percent of Total Variance
Level-1 variance	2.4708	96.6%
Level-2 variance (not significant)	0.0349	1.4%
Level-3 variance	0.0506	2.0%

Table 5.15
Variance in USEFUL for Different Conditional Models

	FAMILIAR and UEDU	FAMILIAR, UEDU, and BEHAVIOR
Level-1 variance		
Value	2.4335	1.6938
% explained	1.5%	31.4%
Level-2 variance		
Value	0.0274	0.0050
% explained	21.5%	85.7%
Level-3 variance		
Value	0.0387	0.0114
% explained	23.5%	77.5%

evidence indicated that the slopes for each librarian did not vary widely between libraries. Furthermore, the random effects were not significant. The remaining unexplained level-3 variance in this unconstrained model was also not determined to be significant. Thus, the further analysis of level-3 predictors was unlikely to predict any significant effects on the level-1 slopes or intercepts.

Four variables were tested as predictors of COMPLETE. In the final model, three variables (FAMILIAR, UEDU, and BEHAVIOR) were determined to have a significant effect in predicting the extent to which a user located any of the information they needed (see Table 5.16). The model explains one-third of the level-1 variance and more than three-fourths of the level-3 variance (see Table 5.17).

5.4.3 The SATISFY Model

Almost all (i.e., −97%) of the variance in the unconditional model is explained at level 1 of the model (see Table 5.18). Differences between

Table 5.16
FAMILIAR, UEDU, and BEHAVIOR as Predictors of USEFUL

$Y = $ COMPLETE Fixed Effects	Coefficient	Std. Error	p Value
Intercept			
	5.7137	0.0643	$p < .05$
FAMILIAR slope	0.0909	0.0357	$p < .05$
UEDU slope	0.0700	0.0211	$p < .05$
BEHAVIOR slope	0.8852	0.0259	$p < .05$
Random Effects	Stand. Dev.	Var. Comp.	p Value
Intercept 1/Intercept 2	0.1066	0.0114	$p > .05$
Intercept 1	0.0707	0.0050	$p > .05$
Level-1 R	1.3015	1.6938	

Table 5.17
Variance in USEFUL for the Final
Conditional Model

	FAMILIAR, UEDU, and BEHAVIOR
Level-1 variance	
Value	1.6938
% explained	31.4%
Level-2 variance (n.s.)	
Value	0.0050
% explained	85.7%
Level-3 variance	
Value	0.0114
% explained	77.5%

Table 5.18
Variance in SATISFY at Different Levels of the
Unconditional Model

	Value	Percent of Total Variance
Level-1 variance	1.3892	96.9%
Level-2 variance	0.0397	2.8%
Level-3 variance (not significant)	0.0044	0.3%

librarians were determined to be significant, although these differences account for a small amount of variance (i.e., 3%). Differences between libraries were not determined to be significant.

As in previous models, three variables (DIFFICULT, FAMILIAR, and UEDU) were entered into the model to test for the effects of user and query characteristics. FAMILIAR and UEDU did not exhibit a significant effect on the outcome variable COMPLETE and were dropped from the model. DIFFICULT exhibited a small but significant positive influence on the outcome. Approximately 0.5% of the level-1 variance was explained by adding DIFFICULT as a predictor. However, after query difficulty was controlled for by entering the variable into the model, the between-librarian differences in SATISFY actually increased (see Table 5.19).

One variable (BEHAVIOR) was then entered in the model to account for the effect that the librarian's actions during the transaction may have had on the outcome. After BEHAVIOR was entered into the model, the variable DIFFICULT no longer exhibited a significant effect on the outcome and was dropped from the model. Entering BEHAVIOR alone explained almost two-thirds of the level-1 variance (see Table 5.19).

Before any level-2 predictors were entered, the slopes for BEHAVIOR were allowed to vary randomly between librarians in the model. This determined the amount of variance in the level-2 model that was attributable to BEHAVIOR and the amount of level-2 variance that remained unexplained. After BEHAVIOR slopes were entered as random, the model only explained approximately two-thirds of the variance at level 2 (see Table 5.20). The remaining unexplained variance was significant.

Four variables were used to measure the effects of the characteristics of the librarian on the outcome variable: the librarian's reference experience (EXP), the librarian's level of education (LEDU), the librarian's job motivation (MOTIVE), and the librarian's job distress (DISTRESS). Each variable was entered into the

Table 5.19
Variance in SATISFY for Different Conditional Models

	DIFFICULT	BEHAVIOR
Level-1 variance		
Value	1.3821	0.5282
% explained	0.5%	62.0%
Level-2 variance		
Value	0.0425	0.0011
% explained	−7.1%	97.2%
Level-3 variance (n.s.)		
Value	0.0036	0.0026
% explained	18.2%	40.9%

Table 5.20
Variance in SATISFY for Different Conditional Models

	BEHAVIOR	BEHAVIOR with Random Slopes
Level-1 variance		
Value	0.5282	0.5065
% explained	62.0%	63.5%
Level-2 variance		
Value	0.0011	0.0122
% explained	97.2%	69.3%
Level-3 variance (n.s.)		
Value	0.0026	0.0000
% explained	40.9%	100.0%

Table 5.21
BEHAVIOR as a Predictor of SATISFY

$Y =$ COMPLETE Fixed Effects	Coefficient	Std. Error	p Value
Intercept	6.3538	0.0309	$p < .05$
BEHAVIOR slope	0.9355	0.0375	$p < .05$

Random Effects	Stand. Dev.	Var. Comp.	p Value
Intercept 1/Intercept 2	0.0031	0.0000	$p > .05$
Intercept 1	0.1104	0.0122	$p < .05$
BEHAVIOR slope	0.1205	0.0145	$p < .05$
Level-1 R	0.7117	0.5065	

model individually. None of the variables exhibited a significant effect when entered as a predictor of the level-1 intercept. None of the variables exhibited a significant effect when entered as a predictor of the BEHAVIOR slopes.

Eight variables were tested as predictors of SATISFY. In the final model, only one variable was determined to have any significant ability to predict user satisfaction (see Table 5.21). The model explains almost two-thirds of the level-1 variance and just over two-thirds of the level-2 variance (see Table 5.22).

5.4.4 The ACCURATE Model

Almost all (i.e., −99%) of the variance in the unconditional model is explained at level-1 of the model (see Table 5.23). Differences between librarians were determined to be significant, although these differences account

Table 5.22
Variance in SATISFY for the Final
Conditional Model

	BEHAVIOR with Random Slopes
Level-1 variance	
Value	0.5065
% explained	63.5%
Level-2 variance	
Value	0.0122
% explained	69.3%
Level-3 variance (n.s.)	
Value	0.0000
% explained	100.0%

Table 5.23
Variance in ACCURATE at Different Levels of the
Unconditional Model

	Value	Percent of Total Variance
Level-1 variance	0.8586	98.9%
Level-2 variance	0.0082	0.9%
Level-3 variance	0.0016	0.2%
(not significant)		

for a small amount of variance (i.e., 1%). Differences between libraries were not determined to be significant.

As in previous models, three variables (DIFFICULT, FAMILIAR, and UEDU) were entered into the model to test for the effects of user and query characteristics. FAMILIAR and UEDU did not exhibit a significant effect on the outcome variable COMPLETE and were dropped from the model. DIFFICULT exhibited a small but significant positive influence on the outcome. Almost a tenth of the level-1 variance was explained by adding DIFFICULT as a predictor (see Table 5.24).

One variable (BEHAVIOR) was then entered in the model to account for the effect that the librarian's actions during the transaction may have had on the outcome. BEHAVIOR did not exhibit a significant effect on the outcome when entered into the model with DIFFICULT. Unlike the previous three models, adding BEHAVIOR did not explain a substantial portion of the variance.

Table 5.24
Variance in ACCURATE for Different Conditional Models

	DIFFICULT	DIFFICULT with Random Slopes
Level-1 variance		
Value	0.7834	0.7171
% explained	8.8%	16.5%
Level-2 variance		
Value	0.0070	0.0090
% explained	14.6%	−9.8%
Level-3 variance (n.s.)		
Value	0.0018	0.0000
% explained	−12.5%	100.0%

Before any level-2 predictors were entered, the slopes for DIFFICULT and BEHAVIOR were allowed to vary randomly between librarians in the model. This determined the amount of variance in the level-2 model that was attributable to BEHAVIOR and the amount of level-2 variance that remained unexplained. After BEHAVIOR slopes were entered as random, the model only explained approximately two-thirds of the variance at level 2 (see Table 5.24). The remaining unexplained variance was not significant.

As with the SATISFY model, four variables were used to measure the effects of the librarian's characteristics (EXP, LEDU, MOTIVE, and DISTRESS). Each variable was entered into the model individually. None of the variables exhibited a significant effect when entered as predictors of the level-1 intercepts. None of the variables exhibited a significant effect when entered as predictors of either the DIFFICULT or BEHAVIOR slopes.

Table 5.25
DIFFICULT as a Predictor of ACCURATE

$Y =$ ACCURATE Fixed Effects	Coefficient	Std. Error	p Value
Intercept	6.5691	0.0389	$p < .05$
DIFFICULT slope	−0.3260	0.0528	$p < .05$

RANDOM EFFECTS	Stand. Dev.	Var. Comp.	p Value
Intercept 1/Intercept 2	0.0015	0.0000	$p > .05$
Intercept 1	0.0946	0.0090	$p > .05$
DIFFICULT slope	0.2914	0.0849	$p < .05$
Level-1 R	0.8468	0.7171	

Table 5.26
Variance in ACCURATE for the Final
Conditional Model

	DIFFICULT with Random Slopes
Level-1 variance	
Value	0.7171
% explained	16.5%
Level-2 variance	
Value	0.0090
% explained	−9.8%
Level-3 variance (n.s.)	
Value	0.0000
% explained	100.0%

Eight variables were tested as predictors of ACCURATE. In the final model, two variables (DIFFICULT and BEHAVIOR) were determined to have any significant ability to predict accuracy (see Table 5.25). The model explains approximately one- sixth of the level-1 variance and one-tenth of the level-2 variance (see Table 5.26).

References

1. Richard N. MacLennan, "Interrater Reliability with SPSS for Windows 5.0," *American Statistician* 47 (November 1993): 292–294.
2. Mary E. Lunz and John A. Stahl, "Interjudge Reliability and Decision Reproducibility," *Educational and Psychological Measurement* 54 (Winter 1994): 919.
3. Jo Bell Whitlatch, *The Role of the Academic Reference Librarian* (New York: Greenwood Press, 1990), 71–73.

6

Conclusions and Implications

6.1

General Observations

Each reference service outcome is driven by different elements that affect the reference transaction. Library users indicate high satisfaction even when they do not find what they want or are not given accurate information. Library users indicate that they find the service useful even when they are not given accurate information.

The distribution of scores for the accuracy outcome measure (ACCURATE) sharply contradicts the conventional finding that reference queries are answered correctly only just over 50% of the time. In this study, over 90% of the reference queries were judged to be completely accurate or partially accurate or provided the user with an accurate referral to another agency. Previous studies of reference accuracy used test sets composed of "typical" reference queries, but failed to assess whether or not those sets of queries were proportionally representative of the actual population of reference queries. The field sample used in this study presents strong evidence that the expectation of "half-right reference" is not supported when a large, random sample of actual reference queries is examined.

The distributions of scores for the two utility outcome measures (COMPLETE and USEFUL) examined in this study are substantially less skewed than the distributions of scores for measures of user satisfaction or accuracy. Consequently, these outcome measures have greater ability to discriminate between levels of good and poor reference service than the satisfaction or accuracy measures used in this study. In the future, prediction models based on utility outcomes may be more likely to enable researchers to identify predictors of reference service performance than satisfaction or accuracy outcomes.

The COMPLETE Model

Users who are assisted by a librarian who follows the RUSA *Behavioral Guidelines* in regular reference practice are more likely to find all the information they need than those users who are assisted by a librarian who does not follow the guidelines. The data from this study provide statistical evidence indicating that the guidelines encapsulate principles of good reference desk practice and do contribute to high-quality service.

Differences in the extent to which the librarians at each institution adhered to the behavioral guidelines predicted a portion of the level-3 variance. An individual librarian's reference desk behavior may be influenced by the culture of the institution in which he or she works. The measure of reference desk behaviors is just as much an assessment of the institution as it is a characteristic of the individual librarian. Examining the between-library differences in terms of reference desk behavior provides a more complete understanding of the total effect of librarian behavior on the outcome variable.

The user's familiarity with using the library also contributes to the likelihood of the user finding all the information he or she requires. Individuals who frequently ask questions at the reference desk are more likely to understand the query negotiation process and be more comfortable discussing their information needs with a librarian than individuals who rarely ask questions at the reference desk. In addition such users might also be more demanding in terms of the amount of service they expect from the librarian based on their previous experiences. Both attributes increase the likelihood that a user will continue the transaction process until the desired information is obtained.

The level of service explained a small amount of the differences between libraries. This effect can be viewed as an attribute of the culture of the library. In libraries that provide a high level of service to users, the user's familiarity with using the library is less important in terms of guaranteeing that all the required information is obtained. Even if the user is a novice in library research, the reference staff will compensate by doing more for the user.

In the model, the level of service also lessened the importance of the librarian's behavior in predicting whether or not the user received all the information he or she needed. Although this would seem to be contradictory, one explanation may be that the variables used to measure these constructs are measuring a similar phenomenon. In libraries that provide a high level of service, most librarians in that library are likely to follow the RUSA *Behavioral Guidelines* more closely.

6.3

The USEFUL model

As in the COMPLETE model, users who are assisted by a librarian who follows the RUSA *Behavioral Guidelines* in regular reference practice are more likely to find any of the information they need than those users who are assisted by a librarian who does not follow the guidelines. Also, as in the COMPLETE model, the user's familiarity with using the library also contributes to the likelihood of the user finding any useful information.

In addition to these two factors, the user's level of education increases the probability of finding any useful information. Logically, individuals with greater levels of education are able to utilize a greater proportion of the available information resources. For example, someone with high reading ability and a large vocabulary is more likely to be capable of using a wider range of information sources effectively than someone with low reading ability and limited vocabulary. Consequently, one reason individuals reporting higher levels of education were more likely to obtain at least some of the information they required may be because they could draw from a greater range of materials, formats, and reading levels. One might also infer that individuals reporting higher education levels would be generally more familiar with using libraries and thus be able to locate information more effectively.

6.4

The SATISFY Model

The extent to which a librarian follows the principles outlined in the RUSA *Behavioral Guidelines* was the strongest predictor of whether or not a user would be satisfied with the service he or she received. Also, the librarian's behavior predicted user satisfaction to a greater extent than it predicted any of the other reference service outcomes. One inference is that librarians can deliver good customer service even in cases where the individual does not obtain desired information.

Unlike the previous two models, differences between librarians were important in predicting the relationship between librarian behavior and user satisfaction, while the differences between libraries were not important. Although libraries develop their own individual service culture, the factors influencing user satisfaction are much more personal. The librarian's own individual level of professionalism in delivering reference service plays a greater role than the level of professionalism demanded by the institution.

6.5

The ACCURATE model

The only variable that was found to predict the accuracy of the librarian's response was the difficulty of the query. The responses provided to users by librarians for difficult queries were less likely to exhibit a high degree of accuracy than responses provided to users posing simple queries. Although this logical finding is consistent with theory, it might also be the result of the study design since both measures are drawn from the same instrument. Judges may have subconsciously indicated that queries which exhibited low levels of accuracy also exhibited high levels of difficulty.

None of the other variables in this study exhibited a significant ability to predict the degree of response accuracy. As with the SATISFY model, the high degree of skewness may be responsible for inhibiting the power of the independent variables to discriminate outcomes. The suggestion that factors such as the experience or education of the librarian have no influence on the accuracy of the transaction response is not logical and requires further investigation before any sensible explanation can be proposed.

6.6

Other Independent Variables

The variables describing experience and education of the librarian failed to predict any of the outcome variables. This finding contradicts conventional theory. One possible explanation is that the measures used in this study for each of these phenomena exhibited low construct validity. In other words, the operational definition failed to capture the essence of the phenomena in terms of the effect it may have on the outcome variables. Creating a new scale for the data gathered in this study may yield different results.

The variables describing the size and service policy of the library failed to predict any of the outcome variables. One explanation is that the sample did not exhibit enough variation in these variables to be able to predict differences in the outcome variable. All the libraries taking part in the study were of similar size. The range of scores for this variable was restricted. Recalibrating the scale for collection size might improve the results.

6.7

Comparison to Previous Studies

All of the earlier studies of reference service that examined accuracy as an outcome variable utilized questionnaires of ready-reference queries to test librarians' abilities. Research reference queries and frequently asked questions were not included. Consequently, these studies were based on queries that only represented about half of the total query population.

Earlier field studies of reference service that utilized a user survey as the instrument did not assess reference services provided by telephone. Based on the sample obtained in this study, one implication is that earlier studies may have ignored approximately a third of the query population by failing to survey telephone users.

The sample contains approximately the same number of reference queries and directional queries. This observation may suggest one reason for high levels of satisfaction indicated by earlier studies. Library users may not make a distinction between reference queries and directional queries when they ask for assistance. If directional queries are easier to answer, then satisfaction scores should be high.

6.8

Implications for Practice

Staff development activity should focus on the principles outlined in the RUSA *Behavioral Guidelines*. While many staff training events focus on specific reference tools for various subjects or on developing stronger online publishing, Web development, or computer skills, the most important factor contributing to good service in this study was the fundamental practices associated with interviewing library users. Reinforcement of these behavioral practices will help new librarians become more effective practitioners quickly as well as helping veteran staff members resist developing less desirable performance habits or adopting poor practices associated with "burnout."

The planning and design of virtual or remote reference services should also reflect the principles outlined in the RUSA *Behavioral Guidelines*. Librarians often evaluate Web sites or digital reference products in terms of their user-friendliness or ease of use. In designing digital reference services, librarians should look beyond such basic elements of good interface design and strive to design tools that can simulate expressing interest in the user query and also attempt to verify whether or not the user received the information they wanted.

6.9

Implications for Research

Instead of satisfaction or accuracy measures, utility measures are more likely to become the critical outcome measure for assessment of reference services in the future. As seen in this study, the same users who almost uniformly indicated they were satisfied with service indicated a wider range of responses when they were asked if they found the information they needed. Accordingly, utility scores will most likely be more useful when investigators attempt to distinguish between good and poor service. Also, these measures may also enable researchers to evaluate remote reference services where a librarian may only be indirectly involved in the mediation of a reference query. Utility measures enable the user to assess the value for the information as opposed to the quality of the customer service they received from the librarian.

Both utility measures in this study were predicted by three of the same variables. Creating new scales for measuring utility that could assess the outcome in a single variable might provide a more accurate estimate of how useful the service was to the user. If researchers can continue to gather large samples, then latent variable analysis may prove a viable means for developing and testing new measures.

The behavioral guidelines developed by RUSA are detailed. The four variables used in this study are in no way capable of assessing the full extent of all the criteria listed in the guidelines. Whereas this study employed one variable to stand for each major section of the guidelines, future studies might develop a series of measures to describe each concept more precisely. Can we devise more effective constructs that are better predictors of outcomes than those used in this study?

Why did measures of librarian experience and education fail to predict service outcomes? Did these measures suffer from low construct validity, or do the librarian's background characteristics actually produce little effect on the outcome? Developing more precise measures for these variables may prove to resolve the questions posed by the evidence in this study. Another possibility for resolution might be that these variables are indirect predictors of the outcome variables. To what degree does the librarian's experience and education predict the extent to which the librarian follows the behavioral guidelines?

In assessing accuracy, this study only examined negotiated queries. Further research is required regarding the quality of the negotiation process. How well do librarians perceive the true need of the user? Since query negotiation and query resolution are two overlapping processes, better understanding of this process is likely to inform service outcomes.

Users who participated in this study were asked about the transaction as soon as it was finished. Consequently, this study obtained data regarding only the short-term satisfaction of users and the users' immediate perceptions as to the usefulness of the information they received. What are the differences between the user's short-term and long-term perceptions of satisfaction and utility? To what extent can short-term perceptions predict long-term perceptions? Although the research design would have to overcome many difficulties related to contacting library users some period of time after the transaction, investigation would provide a better context for research in reference service evaluation.

6.10

Implications for Education

Students in the field of library and information science need to learn about the existence of multiple outcomes in the reference process and to recognize that each outcome is driven by different factors. By understanding these different components, novice librarians will be in a stronger position to assess and diagnose both their own performance on the reference desk and that of their colleagues. They will also be more sophisticated consumers of research in the field and will be able to evaluate the limitations of published studies more effectively.

Students also need to conceptualize reference work as being an inter-personal process. Three of the four outcomes examined in this study were predicted by the individual behavior of the librarian. As the profession looks to the implementation of new technologies to increase efficiency, providing the greatest amount of benefit to the largest number of people with the available resources, novice librarians should remember that maintaining high quality in their work is based on providing the maximum benefit possible to each individual, rather than mediocre service to many.

Educators need to reexamine curriculum in the area of information services. For students specializing in reference work, traditional curriculum is based on an introductory course which is then supplemented by a series of electives that specialize in the literature and resources of some subject area. This traditional approach places a heavy emphasis on information sources. If good service is more greatly influenced by librarian behavior than other factors, then more emphasis needs to be placed on developing these behavioral skills in more than one course to prepare students for providing good service in multiple contexts and environments.

7

Systems Analysis of the Reference Process

This chapter presents a model of the reference process derived from a formal systems analysis in an attempt to improve the field's understanding of this important transactional system. More specifically, this article (1) identifies the reference process' goals, functional as well as nonfunctional requirements, related system events, and fit criteria; (2) posits several competing graphical models of the reference process including context diagrams and flowcharts; and (3) proposes tests for their goodness of fit.

7.1

The Need for Systems Analysis

The process that occurs when an individual solicits assistance from an information professional to find the answer to a question, technically called the reference transaction in the field of library and information science, can be defined as a face-to-face (or face-to-interface-to-face) process involving an inquirer and an information professional (e.g., a librarian) within an information-seeking environment (e.g., a library). Although the process can readily be defined as such, reference practitioners and research have encountered difficulties in clearly conceptualizing or successfully modeling this process. Furthermore, several different graphical representations have been proposed, but often without any explicit justifications or explanations of their inherent biases. Hence, in order to possess a comprehensive, robust, and multipurpose visualization of the reference process, practitioners and researchers require a stronger theoretical resolution using new knowledge.

Without a doubt, the process of question answering, with a long history of discussion since its introduction as a recognized professional practice in 1876 by Samuel S. Green, is an important one to understand. For example, the several thousand new practitioners who enter the information field each year need to be able to visualize this process accurately if they are to engage in it successfully.

Such visualization would also offer insight into other question-and-answer settings such as help desk situations, counseling sessions, or interviews more generally. An effective model that is applicable to a wide range of environments and contexts would be a useful teaching aid for instructors. Furthermore, the inquirers who ask more than 295 million reference questions in libraries in the United States each year[1] would benefit directly by having their questions answered more accurately, more efficiently, and more attentively by reference librarians who clearly understand the process. A model could make the question answering process more systematic.

At present, one could argue the profession faces a serious situation because the system requirements for question-answering services have never been codified and diffused as such. Standards for performance have been discussed, most recently in the context of online information services. Organizations such as the Virtual Reference Desk have posted criteria articulating the characteristics of a well-managed digital reference service.[2] However, this falls short of stipulating and justifying, from a theoretical basis, the elements that must be present for a question-answering service to function.

Starting in the early to mid-1960s, the flowcharting model (also known as the block diagram or logic diagram) of the reference transaction became the predominant approach to understanding the process. This shift occurred because of the pioneering work of at least seven people: Alan Rees and Tefko Saracevic, Robert Hayes and Gary Carlson, Jesse Shera, F. S. Stych, and Charles Bunge.[3] Today, this model still influences how the process is taught to novice practitioners. Hence, it is important to examine its implications. Coming out of business data processing, flowcharting merges data and process and graphically represents functions over time. Depending on the level of granularity, the flowcharting approach accentuates the linearity of the system, its discrete elements or components, and the procedural detail of the process. Furthermore, the flowchart approach examines the transaction itself as a closed system that exists independently of all other transactions. In other words, it is a good technique for seeking the individual trees, but not the forest. By the 1960s, some people recognized the necessity of distinguishing between data and process.[4]

In seeking a new approach, the following discussion introduces an alternative problem-solving paradigm, that of systems analysis. Throughout this chapter, an information service will be examined as a system that includes persons, events, and dataflows. The terms "system" and "service" will be used interchangeably. This analytical approach is different in its assumptions and constitutes a new and unique way to think about the reference process. For example, systems analysis encourages one to identify explicitly the system's users, goals, and requirements in contrast to process. Although the reference literature mentions such things in passing, no one has brought together in one place a complete list of the requirements. Second, systems analysis encourages the graphic representation of data flows (see the four diagrams given later) and begins to suggest how the inputs are transformed into outputs. Thus, it is a unique way of representing the problem and leads to new insights as mentioned later.

The advantage of the systems analysis perspective is that it provides a top-level view of the process. In that sense, it reveals the forest rather than the trees, so that one can see how the subsystems interact. Although the diagrams may seem rather intuitively obvious, these are original because the previous work has always approached the process in a piecemeal fashion.

For instance, the system's log requirement (see R2.1 later) encourages continuous quality improvement, an element of the process that was not easily recognized before. Rather than merely making a tick mark that a question was attempted, the librarian can check to see what percentage of questions are unanswered because of inadequate resources, poor communication, or other cause. Administrators can examine the economic implications and decide to allocate reference funds based on data. This is only one example of the benefits from using a systems analysis approach.

7.2

Theoretical Framework

Applying systems analysis to the problem of visualizing and modeling reference service can be described further as the interaction between what exists (i.e., the idea of the reference transaction as a process) and what is unknown (i.e., the system requirements and various models including context diagrams, data flow diagrams, and flowcharts). In this discussion, the reference process is treated as a system following

> the definition of a system as (1) something consisting of a set (finite or infinite) of entities (2) among which a set of relations is specified, so that (3) deductions are possible from some relations to others or from the relations among the entities to the behavior or the history of the system.[5]

In systems analysis, the overall strategy in dealing with a large system is to partition it into a number of smaller, manageable pieces. In this case, the individual pieces are diagrammatically represented as data flow diagrams and events. Furthermore, the discussion is predicated on the assumptions that the reference process is: (1) goal directed in that the inquirer and librarian are both engaged in solving or resolving[6] an information problem and (2) well bounded in that the problem–solution boundaries (i.e., the number of reference questions asked and reference questions answered) are finite.[7]

Systems analysis, including its attendant concepts such as goals, events, requirements, and criteria of fit (defined below), is a useful theoretical bridge between these known and unknown states. As a general problem-solving technique, systems analysis is the "craft of understanding and specifying systems by building models of them"[8] and contains techniques such as structured systems analysis and design.

An event is a response to a stimulus, such as an inquirer requesting service. Furthermore, there are three types of events: (1) external to the system, (2) internal to the system, and (3) temporal. For example, an inquirer with an information need coming into contact with an information professional who is a member of the system is an external event; the information need exists whether or not the system is utilized to resolve it. Internal events occur when predefined conditions within the system have been reached, such as when a visceral information need has been expressed in the form of a statement. Temporal events are those that are time dependent, such as following up on user satisfaction, for instance.

When used within the context of systems analysis, the word "requirement" refers to the real (i.e., essential or logical) activity of the system without regard to its actual physical implementation. By contrast, a nonfunctional requirement is any property of the system such as its performance or usability.

The key questions this investigation seeks to address are: (1) who are the system's users; (2) what are the system's goals, requirements, and criteria of fit; and (3) what models might be usefully employed? Answering these questions will improve as well as advance our understanding of the reference transaction because they are fundamental questions about the nature of the system and its boundaries. The explicit hypothesis is that the user requirements fall under three system responses: query negotiation, query resolution, and satisfaction assessment.

This deductive analysis is based on three sources of evidence: the experience of the authors in performing reference work in a variety of settings (University of Kentucky, Simon Wiesenthal Center Library and Archives (Los Angeles, California), Beverly Hills Public Library (California), Anaheim Public Library (California), Santa Ana Community College (California), and University of Washington); obtrusive and unobtrusive observation of reference work (Santa Monica Public Library (California) and University of California, Los Angeles); an extensive review of the research literature as well as introductory reference textbooks; and a review of professional statements regarding normative standards of practice.[9] In this sense, then, the research reported here is based on what is done in practice as well as what is said (the reported research on the reference process). Finally, the findings draw heavily upon the analytical techniques of systems design and analysis.[10]

7.3

The System Analysis Model

Following the common process of analysis, this section discusses (1) the users in order to create (2) a context diagram, followed by (3) an explicit statement of the goal and (4) system requirements as well as a set of (5) event diagrams.

The two primary users of the question answering system are (a) inquirers and (b) librarians. Inquirers can be characterized on a variety of attributes such as age, appearance, gender, education, educational plans, employment status, ethnicity, family size, geographical mobility, income, language ability, marital status, occupation, reading skill, and place of residency (including urban vs rural). A common approach is to set a default stereotype model of the inquirer that would consist of a set of "clusters of characteristics."[11] Librarians and other information professionals constitute a second primary user group. The identified attributes of librarians are personality traits, education, specific course work, and subject expertise. A secondary set of users is information service managers, those who will use data provided by the system to support decision making that affects system processes.

As mentioned earlier, the primary system goal is to resolve or solve the user's information problem by providing an answer to the inquirer's question, the sine qua non of all reference service in libraries. Stated negatively, it is not supposed to make the user go away uninformed or unsatisfied. A secondary system goal is to create information that will facilitate the process of providing answers to inquirers in the future.

A graphic abstraction of the question answering system context appears as Fig. 7.1. As a model, its purpose is to aid in understanding the process and its boundaries. Data flows into the process from two sources: the inquirer and the reference collection. The process terminates with (1) a return of information to the user or a referral to another agent, (2) an assessment of user satisfaction, and (3) a record in the reference log.

Requirements are a set of user specifications indicating what the system is supposed to do.[12] Requirements tell someone (usually, the system analyst or designer) what needs to be done rather than how to do it. Often, requirements are divided into two categories: those requirements that are functional (i.e., a must-do list) and nonfunctional ones (i.e., system constraints or properties). Unfortunately, many if not most reference departments do not have written mission statements[13]; if they did, it would make it easier to identify the system requirements. Hence, it is unclear whether all reference librarians would subscribe to the following system requirements.

In this model, three events are identified (see Table 7.1). The first event is external and occurs when an inquirer expresses an information need that

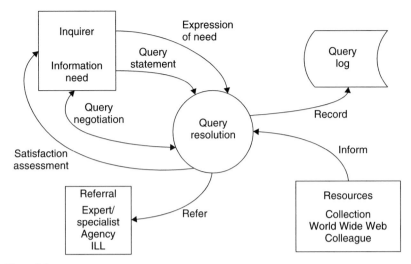

Figure 7.1
Question answering context diagram.

Table 7.1
Event List for Reference Transactions

E1.	Inquirer expresses a need (query negotiation)
	IN: Initial expression of need (EN)
	OUT: Clarifying questions or statements (CQ)
	OUT: Record query in log (RECORD)
E2.	Inquirer confirms statement of need (query resolution)
	IN: Confirmation of query as statement (QS)
	IN: Information resources to answer question (INFORM)
	IN: Human intellect to process data (KNOW)
	OUT: Query response (QR)
	OUT: Verifying questions or statements (VQ)
	IN: Verification statement (VS)
	OUT: Referral if the system is unable to identify a response (REFER)
	OUT: Record query in log (RECORD)
E3.	Satisfaction assessment
	OUT: Follow-up satisfaction query (SQ)
	IN: Satisfaction statement (SS)

initiates the process of query negotiation (see Fig. 7.2). The second event is internal and occurs when the inquirer concurs that the need has been expressed in the form of a statement that initiates the process of query resolution (see Fig. 7.3). The third event is temporal and occurs when the inquirer is asked if he or she is satisfied with the service after some predetermined interval of

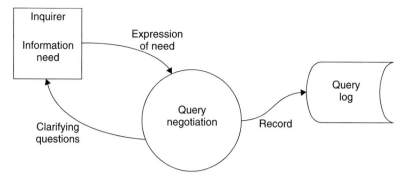

Figure 7.2
Event 1 — Inquirer expresses need (query negotiation).

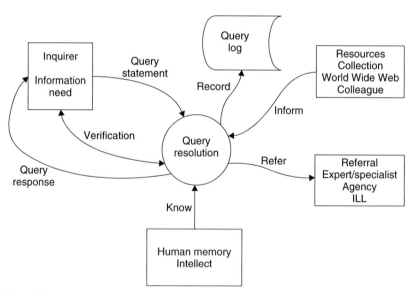

Figure 7.3
Event 2 — Inquirer confirms statement of need (query resolution).

time has passed following the query resolution process (see Fig. 7.4). In the following text, the requirements are discussed as they relate to event 1 (i.e., R1), event 2 (i.e., R2), and event 3 (i.e., R3). Fit criteria measure the ability to know when the system designer is done: in other words, the newly designed system performs as required. Discussion of nonfunctional requirements follows thereafter.

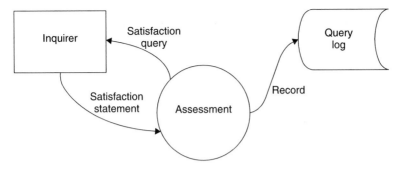

Figure 7.4
Event 3—Satisfaction assessment.

7.3.1 Event 1: Inquirer Expresses Need

R1.1 Answer All Questions

Theoretically, the system must have an "end-product: the information sought by the user."[14] To answer any and every question includes dangerous topics (e.g., how to build a hydrogen bomb, known as "Howard Morland's question" because the FBI arrested him for attempting to gather data on this question), illegal topics (e.g., how to grow marijuana plants or how to pick a lock), politically sensitive topics (e.g., Neo-Nazi literature in Germany or the United States), sexually explicit topics (e.g., how does one download kiddie-porn from alt.binaries.pictures.erotica), legal topics (e.g., which tax form does one need or what does the law mean to my case where selection or interpretation can be considered practicing law), medical topics (e.g., what is the proper drug dosage or is the disease one has fatal), financial topics (e.g., stock quotes in order to determine which stock to purchase), or existential questions (e.g., what is the meaning of life). Practical requirements may exempt these preceding questions as well as "trivial" needs such as newspaper competitions, crossword puzzles, or other games. Some libraries simply limit the number of questions that an individual user can ask per interaction. The reason for stating this requirement is that the goal of the system is to fulfill (i.e., solve the information need) or satisfy (i.e., resolve the need) the inquirer's information problem, perhaps within some limits. One fit criterion would be to pose the service with a question of any of the above types to see if an answer is returned.

R1.2 Question Negotiation Must Be Open-Ended

At the beginning, the system's (e.g., the librarian's) initial question negotiation (i.e., "a process of iterative reformulation and refinement of the initial question"[15]) must be asked as an open-ended, neutral, or selection-type question. Prior research by Geraldine King[16] and Brenda Dervin and Patricia Dewdney[17] reveal that framing questions in that form will result in the maximum of relevant information about the query before attempting to answer it and serves as a narrowing strategy. Highly successful librarians use open-ended questions such as: (1) "What are you trying to do with this information?" or "How are you going to use this?" or (2) "How did this question arise?" or, perhaps best of all, (3) "Give me some context...." Other questions could pertain to the type of information being sought in terms of format, breadth and depth (e.g., difficulty), or language.

R1.3 Record Data Related to Question
The system must record items related to the question in a question log, for only in this way can reference work become data-driven. A log would enable basic statistical information[18] to be generated and could be used in making decisions about librarian deployment, reference collection development work, determining hours of operation, and any subsequent failure analysis. To determine whether the system is successful, examine the log for date and time, question, resolution, or other relevant records.

R1.4 Persistence of System
The system must be persistent during question negotiation. This persistence will result in a more complete clarification of the inquirer's information need. Also, this attribute is necessary to answer the real question, in some cases. All of the reference textbook authors have consistently identified this requirement as desirable.[19] To test the fit, one might ask, Does the system keep asking questions until the inquirer says: "Enough"?

R1.5 Closed-Ended Confirmation
Near the end of question negotiation, a confirming statement about what is meant must be asked as a closed-ended question. Feedback is necessary to identify the negotiated question and to bring about closure as well as to move to the next stage of system. Does the system or librarian say: "If I understand you, you are looking for..." or ask, "Is this what you meant?" This requirement is a type of monitoring.[20]

7.3.2 Event 2: Inquirer Confirms Statement of Need

Figure 7.3 graphically represents the question answering process after the inquirer asks the initial question. By far, this event is the most complicated because it involves both intellectual and physical resources. At this stage of the process, there are additional requirements.

R2.1 Memory Requirement

The system must have a memory (digital or institutional) because the system may encounter recurring questions. Several of the reference textbook authors have commented on the need for the human librarian to have a good memory,[21] and S. D. Neill has written about the three different types of memory devices.[22] Here, the fit criterion might be, Does a log of previously asked questions exist?

R2.2 Obligatory Data Source

The system must have a source of data because the goal of the system is to always cite a source (i.e., make appropriate recommendations based on sources). The fit criteria might be stated as: Does the answer statement come with a print or electronic reference? For example, "How do you spell cat?" in a public library setting could be answered as part of one's common sense knowledge: "c-a-t"? Yet, the question could be about computer-aided tomography or clear-air turbulence, in which case it is capitalized. The reliability of the system is based on the ability of the librarian, not to recall content, but rather to identify a need and locate resources suited to meet that need.

R2.3 Types of Sources

Because the system must respond with an appropriate source, the source of data should be accurate; authoritative (e.g., includes a bibliography); complete; current; appropriate to the user in terms of age, language, and format; easy to use; well-organized and accessible (e.g., includes an index); and revised regularly.[23] The following is a multipart test of the fit. When the system recommends an answer: (1) are the sources prepared by knowledgeable individuals or institutions and published by known publishers, (2) are the materials current, (3) are the sources consistent over time, (4) do the sources match one's personal experience, (5) are the copyright dates within five years or less, (6) does readability match intellectual/mental age, and (7) are there a table of contents, headings, bibliography, and index with cross-references?

R2.4 Complete, Accurate Response

The system must provide "complete, accurate answers"[24] to an inquirer's query because this requirement is the fundamental goal of the system. What would constitute a possible test of fit? Can the system answer a test set ($N = 10$ or 20) of typical questions, similar to what have been done over the past 30 years of reference accuracy studies?[25] Another possibility would be to have a panel of expert judges review the system's recommendations.

R2.5 Timely Response

Ideally, the system must provide "timely answers" because the inquirer can become impatient. In part, user satisfaction depends on receiving an answer within an expected time frame. Since the 1920s, speed has been one of the desirable characteristics in a successful reference librarian.[26] Based on our knowledge of reference practice, reference queries are answered in 2 to 5 minutes; directional questions require less than 1 minute; and instructional (including how to use equipment) and research questions will take longer than 5 minutes.[27] Technically, time performance is a nonfunctional requirement.

R2.6 Determination of Acceptable Response

At the end of the question resolution process, the system must determine what an acceptable answer is by asking a closed-ended question. Feedback is necessary to identify the inquirer's requirements. Does the system ask: "Is this what you need?" or "Is this what you expect?" The former may be more user friendly because it is stated positively. Alan Rees and Tefko Saracevic found certain restrictions on acceptable answers[28] or what Marilyn White refers to as "internal constraints."[29]

R2.7 System Referrals

The system must initiate referral to another individual or institution or interlibrary loan (ILL) if it has exhausted all of its resources (e.g., no source is available in the library to answer question).[30] A test of fit would be whether a colleague (knowledgeable and willing), another collection, or a completed ILL request can match each unanswered question.

R2.8 Question Logging

The system must log the response (e.g., the reference source) to the question. One or two reasons for this requirement is to assess the accuracy of answers as well as prepare reports for management in order to justify resource allocation[31] and service staffing. The fit criterion would be the existence of an accurate and up-to-date log.

7.3.3 Event 3: Satisfaction Assessment

R3.1 Short-Term Customer Satisfaction

The system's answer must fully satisfy the inquirer (based on measures such as relevance and pertinence) in the short term. One of the goals of the system is the ability to review the results and bring about closure. Otherwise, the inquirer goes away and may not come back. The fit criterion might be whether the system asks: "Does this answer your question completely?" or "Do you have what you want?"

R3.2 Long-Term Customer Satisfaction

The system must "create high satisfaction" in the long term because the user may not know if the answer is really useful until it is applied to the information problem (e.g., back home, in the laboratory, or in the study). One appropriate test would be whether the inquirer says yes to "Was the answer useful?" 1 or 2 weeks later. Perhaps a better test is whether the inquirer returns with another question.[32]

7.3.4 Nonfunctional Requirements

As mentioned earlier, nonfunctional requirements are those that operate as constraints upon the system. In this article, these nonfunctional properties are listed seriatim without any detailed elaboration at this point:

1. The system must operate within time/speed tolerances acceptable to the intended users.
2. Ideally, the system should be available for operation any time of day or night (i.e., 7×24). Of course, practically speaking, the historic physical constraint has been twofold: (a) when the library building is open and (b) when the reference staff is available to answer questions.
3. The system must accept new sources as well as simply new editions.
4. The system must protect inquirer confidentiality.
5. The log must be reliable and include error-checking capability (e.g., prevent recording tick marks irresponsibly).
6. The system must perform to standard or normative practice (for example, the system must avoid malpractice and the system must avoid consequential damages).

7.4

Conclusions

With the existence of the data flow diagrams, researchers no longer have to rely solely upon flowcharting as the primary technique of understanding. Of course, while graphic representations of those other dimensions of the reference transaction may still be useful, the data flow diagram explains how librarians collect enough information to increase the chances of a good outcome (i.e., a correct and useful response that satisfies the user). This new perspective shifts the focus onto the dimension of data and time. Furthermore, though it may not be completely exhaustive, this chapter presents the most comprehensive set of requirements to date. Codified and diffused, these can be found in a single convenient place by students in classrooms and by novice librarians.

As mentioned earlier, the fact that this systems analysis perspective is an alternative model to the flowcharting approach suggests that other paradigms may be employed to solve the problem of modeling the reference transaction. At least three other scenarios can be considered: object-oriented, linear programming, and parallel processing, respectively.

Imagine, for instance, an object-oriented approach where the domain would be examined for nouns or things. The nouns would be examined for their properties and what they can do. A linear programming approach could involve the use of matrix transformations. Imagine a set of reference questions expressed as an array or matrix. The matrix of known data (i.e., reference query) could be compared to the solution matrix (i.e., the reference resources). Then, an examination of the shared or common dimensions between the two matrices could yield some useful insights. Similarly, a massive parallel processing approach might result in a nonsequential model. Here, the universe of all known answers could be presented to a filter until an acceptable answer is reached. Though effective, such a model would probably not be efficient. Nonetheless, someone might profitably examine this approach in more detail.

What is the best paradigm for understanding reference transactions? The reference tools have changed from print to digital. The mode of interaction between inquirers and professionals is moving from physical to virtual. Do these facts mean anything in terms of the model we employ to understand the intermediation process? What are some of these proposed models good for and what are they not good for? This is but one of the challenges to be addressed by future research.

References

1. American Library Association, *Library Advocacy Now! Quotable Facts about America's Libraries* (Chicago: American Library Association, Public Information Office, 1996).
2. Abby Kasowitz, Blythe Bennett, and R. David Lankes, "Quality Standards for Digital Reference Consortia," *Reference and User Services Quarterly* 39 (Summer 2000): 355–363.
3. Allan M. Rees and Tefko Saracevic, "Conceptual Analysis of Questions in Information Retrieval Systems," in *Automation and Scientific Communication, Topic 8 Information Storage and Retrieval; Annual Meeting of the American Documentation Institute, Part II*, edited by Hans P. Luhn (Washington, D.C.: American Documentation Institute, 1963): 175–177; Robert Hayes and Gary Carlson, *Search Strategy by Reference Librarians: Part 3 of the Final Report on the Organization of Large Files*, NSF Contract C-280 (Sherman Oaks, CA: Hughes Dynamics, Advanced Information Systems, 17 March 1964); Jesse Shera, "Automation and the Reference Librarian," *RQ* 3 (July 1964): 3–7; F. S. Stych, "Decision Factors in Search Strategy: Teaching Reference Work," *RQ* 12 (Winter 1972): 143–147; and Charles Bunge, "Charting the Reference Query," *RQ* 8 (Summer 1969): 245–250.
4. Flowcharting, American Standard, 1963. As early as 1910, Louis Brandeis brought together Fred W. Taylor, H. L. Gantt, and C. G. Barth, among others; see "Economies Through Scientific Management," in *Evidence Taken by the Interstate Commerce Commission in the Matter of Proposed Advances in Freight Rates by Carriers, August to December 1910, Vol. 8, Briefs of Counsel, Docket No.*

3400 (61st Congress, 3rd Session, Senate Doc. No. 725; U.S. Serial Set 5911) (Washington, D.C.: GPO, 1911), 4758–4803.

5. Anatol Rapport, "Systems Analysis: General Systems Theory," in *International Encyclopedia of Social Sciences*, edited by David L. Sills (New York: Macmillan Company and Free Press, 1968), Vol. 15, 453.

6. Problems can be resolved (i.e., a good enough answer), solved (i.e., the best possible answer), or dissolved (i.e., changed), according to Russell L. Ackoff, "The Art and Science of Mess Management," *Interfaces* 11 (February 1981): 20–21.

7. Noam Chomsky argues that the number of sentences is infinite and so although it is true that a finite number of reference questions are asked, one might wish to pursue the unasked questions of inquirers as well. In his *Tractatus Logico-Philosophicus* (London, Routledge, and Kegan Paul, 1921), Wittgenstein argued within the context of his system that an askable question was an answerable question; see paragraph 6.5. So, even existential questions such as "Why do we exist?" might be answerable.

8. James Robertson and Suzanne Robertson, *Complete Systems Analysis* (New York: Dorset House Publishing, 1994), 314.

9. For example, see American Library Association. Reference and Adult Services Division. Standards and Guidelines Committee. *Information Services for Information Consumers: Guidelines for Providers* (Chicago: ALA, June 1990); reprint ed., *RQ* 30 (Winter 1990): 262–265.

10. Jerry Fitzgerald, Ardra Fitzgerald, and Warren D. Stallings, *Fundamentals of Systems Analysis* (New York: Wiley, 1987), 7–8.

11. Elaine A. Rich, "Building and Exploiting User Models," Ph.D. dissertation, Carnegie Mellon University, April 1979. More recently, this idea has been expanded by Robert B. Allen, "User Models: Theory, Method, and Practice," *International Journal of Man–Machine Studies* 32 (May 1990): 511–543.

12. Alan M. Davis, *Software Requirements: Objects, Functions, and States*, 2nd ed. (Englewood Cliffs, NJ: PTR Prentice Hall, 1993).

13. William A. Katz, *Reference and Online Services Handbook: Guidelines, Policies, and Procedures for Libraries* (New York: Neal-Schuman, 1982).

14. Guidelines for Providers, section 1.1.

15. Norman J. Crum, "The Librarian–Customer Relationship Dynamics of Filling Requests for Information," *Special Libraries* 60 (May/June 1969): 269–277.

16. Geraldine B. King, "The Reference Interview: Open and Closed Questions," *RQ* 12 (Winter 1972): 157–160.

17. Brenda Dervin and Patricia Dewdney, "Neutral Questioning: A New Approach to the Reference Interview," *RQ* 25 (Summer 1986): 506–513.

18. *Guidelines for Providers*, section 5.6.

19. John V. Richardson Jr., *Knowledge-Based Systems for General Reference Work. Applications, Problems, and Progress* (San Diego: Academic Press, 1995), 25.

20. Marcia Bates, "Information Search Tactics," *Journal of the American Society for Information Science* 30 (July 1979): 205–214.

21. Richardson, 25.

22. S. D. Neill, "The Reference Process and Certain Types of Memory: Semantic, Episodic, and Schematic," *RQ* 23 (Summer 1984): 417–423.

23. Many of these criteria appear in the incomplete and now outdated *Reference Books Bulletin Manual* (Chicago: ALA, 1990). Criteria for digital sources are well addressed in James Rettig, "Beyond Cool: Analog Models for Reviewing Digital Resources," *Online* 20 (October 1996): 52–54, available online at http://www.onlineinc.com/onlinemag/SeptOL/rettig9.html.

24. *Guidelines for Providers*, section 1.3.

25. Matthew L. Saxton, "Reference Service Evaluation and Meta-analysis: Findings and Methodological Issues," *Library Quarterly* 67 (July 1997): 267–289.

26. Richardson, 25.

27. Peter Hernon and Charles R. McClure, "Unobtrusive Reference Testing: The 55 Percent Rule," *Library Journal* 111 (15 April 1986): 37–41.

28. Rees and Saracevic, 175–177.

29. Marilyn D. White, "Evaluation of the Reference Interview," *RQ* 24 (Fall 1985): 76–84.

30. *Guidelines for Providers*, 1.11 and 1.13. The factors influencing referral are covered in George S. Hawley, *Referral Process in Libraries: Characterization and an Exploration of Related Factors* (Metuchen, NJ: Scarecrow Press, 1987).

31. This requirement was suggested as early as the 1940s; see Elizabeth O. Stone, "Methods of Evaluating Reference Service," *Library Journal* 67 (1 April 1942): 296–298.

32. On use and nonuse, see John Lubans, "Nonuse of the Academic Library," *College & Research Libraries* 32 (September 1971): 362–367.

Appendix A:
Instruments

Library Environment Assessment Instrument

Worksheet 1

DESCRIBING THE REFERENCE ENVIRONMENT

Part 1

Directions: Please check the box next to the statement that you feel best describes the general level of reference service your library provides to readers. Although all librarians often "go the extra mile" in helping someone, please select the statement that you feel best describes the average level of service provided.

Please mark only one (Example: ☒).

☐ Librarians direct readers to the catalog, indices, and other reference sources.

☐ Librarians direct readers to the catalog, indices, reference sources, and provide some instruction on how to use them efficiently.

☐ Librarians answer ready-reference questions, consult reference sources, and provide instruction in using sources efficiently.

☐ Librarians guide readers to the stacks, recommend particular works, answer ready-reference questions, consult sources, and provide instruction in using sources efficiently.

☐ Librarians locate excerpts and passages in sources for readers, guide readers to the stacks, recommend particular works, answer ready-reference questions, consult sources, and provide instruction in using sources efficiently.

☐ Librarians perform some limited research for readers, regularly search indices and abstracts (print and/or online) to find materials, locate excerpts and passages for readers, and answer ready-reference questions.

☐ Librarians actively perform research and package information for readers.

Part 2

Directions: Please check the box next to the statement that you feel best describes how policies on reference service and job expectations are generally communicated to staff. Please mark only one (Example: ☒).

☐ The library has developed a comprehensive written reference policy that clearly establishes job expectations.

☐ The library has developed some written guidelines which provide a general sense of job expectations.

☐ Library supervisors frequently issue memos in response to problems as they arise.

☐ Library supervisors frequently make spoken announcements in response to problems as they arise.

☐ Traditions of service are passed word-of-mouth among staff members with a high degree of uniformity in the understanding of policy.

☐ Traditions of service are passed word-of-mouth among staff members with a low degree of uniformity in understanding regarding policy.

☐ The library has no service policy of any kind.

Librarian Profile Instrument

Worksheet 2

JOB SATISFACTION AND REFERENCE EXPERIENCE

Part 1

Directions: Please indicate how strongly you agree or disagree with the following statement by **circling** a number on a scale of 1 to 7. Higher numbers indicate stronger agreement.

	Strongly Disagree						Strongly Agree
Example: I enjoy reading.	1	2	3	4	5	6	⑦
I frequently think of quitting this job.	1	2	3	4	5	6	7
I am generally satisfied with the kind of work I do on this job.	1	2	3	4	5	6	7
I get a feeling of personal satisfaction from doing my job well.	1	2	3	4	5	6	7
I feel bad when I do a poor job.	1	2	3	4	5	6	7
Doing my job well gives me a good feeling.	1	2	3	4	5	6	7
Generally speaking, I am very satisfied with this job.	1	2	3	4	5	6	7

Part 2

Directions: For every library you have worked in, please write down the approximate number of years and months you worked there. Then indicate the average number of hours per week you spent working at the reference desk for that library. On a separate piece of scratch paper, you may wish to begin by listing all the libraries in which you have worked. Please list all sites where you performed reference work, regardless of your job title or educational attainment at that time.

	Length of Employment (Years, Months)	Average Amount of Desk Hours per Week
First Library		
Second Library		
Third Library		
Fourth Library		
Fifth Library		
Sixth Library		
Seventh Library		

EXAMPLE: Matthew Saxton, the principal investigator for this study, would fill out the worksheet as follows. Notice that at no time does he actually write down the name of the libraries in which he works.

	Length of Employment (Years, Months)	Average Amount of Desk Hours per Week
First Library	1 month	12 hours
Second Library	3 years, 10 months	20 hours
Third Library	6 months	35 hours
Fourth Library	1 year, 4 months	25 hours
Fifth Library		
Sixth Library		
Seventh Library		

Part 3

Directions: Please answer each of the questions by **circling** yes or no.

Do you have a graduate degree in library and information science?	Yes	No
Do you have a graduate degree in a field other than library and information science?	Yes	No
Have you taken any graduate-level courses in library and information science but not completed a graduate degree?	Yes	No
Have you taken any graduate-level courses in a field other than library and information science but not completed a graduate degree in that field?	Yes	No

FAQ Survey Instrument

Worksheet 3

FREQUENTLY ASKED QUESTIONS (FAQs)

Directions: Please write down the five questions most frequently asked at your library. Once you have listed them, please rank them 1–5 from most frequently asked to least frequently asked.

QUESTION	RANK

Transaction Record Instrument

LIBRARIAN #:

Query:

Response:

Source:

FAQ:
☐ Kelly Blue Book   ☐ Daily Graphs   ☐ SAMS   ☐ Criss-Cross
  Directory

Do you have a copy of:

User Response Instrument

Reference Service Survey

Please help us to improve library service by answering this brief survey. All responses are anonymous.

Directions: Please indicate whether or not you agree with the following statements by circling a number on a scale of 1 to 7. Higher numbers indicate stronger agreement.

	Disagree			Agree			Strongly Agree
Example:	1	2	3	④	5	6	7
I found useful information today.	1	2	3	4	5	6	7
I found everything I needed.	1	2	3	4	5	6	7
The librarian was ready to help me.	1	2	3	4	5	6	7
The librarian was interested in my question.	1	2	3	4	5	6	7
The librarian understood my question.	1	2	3	4	5	6	7
The librarian made sure I found what I wanted.	1	2	3	4	5	6	7
I am satisfied with the service I received.	1	2	3	4	5	6	7

Directions: Please check the box next to the best answer for each question (Example:☒). Only mark one.

How often do you use the library?	How often do you ask questions at the reference desk?	How much formal education have you received?
☐ First time	☐ First time	☐ Some high school
☐ Once a year	☐ Once a year	☐ High school graduate
☐ 2–3 times each year	☐ 2–3 times each year	☐ Some college
☐ Once a month	☐ Once a month	☐ Associate degree
☐ Twice a month	☐ Twice a month	☐ Bachelor's degree
☐ Once a week	☐ Once a week	☐ Some graduate school
☐ 2–3 times each week	☐ 2–3 times each week	☐ Graduate degree

Who is this information for?

☐ Myself   ☐ Spouse   ☐ Child   ☐ Boss   ☐ Instructor   ☐ Other _____

Please place completed surveys in the box behind the information desk.

Transaction Assessment Instrument

Query:

Response:

Sources:

Circle the appropriate response.

Accuracy Score: **1   2   3   4   5   6   7**

Difficulty Score: **1   2   3   4   5   6   7**

Was the query recorded well?   Yes   No

Questions:

Comments:

Job Description for Panel Recruitment

★★★ WANTED ★★★

Experienced reference librarians are invited to apply to serve on a panel of experts. The panel will be reviewing recorded reference transactions gathered during a recent study of reference service in public libraries. Panelists will be asked to assess the accuracy of responses and the difficulty of queries. Successful applicants will have extensive experience performing general reference work in public libraries and demonstrate a high level of professional knowledge.

Panelists will be awarded the sum of $500 as compensation for their time.

Panelists will be required to:

• Attend a one-hour orientation session.

• Dedicate 15 to 20 hours reviewing and scoring reference queries.

How to apply:

Please write a brief statement (1–2 paragraphs) that addresses the following:

• Why are you interested in taking part in this project?

• How long have you been doing general reference work in public libraries?

• Do you have any special subject expertise (business, genealogy, etc.)?

Statements on interest should be submitted via e-mail or fax to:

> Matthew Saxton
> msaxton@ucla.edu
> FAX: (714) 564–6729

Be sure to include information regarding how you can be contacted.

Your statement of interest must be received by November 6, 1998.

Appendix B: Descriptive Statistics

Table B.1

Descriptive Statistics for Level-1 Predictors

Variable	N	Mean	Med	SD	Mi	Max	Skew
COMPLETE	696	5.14	6.00	1.97	1.00	7.00	−0.70
USEFUL	696	5.72	6.00	1.60	1.00	7.00	−1.17
SATISFY	696	6.35	7.00	1.20	1.00	7.00	−1.95
ACCURATE	696	6.57	7.00	0.93	1.00	7.00	−3.10
DIFFICULT	696	1.36	1.00	0.84	1.00	6.00	2.55
CURRENT	696	1.45	1.00	0.84	1.00	7.00	3.81
FAMILIAR	696	0.00	0.07	1.00	−2.05	2.20	−0.11
UEDU	696	4.43	4.00	1.72	1.00	7.00	−0.01
BEHAVIOR	696	0.00	0.61	1.00	−5.11	0.61	−2.02

Table B.2

Descriptive Statistics for Level-2 Predictors

Variable	N	Mean	Med	SD	Mi	Max	Skew
EXP	52	4.38	4.00	1.89	1.00	7.00	0.05
LEDU	52	4.85	5.00	1.75	1.00	7.00	−1.03
MOTIVE	52	0.00	0.12	1.00	−3.38	0.98	−1.70
DISTRESS	52	0.00	0.36	1.00	−4.24	0.66	−2.50

Table B.3

Descriptive Statistics for Level-3 Predictors

Variable	N	Mean	Med	SD	Mi	Max	Skew
SIZE	12	3.50	3.50	0.67	3.00	5.00	0.64
SERVICE	12	4.75	5.00	0.62	4.00	6.00	0.64
POLICY	12	5.75	5.50	0.97	4.00	7.00	0.64

Appendix C:
Correlation Matrices

Table C.1
Correlation Matrix for Outcome Variables

$n = 696$	COMPLETE	USEFUL	SATISFY	ACCURATE
COMPLETE				
r	1.00			
p	—			
USEFUL				
r	0.69	1.00		
p	0.001	—		
SATISFY				
r	0.47	0.57	1.00	
p	0.001	0.001	—	
ACCURATE				
r	0.12	0.02	0.02	1.00
p	0.003	0.594	0.645	—

Table C.2
Correlation Matrix for Variables Measuring Behavioral Guidelines

$n = 696$	READINESS	INTEREST	UNDERSTAND	VERIFY
READINESS				
r	1.00			
p	—			
INTEREST				
r	0.80	1.00		
p	0.001	—		
UNDERSTAND				
r	0.83	0.81	1.00	
p	0.001	0.001	—	
VERIFY				
r	0.65	0.61	0.65	1.00
p	0.001	0.001	0.001	—

Table C.3

Correlation Matrix for Variables Measuring User Characteristics

$n = 696$	UEDU	LIB-USE	REF-USE
UEDU			
r	1.00		
p	—		
LIB-USE			
r	0.13	1.00	
p	0.001	—	
REF-USE			
r	0.08	0.64	1.00
p	0.048	0.001	—

Table C.4

Correlation Matrix for Variables Measuring Librarian Characteristics

$n = 52$	EXP	LEDU	MOTIVE	DISTRESS
EXP				
r	1.00			
p	—			
LEDU				
r	0.01	1.00		
p	0.929	—		
MOTIVE				
r	−0.00	0.24	1.00	
p	0.992	0.100	—	
DISTRESS				
r	0.03	−0.09	0.54	1.00
p	0.858	0.555	0.001	—

Table C.5

Correlation Matrix for Variables Describing Library Characteristics

$n = 12$	SIZE	SERVICE	POLICY
SIZE			
r	1.00		
p	—		
SERVICE			
r	−0.52	1.00	
p	0.125	—	
POLICY			
r	−0.76	0.48	1.00
p	0.011	0.163	—

Appendix D:
Dependent and Independent Variables Used in the Study of Reference Service

The purpose of these two appendices is to provide a resource for studying reference performance. In particular, this goal includes: (1) identifying all the literature in this area of study and (2) describing the literature by (a) identifying all factors which have been considered; (b) identifying all the operational definitions for these factors; and (c) providing a summary of the findings, which will allow any interested reader to compare and contrast this literature.

The first appendix is a summary chart, listing in chronological order the reference performance studies and their main characteristics. As Kinnucan *et al.* observed, "The presence of statistics in an article is rarely mentioned in the article's abstract. It is even more rare for articles to be indexed by the statistics used." Nonetheless, the purpose of this appendix is exactly that — to describe all of the published research literature according to the concept and variables used.

In the following chart, we provide the principal investigator's name and year (both when it was conducted and when it was published); for complete bibliographical information on those citations that are not discussed in the preceding text (see http://purl.org/net/reference). In addition, we summarize the method, the size of the population (N), the subject's studied, the statistic employed, and the dependent variable (d.v.) for each study. If you would like to find similar information on an interactive Web page (which is searchable by PI, year of study, data collection method, data analysis method, query type, and outcome variable), point your browser to http://purl.org/net/reftest. Our intent is to keep the Web page more up-to-date than this appendix.

In brief, the dependent variables are accuracy and user satisfaction broadly defined. And, of course, researchers have identified a host of independent variables. We have summarized the dependent variables into the following categories:

130

I. Dependent Variables: Measures of Question-Answering Performance
   A. Accuracy: Answering Success
      1. Percent of questions answered correctly out of total number of questions
      2. Percent of questions answered correctly out of those that were possible to answer
      3. Percent of questions answered correctly out of those attempted
      4. Answers grouped into categories
      5. Answers ranked on a scale
      6. Answering success as reported by the client
   B. Client Satisfaction
      1. Process
      2. Value of information received
   C. Successful Probe
   D. Efficiency = Accuracy/Time
   E. Librarian Satisfaction
   F. Cost benefit analysis = US$/Unit of Service
   G. Unique dependent variables
      1. Bunge's Composite
      2. Illinois Index of Reference Performance

Likewise, we can summarize the independent variables as follows:

II. Independent Variables
   A. The Reference Environment
      1. Size of collection
      2. Type of library
      3. Size of staff
      4. Size of professional staff
      5. Size of nonprofessional staff
      6. Number of volunteers
      7. Library expenditures
      8. Library income
      9. Hours of service
      10. Size of service population
      11. Circulation
      12. Fluctuation in collection
      13. Institution's bureaucratic service orientation
      14. Staff availability
      15. Level of referral service
      16. Arrangement of service points
      17. Administrative evaluation of services
      18. Use of paraprofessionals at the reference desk
      19. Volume of questions

    B. The Librarian
        1. Experience of librarian
        2. Education of librarian
        3. For paraprofessionals, amount of in-service training
        4. Question-answering duties
        5. Librarian's attitude toward question-answering duties
        6. Duties other than question answering
        7. Librarian's service orientation
        8. Librarians' perception of the collection adequacy
        9. Librarian's perception of personal education
       10. Librarian's perception of other duties
       11. Outside reading
       12. Memberships in associations and committees
       13. Age of librarian
       14. Sex of librarian
    C. The Client
        1. User participation in process
        2. User perception of librarian's service orientation
    D. The Question
        1. Subject knowledge of librarian
        2. Subject knowledge of client
        3. Number of sources used to answer question
        4. Source of answer named
        5. Type of question
    E. The Dialogue
        1. Business at the reference desk
        2. Communication effectiveness between patron and librarian
        3. Amount of time spent with user by reference librarian
        4. Type of assistance provided
        5. Amount of time willing to be spent by patron

How to Use This Appendix

The data on the independent variable are organized in the following fashion:

Variable Concept
   Operational Definition
     Dependent Variable
       Study Findings
       Study Findings

Dependent Variable
    Study Findings
    Study Findings
Operational Definition
Dependent Variable
    Study Findings
Variable Concept
    Operational Definition
    Dependent Variable
        Study Findings
        Study Findings
        Study Findings

In this manner, all the operational definitions for a particular concept are brought together. Under each operational definition, all the findings utilizing the same dependent variable are also brought together for meaningful comparison.

Many different symbols and abbreviations have been used throughout the studies to represent the same statistical evidence. The results reported here will adhere to the following notation.

r = The Pearson product-moment correlation coefficient

r_S = The Spearman rank order correlation coefficient

R = Multiple R, also known as the zero-order correlation coefficient

R^2 = The regression sum of squares. The percentage of variation explained by the joint effect of all the independent variables in the regression equation.

B = Unstandardized regression coefficient

Beta = Standardized regression coefficient

F = According to the Internet Glossary of Statistical Terms, "the ratio of two s squares (i.e. estimates of a population variance, based on the information in two or more random samples). "When employed in the procedure entitled ANOVA, the obtained value of F provides a test for the statistical significance of the observed differences among the means of two or more random samples."

p = Measure of strength of association; usually set at 0.01 or 0.05, depending on whether a type I or type II error is desired.

N = Number in the population or sample

Exp.X^2 = Expected chi-square critical value

Obs.X^2 = Observed chi-square value

Zcrit = Z critical value

Z = Observed Z value

E^2 = Correlation ratio in an ANOVA design

ε^2 = Unbiased correlation ratio in an ANOVA design t = According to the Internet Glossary of Statistical Terms, "This statistic is a measure on a random sample (or pair of samples) in which a mean (or pair of means) appears in the numerator and an estimate of the numerator's standard deviation appears in the denominator. The latter, estimate is based on the calculated s square or s squares of the samples."

d.v. = dependent variable

A

The Reference Environment

A1 Size of collection

1. Number of volumes broken into three categories
(Small, Medium, Large)

d.v. = Answering Success 6
     Bunge (1990), 44   Percent
                               Success Rate for Small Libraries =
                                 59.49%
                                 Success Rate for Medium Libraries =
                                 60.93%
                                 Success Rate for Large Libraries =
                                 63.65%

2. Number of volumes in total collection

d.v. = Answering Success 1
     Benham (1987), 122–123   Multiple Regression
                                 $N = 244$, $F = 13.4323$, $p \leq .001$,
                                 $r^2 = .4319$
                                 $B = .043$, Beta $= .058$
     Powell (1987), 210   Pearson's Product
                                 Correlation coefficient not reported
     Childers (1971), 183   Pearson's Product
                                 $N = 25$, $p < .01$, $r = .46$
     Myers (1983), 73–75   Spearman Rank Order Correlation
                                 $N = 40$, $r_S = .55$, $p \leq .01$
     Jirjees (1983), 201   Spearman Rank Order Correlation
                                 $N = 5$, $r_S = .20$, $p < .374$
                                    (Finding not significant)

d.v. = Answering Success 3
     Childers (1971), 183   Pearson's Product
                                 $N = 25$, $p < .01$, $r = .33$

d.v. = Answering Success 5 (0, 3)
    Childers (1971), 183   Pearson's Product
                                 $N = 25$, $p < .01$, $r = .43$

d.v. = Answering Success 5 (0, 2)
    Childers (1971), 183   Pearson's Product
                                 $N = 25$, $p < .01$, $r = .40$

3. Number of volumes in the reference collection

d.v. = Answering Success 1
    Benham (1987), 120   Multiple Regression
                                 $N = 244$, $F = 10.7438$, $p \leq .01$,
                                    $r^2 = .3494$
                                 $B = -.00006$, Beta $= .048$
    Powell (1987), 219,   a. Pearson's Products
       227–228 $N = 51$, $r = .49$, $p < .001$
                               b. Multiple Regression
                                 $N = 51$, $F = 5.606$,
                                    $p < .01$, $R^2 = .384$
                                 $B = .001$, Beta $= .330$
                               c. Multiple Regression (p. 228)
                                 $N = 51$, $F = 4.176$,
                                     $p < .05$, $R^2 = .317$
                               $B = .002$, Beta $= .447$
    Myers (1983), 93   Spearman Rank Order Correlation
                                 $N = 33$, $r_s = .67$, $p \leq .05$

d.v. = Answering Success 2
    Powell (1987), 219,   a. Pearson's Products
       229–230 $N = 51$, $r = .24$, $p < .047$
                               b. Multiple Regression
                                   $N = 51$, $F = 2.232$,
                                   $p <?$, $R^2 = .199$
                               $B = .000$, Beta $= .190$
                               c. Multiple Regression (p. 228)
                                 $N = 51$, $F = .492$,
                                 $p <?$, $R^2 = .052$
                               $B = .00001$, Beta $= .2254$

4. Collection strength in the topic of the given question (Bunge, 1990)

5. Number of current periodical subscriptions

d.v. = Answering Success 1
    Childers (1971), 183   Pearson's Product
                                   $N = 25$, $p < .01$, $r = .35$

d.v. = Answering Success 3
    Childers (1971), 183   Pearson's Product
                                   $N = 25, p < .01, r = .18$

d.v. = Answering Success 5 (0, 3)
    Childers (1971), 183   Pearson's Product
                                   $N = 25, p < .01, r = .33$

d.v. = Answering Success 5 (0, 2)
    Childers (1971), 183   Pearson's Product
                                   $N = 25, p < .01, r = .31$

6. Periodicals held more than 5 years

d.v. = Answering Success 1
    Childers (1971), 183   Pearson's Product
                                   $N = 25, p < .01, r = .41$

d.v. = Answering Success 3
    Childers (1971), 183   Pearson's Product
                                   $N = 25, p < .01, r = .38$

d.v. = Answering Success 5 (0, 3)
    Childers (1971), 183   Pearson's Product
                                   $N = 25, p < .01, r = .38$

d.v. = Answering Success 5 (0, 2)
    Childers (1971), 183   Pearson's Product
                                   $N = 25, p < .01, r = .36$

7. Number of nonbook items

d.v. = Answering Success 1
    Childers (1971), 183   Pearson's Product
                                   $N = 25, p < .01, r = .39$

d.v. = Answering Success 3
    Childers (1971), 183   Pearson's Product
                                   $N = 25, p < .01, r = .33$

d.v. = Answering Success 5 (0, 3)
    Childers (1971), 183   Pearson's Product
                                   $N = 25, p < .01, r = .38$

d.v. = Answering Success 5 (0, 2)
    Childers (1971), 183   Pearson's Product
                                   $N = 25, p < .01, r = .37$

8. Number of books owned per capita

d.v. = Answering Success 1
    Childers (1971), 184   Pearson's Product
                                   $N = 25, p < .01, r = -.44$

d.v. = Answering Success 3
    Childers (1971), 184   Pearson's Product
                                   $N = 25, p < .01, r = -.14$

d.v. = Answering Success 5 (0, 3)
    Childers (1971), 184   Pearson's Product
                                   $N = 25, p < .01, r = -.42$

d.v. = Answering Success 5 (0, 2)
    Childers (1971), 184   Pearson's Product
                                   $N = 25, p < .01, r = -.40$

9. Size of reference collection as percent of total collection

d.v. = Answering Success 1
      Benham (1987),   Pearson's Product
                                    Unreported correlation coefficient not
                                      considered significant enough to in-
                                      clude this variable in regression
                                      calculations
      Powell (1987), 210   Pearson's product
                                        Correlation coefficient not reported

10. Number of volumes in adult collection

d.v. = Composite
      Bunge (1967), 38   Spearman rank order correlation
                                        coefficient
                                        $N = 9$, $r_s = -.533$, Negative value
                                        indicates that the difference in
                                        performance between trained and
                                        untrained personnel continues to
                                        decrease with the increase in
                                        collection size

11. Number of volumes in ready reference collection

d.v. = Answering Success 1
      Myers (1983), 93   Spearman Rank Order Correlation
                                        $N = 33$, $r_s = .28$, $p \le .10$

12. Number of volumes in reference collection, grouped into five categories
    (0–500, 501–1500, 1501–2500, 2501–4000, 4001 and over)

d.v. = Answering Success 1
      Powell (1987), 235   ANOVA
                                        $N = 51$, $F = 24.198$, $p < .001$
                                        $E^2 = .69$, $\_^2 = .66$

d.v. = Answering Success 2
      Powell (1987), 235   ANOVA
                                          $N = 51$, $F = 44.300$, $p < .001$
                                        $E^2 = .81$, $\_^2 = .79$

A2 Type of library

1. Public or academic

d.v. = Answering Success 1
      Benham (1987), 109   Pearson's Product
                                        Unreported correlation coefficient
                                        not considered significant enough
                                        to include this variable in
                                        regression calculations

A3 Size of staff

1. Total number of FTE professional and nonprofessional staff

d.v. = Answering Success 1
    Childers (1971), 184   Pearson's Product
                               $N = 25$, $p < .01$, $r = .46$

d.v. = Answering Success 3
    Childers (1971), 184   Pearson's Product
                               $N = 25$, $p < .01$, $r = .46$

d.v. = Answering Success 5 (0, 3)
    Childers (1971), 184   Pearson's Product
                               $N = 25$, $p < .01$, $r = .53$

d.v. = Answering Success 5 (0, 2)
    Childers (1971), 184   Pearson's Product
                               $N = 25$, $p < .01$, $r = .49$

2. Total number of FTE professional and nonprofessional staff per capita

d.v. = Answering Success 1
    Childers (1971), 184   Pearson's Product
                               $N = 25$, $p < .01$, $r = -.43$

d.v. = Answering Success 3
    Childers (1971), 184   Pearson's Product
                               $N = 25$, $p < .01$, $r = .01$

d.v. = Answering Success 5 (0, 3)
    Childers (1971), 184   Pearson's Product
                               $N = 25$, $p < .01$, $r = -.42$

d.v. = Answering Success 5 (0, 2)
    Childers (1971), 184   Pearson's Product
                               $N = 25$, $p < .01$, $r = -.40$

A4 Size of professional staff

1. Number of FTE professional staff (people in professional slots regardless of degree)

d.v. = Answering Success 1
    Childers (1971), 183   Pearson's Product
                               $N = 25$, $p < .01$, $r = .52$
    Myers (1983), 129   Spearman Rank Order Correlation
                               $N = 40$, $r_s = .31$, $p \leq .027$

d.v. = Answering Success 3
    Childers (1971), 183   Pearson's Product
                               $N = 25$, $p < .01$, $r = .45$

d.v. = Answering Success 5 (0, 3)
    Childers (1971), 183   Pearson's Product
                                   N = 25, p < .01, r = .54

d.v. = Answering Success 5 (0, 2)
    Childers (1971), 183   Pearson's Product
                                   N = 25, p < .01, r = .50

2. Number of professional positions, both filled and vacant

d.v. = Answering Success 1
    Childers (1971), 183   Pearson's Product
                                   N = 25, p < .01, r = .56

d.v. = Answering Success 3
    Childers (1971), 183   Pearson's Product
                                   N = 25, p < .01, r = .47

d.v. = Answering Success 5 (0, 3)
    Childers (1971), 183   Pearson's Product
                                   N = 25, p < .01, r = .59

d.v. = Answering Success 5 (0, 2)
    Childers (1971), 183   Pearson's Product
                                   N = 25, p < .01, r = .56

3. Professional positions per capita

d.v. = Answering Success 1
    Childers (1971), 184   Pearson's Product
                                   N = 25, p < .01, r = −.31

d.v. = Answering Success 3
    Childers (1971), 184   Pearson's Product
                                   N = 25, p < .01, r = .06

d.v. = Answering Success 5 (0, 3)
    Childers (1971), 184   Pearson's Product
                                   N = 25, p < .01, r = −.24

d.v. = Answering Success 5 (0, 2)
    Childers (1971), 184   Pearson's Product
                                   N = 25, p < .01, r = −.23

4. Number of staff with graduate or undergraduate library degree or library certificate

d.v. = Answering Success 1
    Childers (1971), 183   Pearson's Product
                                   N = 25, p < .01, r = .52

d.v. = Answering Success 3
    Childers (1971), 183   Pearson's Product
                                   N = 25, p < .01, r = .31

d.v. = Answering Success 5 (0, 3)
  Childers (1971), 183   Pearson's Product
                          $N = 25$, $p < .01$, $r = .53$

d.v. = Answering Success 5 (0, 2)
  Childers (1971), 183   Pearson's Product
                          $N = 25$, $p < .01$, $r = .50$

5. Professional degrees per capita

d.v. = Answering Success 1
  Childers (1971), 184   Pearson's Product
                          $N = 25$, $p < .01$, $r = -.09$

d.v. = Answering Success 3
  Childers (1971), 184   Pearson's Product
                          $N = 25$, $p < .01$, $r = -.04$

d.v. = Answering Success 5 (0, 3)
  Childers (1971), 184   Pearson's Product
                          $N = 25$, $p < .01$, $r = -.06$

d.v. = Answering Success 5 (0, 2)
  Childers (1971), 184   Pearson's Product
                          $N = 25$, $p < .01$, $r = -.06$

6. Paid professionals/Paid nonprofessionals

d.v. = Answering Success 1
  Childers (1971), 184   Pearson's Product
                          $N = 25$, $p < .01$, $r = .13$

d.v. = Answering Success 3
  Childers (1971), 184   Pearson's Product
                          $N = 25$, $p < .01$, $r = .08$

d.v. = Answering Success 5 (0, 3)
  Childers (1971), 184   Pearson's Product
                          $N = 25$, $p < .01$, $r = .17$

d.v. = Answering Success 5 (0, 2)
  Childers (1971), 184   Pearson's Product
                          $N = 25$, $p < .01$, $r = .18$

7. Professional degrees/Paid nonprofessionals

d.v. = Answering Success 1
  Childers (1971), 184   Pearson's Product
                          $N = 25$, $p < .01$, $r = .25$

d.v. = Answering Success 3
  Childers (1971), 184   Pearson's Product
                          $N = 25$, $p < .01$, $r = .04$

d.v. = Answering Success 5 (0, 3)
  Childers (1971), 184   Pearson's Product
                          $N = 25$, $p < .01$, $r = .28$

d.v. = Answering Success 5 (0, 2)
    Childers (1971), 184   Pearson's Product
                                 N = 25, p < .01, r = .26

8. Number of full-time staff with MLS

d.v. = Answering Success 1
    Benham (1987), 119   Multiple Regression
                                 N = 244, F = 13.6918, p ≤ .001,
                                   r^2 = .3732
                                 B = .003, Beta = .042

9. Total FTE reference staff

d.v. = Answering Success 1
    Powell (1987), 221   Pearson's Product
                                 N = 51, r = .31, p < .023
    Jirjees (1983), 201   Spearman Rank Order
                                   Correlation
                                 N = 5, r_s = .67, p < .109
                                 (Finding not significant)

d.v. = Answering Success 2
    Powell (1987), p. 221   Pearson's Product
                                 N = 51, r = .03, p < .439

10. Total FTE professional staff with graduate degree

d.v. = Answering Success 1
    Myers (1983), 73   Spearman Rank Order
                                   Correlation
                                 N = 40, r_s = .48, p ≤ .01

11. Number of reference staff who are personal members of ALA

d.v. = Answering Success 1
    Myers (1983), 129   Spearman Rank Order
                                   Correlation
                                 N = 40, r_s = .40, p ≤ .007

A5 Size of nonprofessional staff

1. Number of FTE nonprofessional staff

d.v. = Answering Success 1
    Childers (1971), 183   Pearson's Product
                                 N = 25, p < .01, r = .48
    Myers (1983), 129   Spearman Rank Order Correlation
                                 N = 40, r_s = −.25, p ≤ .068

d.v. = Answering Success 3

  Childers (1971), 183   Pearson's Product

             $N = 25$, $p < .01$, $r = .38$

d.v. = Answering Success 5 (0, 3)

  Childers (1971), 183   Pearson's Product

             $N = 25$, $p < .01$, $r = .43$

d.v. = Answering Success 5 (0, 2)

  Childers (1971), 183   Pearson's Product

             $N = 25$, $p < .01$, $r = .41$

2. Number of nonprofessional positions, filled or not

d.v. = Answering Success 1

  Childers (1971), 183   Pearson's Product

             $N = 25$, $p < .01$, $r = .48$

d.v. = Answering Success 3

  Childers (1971), 183   Pearson's Product

             $N = 25$, $p < .01$, $r = .38$

d.v. = Answering Success 5 (0, 3)

  Childers (1971), 183   Pearson's Product

             $N = 25$, $p < .01$, $r = .43$

d.v. = Answering Success 5 (0, 2)

  Childers (1971), 183   Pearson's Product

             $N = 25$, $p < .01$, $r = .41$

A6 Number of volunteers

1. Number of volunteers

d.v. = Answering Success 1

  Childers (1971), 183   Pearson's Product

             $N = 25$, $p < .01$, $r = .11$

d.v. = Answering Success 3

  Childers (1971), 183   Pearson's Product

             $N = 25$, $p < .01$, $r = .09$

d.v. = Answering Success 5 (0, 3)

  Childers (1971), 183   Pearson's Product

             $N = 25$, $p < .01$, $r = .19$

d.v. = Answering Success 5 (0, 2)

  Childers (1971), 183   Pearson's Product

             $N = 25$, $p < .01$, $r = .20$

A7 Library expenditures

1. High versus low based on total amount of expenditure and per capita expenditure

d.v. = Answering Success
        Crowley (1971), 30–32   One-tailed test
                              $N = 12$, $p > .05$
                              Zcrit. $= 1.645$, $Z = 1.373$
                              No significant difference in
                                  performance

2. Total expenditures

d.v. = Answering Success 1
        Childers (1971), 183   Pearson's Product
                              $N = 25$, $p < .01$, $r = .62$
        Powell (1987), 219   Pearson's Product
                              $N = 51$, $r = .59$, $p < .001$
        Myers (1983), 73   Spearman Rank Order Correlation
                              $N = 40$, $r_s = .46$, $p \leq .01$
        Jirjees (1983), 201   Spearman Rank Order Correlation
                              $N = 5$, $r_s = ..20$, $p < .374$
                                  (Finding not significant)

d.v. = Answering Success 2
        Powell (1987), 219   Pearson's Product
                              $N = 51$, $r = .26$, $p < .36$

d.v. = Answering Success 3
        Childers (1971), 183   Pearson's Product
                              $N = 25$, $p < .01$, $r = .46$

d.v. = Answering Success 5 (0, 3)
        Childers (1971), 183   Pearson's Product
                              $N = 25$, $p < .01$, $r = .59$

d.v. = Answering Success 5 (0, 2)
        Childers (1971), 183   Pearson's Product
                              $N = 25$, $p < .01$, $r = .55$

3. Expenditures for library personnel

d.v. = Answering Success 1
        Childers (1971), 183   Pearson's Product
                              $N = 25$, $p < .01$, $r = .66$

d.v. = Answering Success 3
        Childers (1971), 183   Pearson's Product
                              $N = 25$, $p < .01$, $r = .53$

d.v. = Answering Success 5 (0, 3)
        Childers (1971), 183   Pearson's Product
                              $N = 25$, $p < .01$, $r = .64$

d.v. = Answering Success 5 (0, 2)
        Childers (1971), 183   Pearson's Product
                              $N = 25$, $p < .01$, $r = .61$

4. Expenditures for all personnel (include maintenance and clerical)

d.v. = Answering Success 1
      Childers (1971), 183   Pearson's Product
                                  $N = 25$, $p < .01$, $r = .60$

d.v. = Answering Success 3
      Childers (1971), 183   Pearson's Product
                                    $N = 25$, $p < 0.1$, $r = .45$

d.v. = Answering Success 5 (0, 3)
      Childers (1971), 183   Pearson's Product
                                    $N = 25$, $p < .01$, $r = .57$

d.v. = Answering Success 5 (0, 2)
      Childers (1971), 183   Pearson's Product
                                    $N = 25$, $p < .01$, $r = .54$

5. Expenditures for books

d.v. = Answering Success 1
      Childers (1971), 183   Pearson's Product
                                    $N = 25$, $p < .01$, $r = .42$

d.v. = Answering Success 3
      Childers (1971), 183   Pearson's Product
                                    $N = 25$, $p < .01$, $r = .27$

d.v. = Answering Success 5 (0, 3)
      Childers (1971), 183   Pearson's Product
                                    $N = 25$, $p < .01$, $r = .38$

d.v. = Answering Success 5 (0, 2)
      Childers (1971), 183   Pearson's Product
                                    $N = 25$, $p < .01$, $r = .35$

6. Expenditures for periodicals

d.v. = Answering Success 1
      Childers (1971), 183   Pearson's Product
                                    $N = 25$, $p < .01$, $r = .45$

d.v. = Answering Success 3
      Childers (1971), 183   Pearson's Product
                                    $N = 25$, $p < .01$, $r = .28$

d.v. = Answering Success 5 (0, 3)
      Childers (1971), 183   Pearson's Product
                                    $N = 25$, $p < .01$, $r = .40$

d.v. = Answering Success 5 (0, 2)
      Childers (1971), 183   Pearson's Product
                                    $N = 25$, $p < .01$, $r = .37$

7. Expenditures for all materials

d.v. = Answering Success 1
      Childers (1971), 183   Pearson's Product
                                  $N = 25, p < .01, r = .53$

d.v. = Answering Success 3
      Childers (1971), 183   Pearson's Product
                                  $N = 25, p < .01, r = .35$

d.v. = Answering Success 5 (0, 3)
      Childers (1971), 183   Pearson's Product
                                  $N = 25, p < .01, r = .49$

d.v. = Answering Success 5 (0, 2)
      Childers (1971), 183   Pearson's Product
                                  $N = 25, p < .01, r = .47$

8. Expenditures for all materials/Total expenditures

d.v. = Answering Success 1
      Childers (1971), 184   Pearson's Product
                                  $N = 25, p < .01, r = .22$

d.v. = Answering Success 3
      Childers (1971), 184   Pearson's Product
                                  $N = 25, p < .01, r = -.34$

d.v. = Answering Success 5 (0, 3)
      Childers (1971), 184   Pearson's Product
                                  $N = 25, p < .01, r = .25$

d.v. = Answering Success 5 (0, 2)
      Childers (1971), 184   Pearson's Product
                                  $N = 25, p < .01, r = .24$

9. Expenditures for library personnel/Total expenditures

d.v. = Answering Success 1
      Childers (1971), 184   Pearson's Product
                                  $N = 25, p < .01, r = -.37$

d.v. = Answering Success 3
      Childers (1971), 184   Pearson's Product
                                  $N = 25, p < .01, r = .32$

d.v. = Answering Success 5 (0, 3)
      Childers (1971), 184   Pearson's Product
                                  $N = 25, p < .01, r = -.41$

d.v. = Answering Success 5 (0, 2)
      Childers (1971), 184   Pearson's Product
                                  $N = 25, p < .01, r = -.43$

10. Expenditures for library personnel/Expenditures for all materials

d.v. = Answering Success 1
    Childers (1971), 184   Pearson's Product
        $N = 25, p < .01, r = .34$

d.v. = Answering Success 3
    Childers (1971), 184   Pearson's Product
        $N = 25, p < .01, r = .34$

d.v. = Answering Success 5 (0, 3)
    Childers (1971), 184   Pearson's Product
        $N = 25, p < .01, r = .38$

d.v. = Answering Success 5 (0, 2)
    Childers (1971), 184   Pearson's Product
        $N = 25, p < .01, r = .38$

11. Total expenditures/ Total circulation

d.v. = Answering Success 1
    Childers (1971), 184   Pearson's Product
        $N = 25, p < .01, r = .23$

d.v. = Answering Success 3
    Childers (1971), 184   Pearson's Product
        $N = 25, p < .01, r = .11$

d.v. = Answering Success 5 (0, 3)
    Childers (1971), 184   Pearson's Product
        $N = 25, p < .01, r = .28$

d.v. = Answering Success 5 (0, 2)
    Childers (1971), 184   Pearson's Product
        $N = 25, p < .01, r = .26$

12. Equalized valuation, assessed value of real and personal properties

d.v. = Answering Success 1
    Childers (1971), 183   Pearson's Product
        $N = 25, p < .01, r = .59$

d.v. = Answering Success 3
    Childers (1971), 183   Pearson's Product
        $N = 25, p < .01, r = .39$

d.v. = Answering Success 5 (0, 3)
    Childers (1971), 183   Pearson's Product
        $N = 25, p < .01, r = .56$

d.v. = Answering Success 5 (0, 2)
    Childers (1971), 183   Pearson's Product
        $N = 25, p < .01, r = .54$

13. Equalized valuation per capita

d.v. = Answering Success 1
 Childers (1971), 184   Pearson's Product
                         $N = 25, p < .01, r = -.13$

d.v. = Answering Success 3
 Childers (1971), 184   Pearson's Product
                         $N = 25, p < .01, r = -.01$

d.v. = Answering Success 5 (0, 3)
 Childers (1971), 184   Pearson's Product
                         $N = 25, p < .01, r = -.07$

d.v. = Answering Success 5 (0, 2)
 Childers (1971), 184   Pearson's Product
                         $N = 25, p < .01, r = -.01$

14. Total expenditures for reference wages and salaries

d.v. = Answering Success 1
 Powell (1987), 207   Pearson's Product
                       Correlation coefficient not reported

15. Annual expenditures for new reference collection materials in $

d.v. = Answering Success 1
 Powell (1987), 207   Pearson's Product
                       Correlation coefficient not reported

16. Annual salary of beginning librarian with an MLS and no experience

d.v. = Answering Success 1
 Myers (1983), 129   Spearman Rank Order Correlation
                      $N = 40, r_S = .06, p > .10$
                      (Finding not significant)

A8 Library income

1. Local tax support in $

d.v. = Answering Success 1
 Childers (1971), 183   Pearson's Product
                         $N = 25, p < .01, r = .62$

d.v. = Answering Success 3
 Childers (1971), 183   Pearson's Product
                         $N = 25, p < .01, r = .44$

d.v. = Answering Success 5 (0, 3)
 Childers (1971), 183   Pearson's Product
                         $N = 25, p < .01, r = .59$

d.v. = Answering Success 5 (0, 2)
 Childers (1971), 183   Pearson's Product
                         $N = 25, p < .01, r = .56$

5. Local tax support per capita of service population

d.v. = Answering Success 1
  Childers (1971), 184 Pearson's Product
           $N = 25$, $p < .01$, $r = -.02$

d.v. = Answering Success 3
  Childers (1971), 184 Pearson's Product
           $N = 25$, $p < .01$, $r = .07$

d.v. = Answering Success 5 (0, 3)
  Childers (1971), 184 Pearson's Product
           $N = 25$, $p < .01$, $r = .02$

d.v. = Answering Success 5 (0, 2)
  Childers (1971), 184 Pearson's Product
           $N = 25$, $p < .01$, $r = .03$

6. Local tax support ($)/Total expenditures ($)

d.v. = Answering Success 1
  Childers (1971), 184 Pearson's Product
           $N = 25$, $p < .01$, $r = -.05$

d.v. = Answering Success 3
  Childers (1971), 184 Pearson's Product
           $N = 25$, $p < .01$, $r = -.20$

d.v. = Answering Success 5 (0, 3)
  Childers (1971), 184 Pearson's Product
           $N = 25$, $p < .01$, $r = -.0028$

d.v. = Answering Success 5 (0, 2)
  Childers (1971), 184 Pearson's Product
           $N = 25$, $p < .01$, $r = .02$

A9 Hours of service

1. Number of hours open per week

d.v. = Answering Success 1
  Powell (1987), 208 Pearson's product
           Correlation coefficient not reported
  Childers (1971), 183 Pearson's Product
           $N = 25$, $p < .01$, $r = .67$
  Myers (1983), 73 Spearman Rank Order Correlation
           $N = 40$, $r_s = .55$, $p \leq .01$
  Jirjees (1983), 201 Spearman Rank Order Correlation
           $N = 5$, $r_s = .56$, $p < .161$
           (Finding not significant)

d.v. = Answering Success 3
  Childers (1971), 183 Pearson's Product
           $N = 25$, $p < .01$, $r = .35$

d.v. = Answering Success 5 (0, 3)
    Childers (1971), 183   Pearson's Product
                           $N = 25$, $p < .01$, $r = .59$

d.v. = Answering Success 5 (0, 2)
    Childers (1971), 183   Pearson's Product
                           $N = 25$, $p < .01$, $r = .55$

2. Number of hours reference service is provided per week

d.v. = Answering Success 1
    Benham (1987), 122   Multiple Regression
                           $N = 244$, $F = 13.9557$,
                             $p \leq .001$, $r^2 = .4110$
                           $B = .010$, Beta $= .081$

3. Librarian's estimate of how many hours the library is open to users each week

d.v. = Answering Success 1
    Myers (1983), 92   Spearman Rank Order Correlation
                         $N = 38$, $r_s = .62$, $p \leq .001$

4. Librarian's estimate of how many hours the library provides reference service each week

d.v. = Answering Success 1
    Myers (1983), 92   Spearman Rank Order Correlation
                         $N = 38$, $r_s = .54$, $p \leq .001$

A10 Size of service population

1. Number of persons in target service population

d.v. = Answering Success 1
    Childers (1971), 183   Pearson's Product
                           $N = 25$, $p < .01$, $r = .57$

d.v. = Answering Success 3
    Childers (1971), 183   Pearson's Product
                           $N = 25$, $p < .01$, $r = .38$

d.v. = Answering Success 5 (0, 3)
    Childers (1971), 183   Pearson's Product
                           $N = 25$, $p < .01$, $r = .51$

d.v. = Answering Success 5 (0, 2)
    Childers (1971), 183   Pearson's Product
                           $N = 25$, $p < .01$, $r = .47$

2. Number of FTE students

d.v. = Answering Success 1
    Myers (1983), 73   Spearman Rank Order Correlation
                         $N = 40$, $r_s = .41$, $p \leq .01$

3. Number of FTE students and faculty

d.v. = Answering Success 1

> Jirjees (1983), 201   Spearman Rank Order Correlation
> $N = 5$, $r_s = -.30$, $p < .312$
> (Finding not significant)

A11 Circulation

1. Total circulation for past year

d.v. = Answering Success 1

> Childers (1971), 183   Pearson's Product
> $N = 25$, $p < .01$, $r = .46$
>
> Myers (1983), 73   Spearman Rank Order Correlation
> $N = 40$, $r_s = .46$, $p \leq .01$

d.v. = Answering Success 3

> Childers (1971), 183   Pearson's Product
> $N = 25$, $p < .01$, $r = .33$

d.v. = Answering Success 5 (0, 3)

> Childers (1971), 183   Pearson's Product
> $N = 25$, $p < .01$, $r = .45$

d.v. = Answering Success 5 (0, 2)

> Childers (1971), 183   Pearson's Product
> $N = 25$, $p < .01$, $r = .43$

2. Adult circulation for past year

d.v. = Answering Success 1

> Childers (1971), 183   Pearson's Product
> $N = 25$, $p < .01$, $r = .49$

d.v. = Answering Success 3

> Childers (1971), 183   Pearson's Product
> $N = 25$, $p < .01$, $r = .37$

d.v. = Answering Success 5 (0, 3)

> Childers (1971), 183   Pearson's Product
> $N = 25$, $p < .01$, $r = .45$

d.v. = Answering Success 5 (0, 2)

> Childers (1971), 183   Pearson's Product
> $N = 25$, $p < .01$, $r = .43$

3. Total circulation per capita

d.v. = Answering Success 1

> Childers (1971), 184   Pearson's Product
> $N = 25$, $p < .01$, $r = -.40$

d.v. = Answering Success 3

> Childers (1971), 184   Pearson's Product
> $N = 25$, $p < .01$, $r = -.12$

d.v. = Answering Success 5 (0, 3)
    Childers (1971), 184   Pearson's Product
                                $N = 25$, $p < .01$, $r = -.40$

d.v. = Answering Success 5 (0, 2)
    Childers (1971), 184   Pearson's Product
                                $N = 25$, $p < .01$, $r = -.38$

4. Adult circulation per capita

d.v. = Answering Success 1
    Childers (1971), 184   Pearson's Product
                                $N = 25$, $p < .01$, $r = -.34$

d.v. = Answering Success 3
    Childers (1971), 184   Pearson's Product
                                $N = 25$, $p < .01$, $r = -.08$

d.v. = Answering Success 5 (0, 3)
    Childers (1971), 184   Pearson's Product
                                $N = 25$, $p < .01$, $r = -.36$

d.v. = Answering Success 5 (0, 2)
    Childers (1971), 184   Pearson's Product
                                $N = 25$, $p < .01$, $r = -.35$

5. Adult circulation/total circulation

d.v. = Answering Success 1
    Childers (1971), 184   Pearson's Product
                                $N = 25$, $p < .01$, $r = .21$

d.v. = Answering Success 3
    Childers (1971), 184   Pearson's Product
                                $N = 25$, $p < .01$, $r = .08$

d.v. = Answering Success 5 (0, 3)
    Childers (1971), 184   Pearson's Product
                                $N = 25$, $p < .01$, $r = .08$

d.v. = Answering Success 5 (0, 2)
    Childers (1971), 184   Pearson's Product
                                $N = 25$, $p < .01$, $r = .05$

6. Total circulation/books owned

d.v. = Answering Success 1
    Childers (1971), 184   Pearson's Product
                                $N = 25$, $p < .01$, $r = -.02$

d.v. = Answering Success 3
    Childers (1971), 184   Pearson's Product
                                $N = 25$, $p < .01$, $r = -.03$

d.v. = Answering Success 5 (0, 3)
    Childers (1971), 184   Pearson's Product
                                $N = 25$, $p < .01$, $r = -.04$

d.v. = Answering Success 5 (0, 2)
    Childers (1971), 184   Pearson's Product
                              $N = 25$, $p < .01$, $r = -.05$

A12 Fluctuation in collection

1. Number of books added in the last year

d.v. = Answering Success 1
    Childers (1971), 183   Pearson's Product
                              $N = 25$, $p < .01$, $r = .59$

d.v. = Answering Success 3
    Childers (1971), 183   Pearson's Product
                              $N = 25$, $p < .01$, $r = .36$

d.v. = Answering Success 5 (0, 3)
    Childers (1971), 183   Pearson's Product
                              $N = 25$, $p < .01$, $r = .56$

d.v. = Answering Success 5 (0, 2)
    Childers (1971), 183   Pearson's Product
                              $N = 25$, $p < .01$, $r = .54$

2. Number of books discarded in the last year

d.v. = Answering Success 1
    Childers (1971), 183   Pearson's Product
                              $N = 25$, $p < .01$, $r = .29$

d.v. = Answering Success 3
    Childers (1971), 183   Pearson's Product
                              $N = 25$, $p < .01$, $r = .18$

d.v. = Answering Success 5 (0, 3)
    Childers (1971), 183   Pearson's Product
                              $N = 25$, $p < .01$, $r = .26$

d.v. = Answering Success 5 (0, 2)
    Childers (1971), 183   Pearson's Product
                              $N = 25$, $p < .01$, $r = .25$

3. Number of books added plus the number of books discarded, an absolute measure of change in the last year

d.v. = Answering Success 1
    Childers (1971), 184   Pearson's Product
                              $N = 25$, $p < .01$, $r = .51$

    Jirjees (1983), 201   Spearman Rank Order Correlation
                              $N = 5$, $r_s = .20$, $p < .374$
                              (Finding not significant)

d.v. = Answering Success 3
    Childers (1971), 184   Pearson's Product
                              $N = 25$, $p < .01$, $r = .31$

d.v. = Answering Success 5 (0, 3)
      Childers (1971), 184   Pearson's Product
                                $N = 25$, $p < .01$, $r = .48$

d.v. = Answering Success 5 (0, 2)
      Childers (1971), 184   Pearson's Product
                                $N = 25$, $p < .01$, $r = .45$

4. Proportion of collection change: (Bks add + bks discard)/(bks owned + bks add − bks discard)

d.v. = Answering Success 1
      Childers (1971), 184   Pearson's Product
                                $N = 25$, $p < .01$, $r = .09$

d.v. = Answering Success 3
      Childers (1971), 184   Pearson's Product
                                $N = 25$, $p < .01$, $r = -.14$

d.v. = Answering Success 5 (0, 3)
      Childers (1971), 184   Pearson's Product
                                $N = 25$, $p < .01$, $r = .01$

d.v. = Answering Success 5 (0, 2)
      Childers (1971), 184   Pearson's Product
                                $N = 25$, $p < .01$, $r = .12$

A13 Institutional bureaucratic service orientation

1. Librarian's rating of the degree to which a published service code is used to carry out service
(5-point Likert scale: 1 — Not at all, To a little extent, To some extent, To a great extent, Completely — 5)

d.v. = Answering Success 1
      Myers (1983), 89   Spearman Rank Order Correlation
                                $N = 38$, $r_s = -.33$, $p \le .05$

2. Librarian's rating of the degree to which a service code details the limitations of offered services
(5-point Likert scale: 1 — Not at all, To a little extent, To some extent, To a great extent, Completely — 5)

d.v. = Answering Success 1
      Myers (1983), 89   Spearman Rank Order Correlation
                                $N = 38$, $r_s = -.32$, $p \le .05$

3. Librarian's rating of the degree to which staff meetings are held with reference personnel
(5-point Likert scale: 1 — Never, Rarely, Occasionally, Regularly, Always — 5)

d.v. = Answering Success 1

        Myers (1983), 128   Spearman Rank Order Correlation

                                $N = 40$, $r_s = .09$, $p > .10$

                                (Finding not significant)

4. Librarian's rating of the degree to which reference staff are provided a written job description

(5-point Likert scale: 1 — Never, Rarely, Occasionally, Regularly, Always — 5)

d.v. = Answering Success 1

        Myers (1983), 128   Spearman Rank Order Correlation

                                $N = 40$, $r_s = .05$, $p > .10$

                                (Finding not significant)

5. Librarian's rating of the degree to which a specific plan has been developed for instruction in using information aids

(5-point Likert scale: 1 — Not at all, To a little extent, To some extent, To a great extent, Completely — 5)

d.v. = Answering Success 1

        Myers (1983), 127   Spearman Rank Order Correlation

                                $N = 40$, $r_s = -.24$, $p \leq .074$

A14 Staff availability

1. Librarian's rating of the degree to which a librarian is available to users during all hours the library is open

(5-point Likert scale: 1 — Not at all, To a little extent, To some extent, To a great extent, Completely — 5)

d.v. = Answering Success 1

        Myers (1983), 89   Spearman Rank Order Correlation

                                $N = 39$, $r_s = .30$, $p \leq .05$

2. Librarian's rating of the degree to which staffing patterns reflect user needs

(5-point Likert scale: 1 — Not at all, To a little extent, To some extent, To a great extent, Completely — 5)

d.v. = Answering Success 1

        Myers (1983), 127   Spearman Rank Order Correlation

                                $N = 40$, $r_s = .09$, $p > .10$

                                (Finding not significant)

A15 Level of referral service

1. Librarian's rating of the degree to which referrals are a standard level of service

(5-point Likert scale: 1 — Not at all, To a little extent, To some extent, To a great extent, Completely — 5)

d.v. = Answering Success 1
      Myers (1983), 127   Spearman Rank Order Correlation
                               $N = 40$, $r_s = .22$, $p \leq .089$

2. Librarian's rating of the degree to which formal cooperation exists with other agencies to provide for user needs
(5-point Likert scale: 15 — Not at all, To a little extent, To some extent, To a great extent, Completely — 5)

d.v. = Answering Success 1
      Myers (1983), 127   Spearman Rank Order Correlation
                               $N = 40$, $r_s = -.02$, $p > .10$
                               (Finding not significant)

3. Librarian's rating of the degree to which fact-type questions received by phone are answered instead of referring the user to a source which contains the answer
(5-point Likert scale: 1 — Never, Rarely, Occasionally, Regularly, Always — 5)

d.v. = Answering Success 1
      Myers (1983), 128   Spearman Rank Order Correlation
                               $N = 40$, $r_s = .01$, $p > .10$
                               (Finding not significant)

4. Librarian's rating of the degree to which the information for unanswered fact-type questions is obtained from outside sources instead of referring the user to these sources
(5-point Likert scale: 1 — Never, Rarely, Occasionally, Regularly, Always — 5)

d.v. = Answering Success 1
      Myers (1983), 128   Spearman Rank Order Correlation
                               $N = 40$, $r_s = -.13$, $p > .10$
                               (Finding not significant)

5. Librarian's rating of the degree to which unanswered questions are referred to senior staff
(5-point Likert scale: 1 — Never, Rarely, Occasionally, Regularly, Always — 5)

d.v. = Answering Success 1
      Myers (1983), 128   Spearman Rank Order Correlation
                               $N = 40$, $r_s = .01$, $p > .10$
                               (Finding not significant)

6. Librarian's rating of the degree to which a cooperative selection policy has been developed within a given service area

(5-point Likert scale: 1 — Not at all, To a little extent, To some extent, To a great extent, Completely — 5)

d.v. = Answering Success 1
       Myers (1983), 127   Spearman Rank Order Correlation
                                  $N = 40$, $r_s = -.13$, $p > .10$
                                  (Finding not significant)

A16 Arrangement of service points

1. Librarian's rating of the degree to which service points are near the main focus of activity in the library
(5-point Likert scale: 1 — Not at all, To a little extent, To some extent, To a great extent, Completely — 5)

d.v. = Answering Success 1
       Myers (1983), 127   Spearman Rank Order Correlation
                                  $N = 40$, $r_s = -.20$, $p > .10$
                                  (Finding not significant)

2. Librarian's rating of the degree to which the reference collection is near an open area to facilitate access
(5-point Likert scale: 1 — Not at all, To a little extent, To some extent, To a great extent, Completely — 5)

d.v. = Answering Success 1
       Myers (1983), 127   Spearman Rank Order Correlation
                                  $N = 40$, $r_s = -.15$, $p > .10$
                                  (Finding not significant)

3. Librarian's rating of the degree to which provisions are made for quiet concentrated study, i.e., individual carrels
(5-point Likert scale: 1 — Not at all, To a little extent, To some extent, To a great extent, Completely — 5)

d.v. = Answering Success 1
       Myers (1983), 127   Spearman Rank Order Correlation
                                  $N = 40$, $r_s = -.19$, $p > .10$
                                  (Finding not significant)

4. Librarian's rating of the degree to which the reference area is situated so that conversation between librarians and users does not disturb others
(5-point Likert scale: 1 — Not at all, To a little extent, To some extent, To a great extent, Completely — 5)

d.v. = Answering Success 1
       Myers (1983), 127   Spearman Rank Order Correlation
                                  $N = 40$, $r_s = -.09$, $p > .10$
                                  (Finding not significant)

5. Librarian's rating of the degree to which service points are available throughout the library
(5-point Likert scale: 1 — Not at all, To a little extent, To some extent, To a
great extent, Completely — 5)

d.v. = Answering Success 1
       Myers (1983), 127   Spearman Rank Order Correlation
                                   $N = 40$, $r_s = .01$, $p > .10$
                                   (Finding not significant)

6. Number of service points within the main reference area

d.v. = Answering Success 1
       Myers (1983), 128   Spearman Rank Order Correlation
                                   $N = 40$, $r_s = .15$, $p > .10$
                                   (Finding not significant)

A17 Administrative evaluation of services

1. Librarian's rating of the degree to which user data is regularly collected to
determine service effectiveness
(5-point Likert scale: 1 — Not at all, To a little extent, To some extent, To a
great extent, Completely — 5)

d.v. = Answering Success 1
       Myers (1983), 127   Spearman Rank Order Correlation
                                   $N = 40$, $r_s = -.11$, $p > .10$
                                   (Finding not significant)

2. Librarian's rating of the degree to which measurement and evaluation of
services is assigned to staff members with requisite skills
(5-point Likert scale: 1 — Not at all, To a little extent, To some extent, To a
great extent, Completely — 5)

d.v. = Answering Success 1
       Myers (1983), 127   Spearman Rank Order Correlation
                                   $N = 40$, $r_s = -.18$, $p > .10$
                                   (Finding not significant)

3. Librarian's rating of the degree to which statistics are collected systematically
for administrative use
(5-point Likert scale: 1 — Not at all, To a little extent, To some extent, To a
great extent, Completely — 5)

d.v. = Answering Success 1
       Myers (1983), 127   Spearman Rank Order Correlation
                                   $N = 40$, $r_s = -.00$, $p > .10$
                                   (Finding not significant)

4. Librarian's rating of the degree to which the effectiveness of referrals is evaluated
(5-point Likert scale: 1 — Not at all, To a little extent, To some extent, To a great extent, Completely — 5)

d.v. = Answering Success 1
　　Myers (1983), 127　　　　Spearman Rank Order Correlation
　　　　　　　　　　　　　　$N = 40$, $r_s = .05$, $p \le .089$

5. Librarian's rating of the degree to which reference services are regularly reviewed to identify who is being served and how to reach those who are not
(5-point Likert scale: 1 — Not at all, To a little extent, To some extent, To a great extent, Completely — 5)

d.v. = Answering Success 1
　　Myers (1983), 127　　　　Spearman Rank Order Correlation
　　　　　　　　　　　　　　$N = 40$, $r_s = -.22$, $p \le .091$

6. Librarian's rating of the degree to which provision is made for feedback from users about services
(5-point Likert scale: 1 — Not at all, To a little extent, To some extent, To a great extent, Completely — 5)

d.v. = Answering Success 1
　　Myers (1983), 127　　　　Spearman Rank Order Correlation
　　　　　　　　　　　　　　$N = 40$, $r_s = -.15$, $p > .10$
　　　　　　　　　　　　　　(Finding not significant)

A18　Use of paraprofessionals at the reference desk

1. Librarian's rating of the degree to which paraprofessionals answer reference questions
(5-point Likert scale: 1 — Always, Regularly, Occasionally, Rarely, Never — 5)

d.v. = Answering Success 1
　　Myers (1983), 128　　　　Spearman Rank Order Correlation
　　　　　　　　　　　　　　$N = 40$, $r_s = .23$, $p \le .080$

2. Librarian's rating of the degree to which paraprofessionals answer directional questions
(5-point Likert scale: 1 — Always, Regularly, Occasionally, Rarely, Never — 5)

d.v. = Answering Success 1
　　Myers (1983), 128　　　　Spearman Rank Order Correlation
　　　　　　　　　　　　　　$N = 40$, $r_s = .17$, $p > .10$
　　　　　　　　　　　　　　(Finding not significant)

3. Librarian's rating of the degree to which paraprofessionals answer fact-type questions

(5-point Likert scale: 1 — Always, Regularly, Occasionally, Rarely, Never — 5)

d.v. = Answering Success 1
    Myers (1983), 128   Spearman Rank Order Correlation
                             $N = 40$, $r_s = .21$, $p \leq .099$

A19 Volume of questions

1. Number of directional questions answered by the library per week

d.v. = Answering Success 1
    Myers (1983), 129   Spearman Rank Order Correlation
                             $N = 40$, $r_s = .48$, $p \leq .003$

2. Number of reference questions answered by the library per week

d.v. = Answering Success 1
    Myers (1983), 129   Spearman Rank Order Correlation
                             $N = 40$, $r_s = .32$, $p \leq .037$

B

The Librarian

B1 Experience of reference librarian

1. Number of years of experience

d.v. = Answering Success 1
    Benham (1987), 101   Pearson's Product
                             Unreported correlation coefficient
                             not considered significant enough
                             to include this variable in
                             regression calculations
    Powell (1987), 218   Pearson's Product
                             $N = 51$, $r = .11$, $p < .221$

d.v. = Answering Success 2
    Powell (1987), 218   Pearson's Product
                             $N = 51$, $r = .15$, $p < .161$

2. Years in reference work

d.v. = Composite
    Bunge (1967), 30   Spearman Rank Order Correlation
                               Coefficient

N = 9, r_s = .583, Positive value
indicates that the difference in
performance between trained and
untrained personnel continues to
increase regardless of experience

d.v. = Answering Success 1

 Benham (1987), 120   Multiple Regression
          N = 244, F = 10.7438, p ≤ .01,
          r^2 = .3494
          B = −.016, Beta = −.023

 Powell (1987), 218   Pearson's Product
          N = 51, r = −.00, p < .492

 Jirjees (1983), 201   Spearman Rank Order Correlation
          N = 5, r_s = .70, p < .094
          (Finding not significant)

d.v. = Answering Success 2

 Powell (1987), 218, 232   a. Pearson's Product
          N = 51, r = .06, p < .358
         b. Multiple Regression
          N = 51, F = 4.549, p < .05,
          R^2 = .336
          B = .0033, Beta = .360

3. Years in reference work at present library

d.v. = Answering Success 1

 Benham (1987), 102   Pearson's Product
         Unreported correlation coefficient
          not considered significant enough
          to include this variable in
          regression calculations

 Powell (1987), 218, 227   a. Pearson's Product
          N = 51, r = −.10, p < .258
         b. Multiple Regression
          N = 51, F = 5.606, p < .01,
          R^2 = .384
          B = −.396, Beta = −.072

d.v. = Answering Success 2

 Powell (1987), 218, 229   a. Pearson's Product
          N = 51, r = .05, p < .366
         b. Multiple Regression
          N = 51, F = 2.232, p <?,
          R^2 = .199
          B = −.001, Beta = −.022

4. Number of years in reference work after earning MLS

d.v. = Answering Success 1

Benham (1987), 121–124   a. Multiple Regression

$N = 244, F = 13.9557,$
$p \leq .001, r^2 = .4110$
$B = .167, Beta = .122$

b. Multiple Regression

$N = 244, F = 13.4323,$
$p \leq .001, r^2 = .4319$
$B = .186, Beta = .135$

c. Multiple Regression

$N = 244, F = 25.6663,$
$p \leq .001, r^2 = .5273$
$B = .201, Beta = .146$

5. Years elapsed since formal education

d.v. = Efficiency

Bunge (1967), 29   Wilcoxon matched-pairs
                             signed-ranks test
                             $N = 9, p > .05, T = 10$
                             (No significant difference)

d.v. = Answering Success 1

Powell (1987), 218   Pearson's Product
                             $N = 51, r = -.13, p < .439$

Jirjees (1983), 201   Spearman Rank Order Correlation
                             $N = 5, r_s = .10, p < .436$
                             (Finding not significant)

d.v. = Answering Success 2

Powell (1987), 218   Pearson's Product
                             $N = 51, r = .01, p < .477$

6. Years of work experience outside of librarianship

d.v. = Answering Success 1

Benham (1987), 102   Pearson's Product
                             Unreported correlation coefficient
                             not considered significant enough
                             to include this variable in
                             regression calculations

7. (Average number of hours on desk per week) (52) (Number of Years) =
$ee_1 + e_2 + e_3 + \ldots) = E$

It is probable that $520 < E < 83,200$. Break into five classes with an interval of 16,000. (MS)

B2 Education of librarian

1. Professional or paraprofessional

d.v. = Answering Success 3
  Bunge (1967), 23   Wilcoxon matched-pairs
              signed-ranks test
              $N = 9$, $p > .05$, $T = 14$
              (No significant difference)

d.v. = Efficiency
  Bunge (1967), 25   Wilcoxon matched-pairs
              signed-ranks test
              $N = 9$, $p < .025$, $T = 5$
              (Significant difference)

2. Type(s) of degree received (none, bachelor's, master's — subject, BLS, MLS, other)

d.v. = Answering Success 1
  Powell (1987), 218, 228   a. Pearson's Product
               $N = 51$, $r = .40$, $p < .002$
               b. Multiple Regression
                $N = 51$, $F = 4.176$, $p < .05$,
                 $R^2 = .317$
                $B = 2.287$, Beta $= .300$

d.v. = Answering Success 2
  Powell (1987), 218, 230, 232 a. Pearson's Product
               $N = 51$, $r = .11$, $p < .233$
               b. Multiple Regression
                $N = 51$, $F = .492$, $p < .?$,
                 $R^2 = .052$
                $B = .00121$, Beta $= .0220$
               c. Multiple Regression
                $N = 51$, $F = 4.549$, $p < .05$,
                 $R^2 = .336$
                $B = -.0024$, Beta $= . - .044$

3. Second Masters other than MLS (Yes/No)

d.v. = Answering Success 1
  Benham (1987), 99   Pearson's Product
              Unreported correlation coefficient
              not considered significant enough
              to include this variable in
              regression calculations

4. Undergraduate degree major (education, history, English, business and other social sciences, sciences, music, languages, art, religion and other humanities)

d.v. = Answering Success 1

      Benham (1987), 98   Pearson's Product
                                    Unreported correlation coefficient
                                        not considered significant enough
                                        to include this variable in
                                        regression calculations

5. Number and type (accredited/unaccredited, broad/narrow emphasis, considerable/some/slight/little or no attention to technique, use/nonuse of practice questions) of formal reference courses.

d.v. = Efficiency

      Bunge (1967), 35   Not reported
                                        "... The differences on this factor
                                        are not great and would be hard
                                        to score or deal with objectively."

6. Number of library science courses at the undergraduate level

d.v. = Answering Success:

      Benham (1987), 99   a. Multiple Regression
                                        $N = 244$, $F = 13.6918$,
                                            $p \leq .001$, $r^2 = .3732$
                                        $B = -.025$, Beta $= -.044$
                                    b. Multiple Regression
                                        $N = 244$, $F = 13.4323$,
                                            $p \leq .001$, $r^2 = .4319$
                                        $B = -.008$, Beta $= -.01508$

7. Number of library science courses at the master's level

d.v. = Answering Success 1

      Benham (1987), 121   Multiple Regression
                                        $N = 244$, $F = 10.7438$, $p \leq .01$,
                                        $r^2 = .3494$
                                        $B = -.004$, Beta $= -.007$

8. Number of library science courses at the 6th-year specialist level

d.v. = Answering Success 1

      Benham (1987), 99   Pearson's Product
                                        Unreported correlation coefficient
                                        not considered significant enough
                                        to include this variable in
                                        regression calculations

9. Number of reference and bibliography courses

d.v. = Answering Success 1

    Benham (1987), 120   Multiple Regression

                             $N = 244$, $F = 10.7438$, $p \leq .01$,

                             $r^2 = .3494$

                             $B = .112$, Beta $= .102$

                             Powell (1987), 218,227

                             a. Pearson's Product

                                  $N = 51$, $r = .32$, $p < .013$

                             b. Multiple Regression

                                  $N = 51$, $F = 5.606$, $p < .05$,

                                  $R^2 = .384$

                                  $B = .947$, Beta $= .071$

d.v. = Answering Success 2

    Powell (1987), 218, 229   a. Pearson's Product

                                  $N = 51$, $r = -.12$, $p < .211$

                             b. Multiple Regression

                                  $N = 51$, $F = 2.232$, $p <?$,

                                  $R^2 = .199$

                                  $B = -.026$, Beta $= -.266$

10. Total number of library science courses complete

d.v. = Answering Success 1

    Powell (1987), 218   Pearson's Product

                           $N = 51$, $r = .41$, $p < .002$

d.v. = Answering Success 2

    Powell (1987), 218   Pearson's Product

                           $N = 51$, $r = .56$, $p < .001$

11. Number of college/university credit courses completed since degree

d.v. = Answering Success 1

    Benham (1987), 99   Pearson's Product

                           Unreported correlation coefficient

                           not considered significant enough

                           to include this variable in

                           regression calculations

12. Number of continuing education courses completed since degree

d.v. = Answering Success 1

    Benham (1987), 100   Pearson's Product

                           Unreported correlation coefficient

                           not considered significant enough

                           to include this variable in

                           regression calculations

13. Number of workshops or institutes completed since degree

d.v. = Answering Success 1

    Benham (1987), 100   Pearson's Product
                                Unreported correlation coefficient
                                not considered significant enough
                                to include this variable in
                                regression calculations

14. Number of continuing education activities participated in annually

d.v. = Answering Success 1

    Powell (1987), 220, 228   a. Pearson's Product
                                   $N = 51$, $r = .10$, $p < .239$
                                  b. Multiple Regression
                                   $N = 51$, $F = 4.176$, $p < .05$,
                                     $R^2 = .317$
                                   $B = -.369$, $Beta = -.078$

d.v. = Answering Success 2

    Powell (1987), 220, 230   a. Pearson's Product
                                   $N = 51$, $r = .08$, $p < .289$
                                  b. Multiple Regression
                                   $N = 51$, $F = .492$, $p < ?$,
                                   $R^2 = .052$
                                   $B = .00001$, $Beta = .0002$

15. Undergraduate grade point average

d.v. = Answering Success 1

    Benham (1987), 118   Multiple Regression
                                 $N = 244$, $F = 13.6918$, $p \leq .001$,
                                 $r^2 = .3732$
                                 $B = .453$, $Beta = .120$

16. Graduate grade point average

d.v. = Answering Success 1

    Benham (1987), 121   Multiple Regression
                                 $N = 244$, $F = 10.7438$, $p \leq .01$,
                                 $r^2 = .3494$
                                 $B = .112$, $Beta = .017$

17. GRE Verbal score

d.v. = Answering Success 1

    Benham (1987), 122   Multiple Regression
                                 $N = 244$, $F = 13.9557$, $p \leq .001$,
                                 $r^2 = .4110$
                                 $B = .002$, $Beta = .145$

18. GRE Quantitative score

d.v. = Answering Success 1

Benham (1987), 123–124   a. Multiple Regression
$N = 244$, $F = 13.4323$,
$p \leq .001$, $r^2 = .4319$
$B = .003$, Beta $= .208$
b. Multiple Regression
$N = 244$, $F = 25.6663$,
$p \leq .001$, $r^2 = .5273$
$B = .002$, Beta $= .199$

19. Librarian's rating of the degree to which opportunities for continuing education are available

(5-point Likert scale: 1 — Not at all, To a little extent, To some extent, To a great extent, Completely — 5)

d.v. = Answering Success 1

Myers (1983), 127   Spearman Rank Order Correlation
$N = 40$, $r_s = .10$, $p > .10$
(Finding not significant)

20. Librarian's rating of the degree to which individual librarians have training in specific subject fields

(5-point Likert scale: 1 — Not at all, To a little extent, To some extent, To a great extent, Completely — 5)

d.v. = Answering Success 1

Myers (1983), 127   Spearman Rank Order Correlation
$N = 40$, $r_s = .09$, $p > .10$
(Finding not significant)

21. Librarian's rating of the degree to which staff are chosen on both their academic background and their communication skills

(5-point Likert scale: 1 — Not at all, To a little extent, To some extent, To a great extent, Completely — 5)

d.v. = Answering Success 1

Myers (1983), 127   Spearman Rank Order Correlation
$N = 40$, $r_s = -.03$, $p > .10$
(Finding not significant)

22. Number of librarians with a degree outside of library science

Jirjees (1983), 201   Spearman Rank Order Correlation
$N = 5$, $r_s = .30$, $p < .312$
(Finding not significant)

B3 For paraprofessionals, amount of in-service training

1. "Relative amount of in-service training and supervision . . ."

d.v. = Composite

Bunge (1967), 31 — Spearman Rank Order Correlation Coefficient

$N = 9$, $r_s = -.642$, Negative value indicates that the difference in performance between trained and untrained personnel continues to decrease with the increase in in-service training

B4 Question-answering duties

1. Average number of hours per week on the reference desk

d.v. = Answering Success 1

Powell (1987), 221 — Pearson's Product

$N = 51$, $r = .58$, $p < .001$

Jirjees (1983), 201 — Spearman Rank Order Correlation

$N = 5$, $r_s = .60$, $p < .142$

(Finding not significant)

d.v. = Answering Success 2

Powell (1987), 221 — Pearson's Product

$N = 51$, $r = .54$, $p < .001$

2. Number of reference questions answered per week (excluding directional) by librarian

d.v. = Answering Success 1

Benham (1987), 118 — Multiple Regression

$N = 244$, $F = 13.6918$, $p \leq .001$, $r^2 = .3732$

$B = .003$, Beta $= .130$

Powell (1987), 221, 227 — a. Pearson's Product

$N = 51$, $r = .50$, $p < .001$

b. Multiple Regression

$N = 51$, $F = 5.606$, $p < .01$, $R^2 = .384$

$B = .178$, Beta $= .388$

d.v. = Answering Success 2

Powell (1987), 221, 229, 232 — a. Pearson's Product

$N = 51$, $r = .46$, $p < .001$

b. Multiple Regression

$N = 51$, $F = 2.232$, $p < .?$, $R^2 = .199$

B = .001, Beta = .332
c. Multiple Regression
N = 51, F = 4.549, p < .05,
R^2 = .336
B = .0007, Beta = .203

B5 Librarian's attitude toward question-answering duties

1. Librarian's rating of the degree to which reference services are developed to meet current user needs and anticipate future needs
(5-point Likert scale: 1 — Not at all, To a little extent, To some extent, To a great extent, Completely — 5)
d.v. = Answering Success 1
    Myers (1983), 127   Spearman Rank Order Correlation
                                    N = 40, r_s = −.22, p ≤ .091

2. Librarian's rating of the degree to which informational access guides [pathfinders] are developed
(5-point Likert scale: 1 — Not at all, To a little extent, To some extent, To a great extent, Completely — 5)
d.v. = Answering Success 1
    Myers (1983), 127   Spearman Rank Order Correlation
                                    N = 40, r_s = .25, p ≤ .062

3. Librarian's rating of the degree to which service is provided in adaptable settings, i.e., personal contact, correspondence, telephone, or other
(5-point Likert scale: 1 — Not at all, To a little extent, To some extent, To a great extent, Completely — 5)
d.v. = Answering Success 1
    Myers (1983), 127   Spearman Rank Order Correlation
                                    N = 40, r_s = .17, p > .10
                                    (Finding not significant)

B6 Duties other than question-answering

1. Selecting and handling reference books — more duty/less duty in each pair
d.v. = Composite
    Bunge (1967), 33   Spearman rank order correlation
                                    coefficient
                                    N = 9, r_s = .767. Positive value
                                    indicates that the difference
                                    between trained and untrained
                                    personnel continues to increase
                                    with the increase in nonquestion-
                                    answering duties

B7 Librarian's service orientation

1. Attitude about providing services to clients
(4-point Likert scale: Like Very Much—Do Not Do)

d.v. = Answering Success 1
    Benham (1987), 103   Pearson's Product
                                 Unreported correlation coefficient
                                 not considered significant enough
                                 to include this variable in
                                 regression calculations

2. Librarian's rating of the importance of showing a personal interest in user's problems
(7-point Likert scale: Very important—Not at all important)

d.v. = Librarian Satisfaction
    Whitlach (1990), 80, 92   a. Pearson's product
                                    $N = 209$, $p < .05$,
                                       $r = .135$
                                 b. Multiple Regression
                                  $N = 257$, $F = 19.67$,
                                       $p < .001$, adj.$R^2 = .378$
                                  $B = .117$, Beta $= .151$,
                                      $t = 2.79$, $p < .01$

d.v. = Client Satisfaction 1
    Whitlach (1990), 82, 92   Pearson's product
                                    $N = 209$, $p > .05$, $r = -.035$
                                    (Finding not significant)

d.v. = Answering Success 6
    Whitlach (1990), 84, 92   Pearson's product
                                    $N = 209$, $p > .05$, $r = -.071$
                                    (Finding not significant)

3. Librarian's rating of the importance of going beyond library resources
(7-point Likert scale: Very important—Not at all important)

d.v. = Librarian Satisfaction
    Whitlach (1990), 80, 92   a. Pearson's product
                                    $N = 209$, $p > .05$, $r = .088$
                                    (Finding not significant)
                                 b. Multiple Regression
                                  $N = 257$, $F = 19.67$,
                                       $p < .001$, adj.$R^2 = .378$
                                  $B = -.136$, Beta $= -.163$,
                                  $t = -2.75$, $p < .01$

d.v. = Client Satisfaction 1
> Whitlach (1990), 82, 92   Pearson's product
> N = 209, p > .05, r = −.062
> (Finding not significant)

d.v. = Answering Success 6
> Whitlach (1990), 84, 92   Pearson's product
> N = 209, p > .05, r = −.049
> (Finding not significant)

4. Librarian's rating of the degree to which reference staff actively promotes the use of all library services
(5-point Likert scale: 1 — Not at all, To a little extent, To some extent, To a great extent, Completely — 5)

d.v. = Answering Success 1
> Myers 1983, 127   Spearman Rank Order Correlation
> N = 40, r_s = −.09, p > .10
> (Finding not significant)

5. Librarian's rating of the degree to which the accuracy of a source is the responsibility of the user
(5-point Likert scale: 1 — Never, Rarely, Occasionally, Regularly, Always — 5)

d.v. = Answering Success 1
> Myers (1983), 128   Spearman Rank Order Correlation
> N = 40, r_s = .30, p > .10
> (Finding not significant)

6. Librarian's rating of the importance of advising users of all alternative solution to resolve their information needs
(7-point Likert scale: Very important — Not at all important)

d.v. = Librarian Satisfaction
> Whitlach (1990), 80, 92   Pearson's product
> N = 209, p > .05, r = .068
> (Finding not significant)

d.v. = Client Satisfaction 1
> Whitlach (1990), 82, 92   a. Pearson's product
> N = 209, p > .05,
> r = −.161
> b. Multiple Regression
> N = 257, F = 30.13,
> p < .001, adj.R^2 = .412
> B = −.125, Beta = −.151,
> t = −2.83, p < .01

d.v. = Answering Success 6
    Whitlach (1990), 84, 92   a. Pearson's product
                                      $N = 209$, $p < .05$,
                                        $r = -.122$
                          b. Multiple Regression
                                    $N = 257$, $F = 11.95$,
                                        $p < .001$, adj.$R^2 = .266$
                                    $B = -.235$, Beta $= -.151$,
                                    $t = -2.54$, $p < .05$

B8 Librarians' perception of the collection adequacy

1. Adequacy of collection size, relative figure from 1 to 9

d.v. = Answering Success 1
    Powell (1987), 219   Pearson's Product
                                    $N = 51$, $r = .57$, $p < .001$

d.v. = Answering Success 2
    Powell (1987), 219, 232   a. Pearson's Product
                                    $N = 51$, $r = .45$, $p < .001$
                          b. Multiple Regression
                                    $N = 51$, $F = 4.549$,
                                        $p < .05$, $R^2 = .336$
                                    $B = .0309$, Beta $= .477$

2. Adequacy of collection currency, relative figure from 1 to 9

d.v. = Answering Success 1
    Powell (1987), 219   Pearson's Product
                                    $N = 51$, $r = .57$, $p < .001$

d.v. = Answering Success 2
    Powell (1987), 219   Pearson's Product
                                    $N = 51$, $r = .43$, $p < .001$

3. Librarian's rating of the degree to which frequently requested materials are available in multiple copies
(5-point Likert scale: 1 — Not at all, To a little extent, To some extent, To a great extent, Completely — 5)

d.v. = Answering Success 1
    Myers (1983), 89   Spearman Rank Order Correlation
                                    $N = 39$, $r_s = -.29$, $p \leq .05$

4. Librarian's rating of the degree to which a selection policy has been developed to address user needs and anticipated user needs

(5-point Likert scale: 1 — Not at all, To a little extent, To some extent, To a great extent, Completely — 5)

d.v. = Answering Success 1
  Myers (1983), 127   Spearman Rank Order Correlation
                       N = 40, r_s = −.10, p > .10
                       (Finding not significant)

5. Librarian's rating of the degree to which materials are added that reflect a diversity of format and diversity of depth of coverage, and also reflect known user patterns
(5-point Likert scale: 1 — Not at all, To a little extent, To some extent, To a great extent, Completely — 5)

d.v. = Answering Success 1
  Myers (1983), 127   Spearman Rank Order Correlation
                       N = 40, r_s = .04, p > .10
                       (Finding not significant)

6. Librarian's rating of the degree to which the collection is regularly weeded
(5-point Likert scale: 1 — Not at all, To a little extent, To some extent, To a great extent, Completely — 5)

d.v. = Answering Success 1
  Myers (1983), 127   Spearman Rank Order Correlation
                       N = 40, r_s = −.08, p > .10
                       (Finding not significant)

7. Librarian's rating of the degree to which the size of collection is adequate to meet user needs
(5-point Likert scale: 1 — Never, Rarely, Occasionally, Regularly, Always — 5)

d.v. = Answering Success 1
  Myers (1983), 128   Spearman Rank Order Correlation
                       N = 40, r_s = −.09, p > .10
                       (Finding not significant)

8. Librarian's rating of the degree to which the currency of the collection is adequate to meet user needs
(5-point Likert scale: 1 — Never, Rarely, Occasionally, Regularly, Always — 5)

d.v. = Answering Success 1
  Myers (1983), 128   Spearman Rank Order Correlation
                       N = 40, r_s = −.04, p > .10
                       (Finding not significant)

B9 Librarian's perception of personal education

1. Degree of interest in reference/bibliography courses
(5-point Likert scale: Very Interesting — Very Dull)

d.v. = Answering Success 1
   Benham (1987), 121–124 a. Multiple Regression
                $N = 244$, $F = 13.9557$,
                  $p \leq .001$, $r^2 = .4110$
                 $B = .362$, Beta $= .202$
               b. Multiple Regression
                $N = 244$, $F = 13.4323$,
                  $p \leq .001$, $r^2 = .4319$
                 $B = .331$, Beta $= .185$
               c. Multiple Regression
                $N = 244$, $F = 25.6663$,
                  $p \leq .001$, $r^2 = .5273$
                 $B = .249$, Beta $= .139$

2. Perception of degree to which library science education prepared one for reference work
 (4-point Likert scale: Very Well — Very Poorly)

d.v. = Answering Success 1
   Benham (1987), 100 Pearson's Product
              Unreported correlation coefficient
                not considered significant enough
                to include this variable in
                regression calculations

3. Perception of educational preparation for supervision of reference work
(5-point Likert scale: Excellent — Received None)

d.v. = Answering Success 1
   Benham (1987)   Pearson's Product
              Unreported correlation coefficient
                not considered significant enough
                to include this variable in
                regression calculations

4. Perception of awareness of L.S. educators of the reality of library work environment
(5-point Likert scale: Very Well Aware — Not At All Aware)

d.v. = Answering Success 1
     Benham (1987),   Pearson's Product
                             Unreported correlation coefficient
                             not considered significant enough
                             to include this variable in
                             regression calculations

B10 Librarian's perception of other duties

1. Perceived level of responsibility for selecting reference materials
   (4-point Likert scale: None — High)

d.v. = Answering Success 1
     Benham (1987)   Pearson's Product
                             Unreported correlation coefficient
                             not considered significant enough
                             to include this variable in
                             regression calculations

2. Attitude about choosing reference books for purchase
   (4-point Likert scale: Like Very Much — Do Not Do)

d.v. = Answering Success 1
     Benham (1987)   Pearson's Product
                             Unreported correlation coefficient
                             not considered significant enough
                             to include this variable in
                             regression calculations

B11 Outside reading

1. Number of library journals read regularly

d.v. = Answering Success 1
     Benham (1987), 103   Pearson's Product
                             Unreported correlation coefficient
                             not considered significant enough
                             to include this variable in
                             regression calculations
     Powell (1987), 220   Pearson's Product
                             $N = 51$, $r = .48$, $p < .001$
d.v. = Answering Success 2
     Powell (1987), 220   Pearson's Product
                             $N = 51$, $r = .56$, $p < .001$

2. Number of nonlibrary periodicals read regularly

d.v. = Answering Success 1
> Benham (1987), 113   Pearson's Product
> Unreported correlation coefficient
> not considered significant enough
> to include this variable in
> regression calculations

B12 Memberships in associations and committees

1. Number of memberships in associations and committees

d.v. = Answering Success 1
> Powell (1987), 220   Pearson's Product
> $N = 51$, $r = .30$, $p < .016$
> Jirjees (1983), 201   Spearman Rank Order Correlation
> $N = 5$, $r_s = .10$, $p < .436$
> (Finding not significant)

d.v. = Answering Success 2
> Powell (1987), 220   Pearson's Product
> $N = 51$, $r = .40$, $p < .003$

B13 Age of librarian

Operational definition
1. Older or younger in selected pairs

d.v. = Efficiency
> Bunge (1967), 28   Wilcoxon matched-pairs
> signed-ranks test
> $N = 9$, $p > .10$, $T = 13$ (No
> significant difference)

2. Age expressed in years

d.v. = Answering Success 1
> Benham (1987),   a. Multiple Regression
> 118–123 $N = 244$, $F = 10.7438$,
> $p \leq .01$, $r^2 = .3494$
> $B = .029$, Beta $= .118$

b. Multiple Regression
$N = 244$, $F = 13.6918$,
$p \leq .001$, $r^2 = .3732$
$B = .026$, Beta $= .105$
c. Multiple Regression
$N = 244$, $F = 13.9557$,
$p \leq .001$, $r^2 = .4110$
$B = .015$, Beta $= .064$
d. Multiple Regression
$N = 244$, $F = 13.4323$,
$p \leq .001$, $r^2 = .4319$
$B = .019$, Beta $= .079$

Powell (1987), 228   Multiple Regression
$N = 51$, $F = 4.176$, $p < .05$,
$R^2 = .317$
$B = -.045$, Beta $= -.024$

Jirjees (1983), 201   Spearman Rank Order Correlation
$N = 5$, $r_s = -.10$, $p < .436$
(Finding not significant)

d.v. = Answering Success 2
Powell (1987), 230   Multiple Regression
$N = 51$, $F = .492$, $p <$?,
$R^2 = .052$
$B = .00012$, Beta $= .0090$

3. Age in years broken into four categories (Under 18, 18–40, 41–64, 65+)

d.v. = Answering Success 6
Bunge (1990), 44   Percent
Success Rate for Under
18 = 57.56%
Success Rate for Under
18–40 = 61.61%
Success Rate for Under
41–64 = 63.52%
Success Rate for 65+ = 61.18%

B14 Sex of librarian

1. Male or Female
d.v. = Answering Success 1
Jirjees (1983), 201   Spearman Rank Order Correlation
$N = 5$, $r_s = -.10$, $p < .436$
(Finding not significant)

d.v. = Answering Success 6
       Bunge (1990), 44   Percent
                                  Success Rate for Males = 58.87%
                                  Success Rate for Females = 63.01%

C _____

The Client/User

C1 User participation in process

1. A composite of the librarian's ratings of the extent to which the user provided feedback and the degree to which the user played an active role

d.v. = Librarian Satisfaction
       Whitlach (1990), 80, 92   a. Pearson's product
                                  $N = 209, p > .05,$
                                        $r = .159$
                                b. Multiple Regression
                                  $N = 257, F = 19.67,$
                                      $p < .001, adj.R^2 = .378$
                                  $B = .136, Beta = .137,$
                                      $t = 2.44, p < .05$

d.v. = Client Satisfaction 1
       Whitlach (1990), 82, 92   Pearson's product
                                  $N = 209, p > .05, r = -.023$
                                  (Finding not significant)

d.v. = Answering Success 6
       Whitlach (1990), 84, 92   Pearson's product
                                    $N = 209, p > .05, r = -.090$
                                  (Finding not significant)

C2 User perception of librarian's service orientation

1. A composite of the user's ratings of the enthusiasm of the librarian's response, the librarian's interest in finding an answer, and the librarian's interest in resolving the user's information need
    (7-point Likert scale: Enthusiastic — Indifferent)
    (7-point Likert scale: Very interested — Not at all interested)
    (7-point Likert scale: Very interested — Not at all interested)

d.v. = Client Satisfaction 1
    Whitlach (1990), 82, 92   Multiple Regression
                               $N = 257$, $F = 30.13$, $p < .001$,
                               adj.$R^2 = .412$
                               $B = .459$, Beta $= .468$,
                               $t = 8.00$, $p < .001$

D

The Question

D1 Subject knowledge of librarian

1. A composite of the librarian's ratings of personal familiarity with the subject of the query and familiarity with the sources needed to answer the question (7-point Likert scale: Completely — Not at all) (7-point Likert scale: Completely — Not at all)

d.v. = Librarian Satisfaction
    Whitlach (1990), 80, 92   a. Pearson's product
                                  $N = 209$, $p < .05$,
                                 $r = .328$
                              b. Multiple Regression
                                 $N = 257$, $F = 19.67$,
                                    $p < .001$, adj.$R^2 = .378$
                               $B = .208$, Beta $= .208$,
                               $t = 3.68$, $p < .001$

d.v. = Client Satisfaction 1
    Whitlach (1990), 82, 92   Pearson's product
                                  $N = 209$, $p < .05$, $r = .119$

d.v. = Answering Success 6
    Whitlach (1990), 84, 92   a. Pearson's product
                                    $N = 209$, $p < .05$,
                                 $r = .268$
                              b. Multiple Regression
                                 $N = 257$, $F = 11.95$,
                                    $p < .001$, adj.$R^2 = ..266$
                               $B = .318$, Beta $= .171$,
                               $t = 2.81$, $p < .01$

D2 Subject knowledge of client

1. A composite of the user's ratings of personal familiarity with the subject of the query and the familiarity with information sources in this subject

d.v. = Librarian Satisfaction
        Whitlach (1990), 80, 92   Pearson's product
                                  $N = 209$, $p > .05$, $r = .050$
                                  (Finding not significant)

d.v. = Client Satisfaction 1
        Whitlach (1990), 82, 92   Pearson's product
                                  $N = 209$, $p > .05$, $r = .001$
                                  (Finding not significant)

d.v. = Answering Success 6
        Whitlach (1990), 84, 92   a. Pearson's product
                                    $N = 209$, $p > .05$,
                                       $r = -.096$
                                    (Finding not significant)
                                  b. Multiple Regression
                                    $N = 257$, $F = 11.95$,
                                       $p < .001$, $adj.R^2 = .266$
                                    $B = -.248$, $Beta = -.133$,
                                       $t = -2.21$, $p < .05$

D3 Number of sources used to answer question

8. Librarian's rating of the degree to which answers to fact-type questions are verified in more than one source
(5-point Likert scale: 1 — Never, Rarely, Occasionally, Regularly, Always — 5)

d.v. = Answering Success 1
        Myers (1983), 128   Spearman Rank Order
                                    Correlation
                                    $N = 40$, $r_s = -.20$, $p > .10$
                                    (Finding not significant)

D4 Source of answer named

1. Percent of time source for answer is given

d.v. = Answering Success 1
        Benham (1987), 85   Pearson's Product
                                    Unreported correlation
                                      coefficient not considered
                                      significant enough to
                                      include this variable in
                                      regression calculations

Jirjees (1983), 229–231   Percent
Correct: 56.6%, Incorrect: 43.4%
Source Volunteered: 44%, Source
not volunteered: 56%

2. Number of correct sources named on a 12-question test

d.v. = Answering Success 1
Benham (1987), 118–124   a. Multiple Regression
N = 244, F = 10.7438,
p ≤ .01, r^2 = .3494
B = .383, Beta = .550
b. Multiple Regression
N = 244, F = 13.6918,
p ≤ .001, r^2 = .3732
B = .362, Beta = .521
c. Multiple Regression
N = 244, F = 13.9557,
p ≤ .001, r^2 = .4110
B = .363, Beta = .521
d. Multiple Regression
N = 244, F = 13.4323,
p ≤ .001, r^2 = .4319
B = .365, Beta = .524
e. Multiple Regression
N = 244, F = 25.6663,
p ≤ .001, r^2 = .5273
B = .314, Beta = .451

3. Number of sources whose names were volunteered
Jirjees (1983), 229–231 Percent
Correct: 56.6%, Incorrect: 43.4%
Source Not Volunteered: 56%
1 Source Volunteered: 32%
2 Sources Volunteered: 6.3%
3 Sources Volunteered: 2.9%
4 Sources Volunteered: 2.9%

4. Librarian's rating of the degree to which the printed source of an answer is shown to the user
(5-point Likert scale: 1—Never, Rarely, Occasionally, Regularly, Always—5)

d.v. = Answering Success 1
    Myers (1983), 128   Spearman Rank Order Correlation
                            $N = 40$, $r_s = -.06$, $p > .10$
                            (Finding not significant)

5. Librarian's rating of the degree to which source of the answer is cited for telephone queries
(5-point Likert scale: 1 — Never, Rarely, Occasionally, Regularly, Always — 5)

d.v. = Answering Success 1
    Myers (1983), 128   Spearman Rank Order
                            Correlation
                            $N = 40$, $r_s = -.11$, $p > .10$
                            (Finding not significant)

D5 Type of question

1. Van Hoesen's 11 question categories

d.v. = Answering Success 1
    Jirjees (1983), 232   Chi-Square test
                            $N = 11$, $df = 10$, $p < .01$
                            $Exp.X^2 = 23.209$,
                                $Obs.X^2 = 7.121$
                            Category of question exerts no
                            influence on performance

2. Van Hoesen's 11 question categories minus book reviews and illustrations

d.v. = Answering Success 1
    Childers (1971), 142   Chi-Square test
                            $N = 9$, $df = 8$, $p < .01$
                            $Exp.X^2 = 20.09$,
                                $Obs.X^2 = 34.28$
                            Category of question exerts an
                            influence on performance

d.v. = Answering Success 3
    Childers (1971), 142   Chi-Square test
                            $N = 9$, $df = 8$, $p < .01$
                            $Exp.X^2 = 20.09$,
                                $Obs.X^2 = 23.82$
                            Category of question exerts an
                            influence on performance

E ——

Dialogue

E1 Business at the reference desk

1. Librarian's rating of the adequacy of the time available to conduct a full
reference interview
(7-point Likert scale: Completely adequate–Not at all adequate)

d.v. = Librarian Satisfaction
    Whitlach (1990), 80, 92   a. Pearson's product
                                  $N = 209$, $p < .05$,
                                  $r = .426$
                           b. Multiple Regression
                                $N = 257$, $F = 19.67$,
                                  $p < .001$, adj.$R^2 = .378$
                                $B = .189$, Beta $= .284$,
                                $t = 4.77$, $p < .05$

d.v. = Client Satisfaction 1
    Whitlach (1990), 82, 92   Pearson's product
                           $N = 209$, $p > .05$, $r = .084$
                           (Finding not significant)

d.v. = Answering Success 6
    Whitlach (1990), 84, 92   Pearson's product
                           $N = 209$, $p < .05$, $r = .110$

2. Number of questions per hour × difficulty of questions divided by # of
professional staff (MS)

E2 Communication effectiveness between patron and librarian (concept)

1. A composite of the user's ratings of the ease and pleasantness of communication with the librarian
    (7-point Likert scale: Very easy–Very difficult)
    (7-point Likert scale: Pleasant–Unpleasant)

d.v. = Librarian Satisfaction
    Whitlach (1990), 80, 92   a. Pearson's product
                                      $N = 209$, $p < .05$,
                                    $r = .196$
                           b. Multiple Regression
                                $N = 257$, $F = 19.67$,
                                  $p < .001$, adj.$R^2 = .378$

$$B = .086, Beta = .142,$$
$$t = 2.61, p < .01$$

d.v. = Client Satisfaction 1
  Whitlach (1990), 82, 92 a. Pearson's product
             $N = 209, p < .05,$
              $r = .449$
            b. Multiple Regression
             $N = 257, F = 30.13,$
              $p < .001, adj.R^2 = .412$
             $B = .154, Beta = .260,$
              $t = 4.46, p < .001$

d.v. = Answering Success 6
  Whitlach (1990), 84, 92 a. Pearson's product
             $N = 209, p < .05,$
              $r = .284$
            b. Multiple Regression
             $N = 257, F = 11.95,$
              $p < .001, adj.R^2 = .266$
             $B = .327, Beta = .291,$
              $t = 4.87, p < .001$

2. A composite of librarian's ratings of the ease and pleasantness of communication with the user, and the explicitness and sufficiency of information provided by the user
  (7-point Likert scale: Very easy — Very difficult)
  (7-point Likert scale: Pleasant — Unpleasant)
  (7-point Likert scale: Sufficient — Insufficient)
  (7-point Likert scale: Very explicit — Not at all explicit)

d.v. = Librarian Satisfaction
  Whitlach (1990), 80, 92 a. Pearson's product
             $N = 209, p < .05,$
              $r = .433$
            b. Multiple Regression
             $N = 257, F = 19.67,$
              $p < .001, adj.R^2 = .378$
             $B = .354, Beta = .354, t = 6.11,$
              $p < .001$

d.v. = Client Satisfaction 1
  Whitlach (1990), 82, 92 Pearson's product
             $N = 209, p < .05, r = .133$

d.v. = Answering Success 6
  Whitlach (1990), 84, 92 a. Pearson's product

$$N = 209, p < .05,$$
$$r = .183$$
b. Multiple Regression
$$N = 257, F = 11.95,$$
$$p < .001, adj.R^2 = .266$$
$$B = .229, Beta = .124,$$
$$t = 2.05, p < .05$$

E3 Amount of time spent with user by reference librarian

1. Time measured in minutes per question

d.v. = Answering Success
    Bunge (1990), 45   3 minutes or less positively
                          associated with answering success,
                          no figures reported

2. The amount of time in minutes that the user spent with the librarian, broken into four categories
    (0–2 minutes, 3–5 minutes, 6–15 minutes, Over 15 minutes)

d.v. = Librarian Satisfaction
    Whitlach (1990), 80, 92   Pearson's product
                                 $N = 209, p < .05, r = .208$

d.v. = Client Satisfaction 1
    Whitlach (1990), 82, 92   Pearson's product
                                 $N = 209, p > .05, r = .055$
                                 (Finding not significant)

d.v. = Answering Success 6
    Whitlach (1990), 84, 92   a. Pearson's product
                                 $N = 209, p < .05,$
                                 $r = .278$
                                 b. Multiple Regression
                                 $N = 257, F = 11.95,$
                                 $p < .001, adj.R^2 = ..266$
                                 $B = .470, Beta = .186,$
                                 $t = 2.98, p < .01$

E4 Type of assistance provided

1. The librarian provided a direct answer to the query

d.v. = Librarian Satisfaction
    Whitlach (1990), 80, 92   Pearson's product
                                 $N = 209, p < .05, r = -.156$

d.v. = Client Satisfaction 1
    Whitlach (1990), 82, 92   a. Pearson's product
                                    $N = 209$, $p > .05$,
                                         $r = -.145$
                            b. Multiple Regression
                                    $N = 257$, $F = 30.13$,
                                     $p < .001$, $adj.R^2 = .412$
                                     $B = -.443$, Beta $= -.134$,
                                     $t = -2.47$, $p < .05$

d.v. = Answering Success 6
    Whitlach (1990), 84, 92   Pearson's product
                                     $N = 209$, $p < .05$, $r = -.160$

2. Searched with patron for answer or suggested search strategy, bivariate (Bunge, 1990)

E5 Amount of time willing to be spent by patron

1. The amount of time in minutes the user would have been willing to spend with the librarian, broken into five categories
(Less than 5 minutes, 5–10 minutes, 11–15 minutes, 16–30 minutes, Over 30 minutes)

d.v. = Librarian Satisfaction
    Whitlach (1990), 80, 92   Pearson's product
                                     $N = 209$, $p > .05$, $r = .051$
                                     (Finding not significant)
d.v. = Client Satisfaction 1
    Whitlach (1990), 82, 92   a. Pearson's product
                                     $N = 209$, $p > .05$, $r = .063$
                                     (Finding not significant)
                            b. Multiple Regression
                                       $N = 257$, $F = 30.13$, $p < .001$,
                                       $adj.R^2 = .412$
                                       $B = .097$, Beta $= .122$, $t = 2.25$,
                                       $p < .05$
d.v. = Answering Success 6
    Whitlach (1990), 84, 92   a. Pearson's product
                                     $N = 209$, $p < .05$, $r = .239$
                            b. Multiple Regression
                                       $N = 257$, $F = 11.95$, $p < .001$,
                                       $adj.R^2 = .266$
                                       $B = .347$, Beta $= .233$, $t = 3.74$,
                                       $p < .001$

Regression Models

Childers (1971)

y answering success $= -38.309 + 1.070 \times$ hours open $+ 16.884 \times$ professional degrees/capita $+ -1.544 \times$ adult circulation/capita $+ 10.036 \times$ total expenditure/capita $+ -4.747 \times$ books owned/capita $+ 58.620 \times$ proportion of collection change $+ -.002 \times$ nonbook items
$N = 25$, $r^2 = .8983$

Benham (1987)

y answering success $= -3.89 + .31 \times$ total correct sources named $+ .40 \times$ total correct sources available $+ .002 \times$ gre quantitative score $+ .25 \times$ degree to which lib and ref courses were interesting $+ .03 \times$ hours librarian on ref desk/week $+ .20 \times$ #years ref work since mls $+ 40[.40?] \times$ degree to which ref work is satisfying $+ E$
$F = 25.6663$, 7 and 161 degrees of freedom, $p < .001$, $r^2 = .527$

Myers (1983)

$N = 40$, $p \le .05$
$R = .60$, $R^2 = .36$, Adj. $R^2 = .22$
$F = 2.56$
d.v. = Answering Success 1
i.v.'s = Hours open per week, Volumes held, Total expenditures, Net assignable area, Materials circulated, FTE professional staff with graduate degree, FTE students

Myers (1983)

$N = 40$, $p \le .05$
$R = ..82$, $R^2 = .68$, Adj. $R^2 = .53$
$F = 2.08$
d.v. = Answering Success 1
i.v.'s = Reference volumes held, Reference hours, Net assignable area, Reference Librarians, Library Volumes, Library Librarians, Directional Questions, Reference Questions, Library Hours, FTE students, Materials circulated, Total expenditures

Powell (1987)

$N = 51$, $p \leq .001$
$R = .620$, $R^2 = .384$
$F = 5.606$
d.v. = Answering Success 1
i.v.'s = Reference Collection Size, Reference and Bibliography Course, Reference Experience at present library, Reference Questions

Powell (1987)

$N = 51$, $p \leq .05$
$R = .563$, $R^2 = .317$
$F = 4.176$
d.v. = Answering Success 1
i.v.'s = Reference Collection Size, Age, Degree, Continuing Education

Powell (1987)

$N = 51$, $p > .10$ (Finding not significant)
$R = .446$, $R^2 = .199$
$F = 2.232$
d.v. = Answering Success 2
i.v.'s = Reference Collection Size, Reference and Bibliography Courses, Reference Experience at present library, Reference Questions

Powell (1987)

$N = 51$, $p > .10$
$R = .228$, $R^2 = .052$
$F = .492$
d.v. = Answering Success 2
i.v.'s = Reference Collection Size, Age, Degree, Continuing Education

Powell (1987)

$N = 51$, $p \leq .05$
$R = .579$, $R^2 = .336$
$F = 4.549$

d.v. = Answering Success 2
i.v.'s = Adequateness of size,   Degree,   Reference   Experience,   Reference
questions

Ranking of independent variables by strength of association and significance level

Strong Association (.70−1.00)
    p < .001
    p < .01
    p < .05
Moderate Association (.40−.69)
    p < .001
    p < .01
    p < .05
    p < .10
Weak Association (0.00−.39)
    p < .001
    p < .01
    p < .05
    p < .10

Research Issues

Obtrusive−Unobtrusive

"It appears that a slight but statistically significant relationship exists between methods of evaluation and results of evaluation...." (Weech and Goldhor, 1982, 319).

Unobtrusive studies show poorer performance by librarians.

"...Powell's earlier use of obtrusive testing resulted in a level of reference accuracy quite similar to that achieved in the unobtrusive investigations reported by Crowley, Childers (two studies), and Myers... Thus the obtrusive method appeared to be a safe and useful research method for obtaining data about respondents which would otherwise be prohibitively expensive, if not impossible to obtain." Benham (1987), 36.

Referral

Haphazard measurement throughout. Deserves a study all its own.

Client responses

Goldhor notes four studies ask for patron response about questions and answers (Goldhor, 1979, 35).

Two ascertained the degree of patron satisfaction with the reference service they received:

1. *Faculty Appraisal of a University Library*, University of Michigan Library, 1961, 25
2. Committee to evaluate telephone reference service "monitored telephone calls" in "Reports and recommendations" Typescript. Baltimore, MD: Enoch Pratt Free Library, December 1968. Unpublished report, Enoch Pratt Free Library

See Lancaster, *Measurement and Evaluation of Library Services*, 1977, 81.

Lopez and Rubacher (1969) measure satisfaction in encounters with staff on various variables.

"Interpersonal psychology: Librarians and patrons" (*Catholic Library World* 40, 483–487).

Studies Reflected Above

Benham, Frances (1987). *Success in Answering Reference Questions: Two Studies* [Part One]. Metuchen, NJ: The Scarecrow Press, 5–148.

Bunge, Charles A. (1967). *Professional Education and Reference Efficiency*, Research Series no. 11. Springfield, ILL: Illinois State Library.

Bunge, Charles. "Factors Related to Output Measures for Reference Services in Public Libraries: Data from Thirty-Six Libraries." *Public Libraries* 29 (1990): 42–47.

Childers, Thomas (1971) "Telephone information service in public libraries." In *Information Service in Public Libraries: Two Studies*. Metuchen, NJ: Scarecrow Press, 79–204.

Crowley, Terence (1971). "The effectiveness of information service in medium size public libraries." In *Information Service in Public Libraries: Two Studies*. Metuchen, NJ: Scarecrow Press, 1–71.

Goldhor, Herbert. "The Patrons' Side of Public Library Reference Questions." *Public Library Quarterly* 1 (1979): 35–49.

Jirjees, Jassim M. (1983). "Telephone reference/information services in selected northeastern college libraries." In *Telephone Reference/Information Services in Academic Libraries: Two Studies*. Metuchen, NJ: Scarecrow Press.

Lancaster, F. Wilfred. (1977). *Measurement and Evaluation of Library Services*. Washington, DC: Information Resources Press.

Myers, Marcia (1983). "Telephone reference/information services in academic libraries in the Southeast." In *The Accuracy of Telephone Reference/Information Services in Academic Libraries: Two Studies*. Metuchen, NJ: Scarecrow Press.

Powell, Ronald R. (1987). *Success in Answering Reference Questions: Two Studies* [Part Two]. Metuchen, NJ: Scarecrow Press, 151–306.

Weech, Terry, and Goldhor, Herbert. "Obtrusive versus Unobtrusive Evaluation of Reference Service in Five Illinois Libraries: A Pilot Study." *Library Quarterly* 52 (1982): 305–324.

Whitlach, Jo Bell (1990). *The Role of the Academic Reference Librarian*. New York: Greenwood Press.

Bibliography

Journal Articles

Allen, Robert B. "User Models: Theory, Method, and Practice." *International Journal of Man–Machine Studies* 32 (May 1990): 511–543.

American Library Association, Reference and Adult Services Division, Standards and Guidelines Committee. "Information Services for Information Consumers: Guidelines for Providers." *RQ* 30 (Winter 1990): 262–265.

Ackoff, Russell L. "The Art and Science of Mess Management." *Interfaces* 11 (February 1981): 20–26.

Aluri, Rao. "Improving Reference Service: The Case for Using a Continuous Quality Improvement Method." *RQ* 33 (Winter 1993): 220–236.

Brown, Janet Dagenais. "Using Quality Concepts to Improve Reference Services." *College & Research Libraries* 55 (May 1994): 211–219.

Bunge, Charles A. "Charting the Reference Query." *RQ* 8 (Summer 1969): 245–260.

— — —. "Factors Related to Output Measures for Reference Services in Public Libraries: Data from Thirty-six Libraries." *Public Libraries* 29 (January–February 1990): 42–47.

Childers, Thomas. "Using Public Library Reference Collections and Staff." *Library Quarterly* 67 (April 1997): 155–173.

— — —. Cynthia Lopata, and Brian Stafford. "Measuring the Difficulty of Reference Questions." *RQ* 31 (Winter 1991): 237–243.

Crews, Kenneth D. "The Accuracy of Reference Service: Variables for Research and Implementation." *Library and Information Science Research* 10 (July 1988): 331–355.

Crum, Norman J. "The Librarian–Customer Relationship: Dynamics of Filling Requests for Information." *Special Libraries* 60 (May/June 1969): 269–277.

Dewdney, Patricia, and Catherine Sheldrick Ross. "Flying a Light Aircraft: Reference Service Evaluation from a User's Viewpoint." *RQ* 34 (Winter 1994): 217–230.

D'Elia, George, and Eleanor Jo Rodger. "Customer Satisfaction with Public Libraries." *Public Libraries* 35 (September–October 1996): 292–297.

Dervin, Brenda, and Patricia Dewdney. "Neutral Questioning: A New Approach to the Reference Interview." *RQ* 25 (Summer 1986): 506–513.

Douglas, Ian. "Reducing Failures in Reference Service." *RQ* 28 (Fall 1988): 94–101.

Durrance, Joan C. "The Influence of Reference Practices on the Client–Librarian Relationship." *College & Research Libraries* 47 (January 1986): 57–67.

Green, Samuel Swett. "Personal Relations between Librarians and Readers." *American Library Journal* 1 (30 September 1876): 74–81.

Gross, Melissa. "The Imposed Query." *RQ* 35 (Winter 1995): 236–243.

— — —. and Matthew L. Saxton. "Who Wants to Know? Imposed Queries in the Public Library." *Public Libraries* 40 (May–June 2001): 170–175.

Gothberg, Helen M. "Immediacy: A Study of Communication Effect on the Reference Process." *Journal of Academic Librarianship* 2 (July 1976): 126–129.

Guerrier, Edith. "The Measurement of Reference Service." *Library Journal* 61 (July 1936): 529–531.

— — —. "The Measurement of Reference Service in a Branch Library." *Bulletin of the American Library Association* 29 (September 1935): 632–637.

Harris, Roma M., and B. Gillian Michell. "The Social Context of Reference Work: Assessing the Effects of Gender and Communication Skills on Observers' Judgement of Competence." *Library and Information Science Research* 8 (January–March 1986): 85–101.

Hernon, Peter, and Charles R. McClure. "Unobtrusive Reference Testing: The 55 Percent Rule." *Library Journal* 111 (15 April 1986): 37–41.

Jahoda, Gerald, and Mary Culnan. "Unanswered Science and Technology Questions." *American Documentation* 19 (January 1968): 95–100.

Kasowitz, Abby, Blythe Bennett, and R. David Lankes. "Quality Standards for Digital Reference Consortia." *Reference and User Services Quarterly* 39 (Summer 2000): 355–363.

King, Geraldine B. "The Reference Interview: Open and Closed Questions." *RQ* 12 (Winter 1972): 157–160.

Lubans, John. "Nonuse of the Academic Library." *College & Research Libraries* 32 (September 1971): 362–367.

Lunz, Mary E., and John A. Stahl. "Interjudge Reliability and Decision Reproducibility." *Educational and Psychological Measurement* 54 (Winter 1994): 913–925.

Murfin, Marjorie E., and Gary M. Gugelchuck. "Development and Ttesting of a Reference Prediction Assessment Instrument." *College & Research Libraries* 48 (July 1987): 314–338.

Perry, James W. "Defining the Query Spectrum — The Basis for Designing and Evaluating Retrieval Methods." *IEEE Transactions on Engineering Writing and Speech* 6 (September 1963): 20–27.

Powell, Ronald R. "An Investigation of the Relationships between Quantifiable Reference Service Variables and Reference Performance in Public Libraries." *Library Quarterly* 48 (January 1978): 1–19.

— — —. "Reference Effectiveness: A Review of the Research." *Library and Information Science Research* 6 (July–September 1984): 3–19.

RASD Ad Hoc Committee on Behavioral Guidelines for Reference and Information Services. "Guidelines for Behavioral Performance of Reference and Information Services Professionals." *RQ* 36 (Winter 1996): 200–203.

Rettig, James. "A Theoretical Model and Definition of the Reference Process." *RQ* 18 (Fall 1978): 19–29.

Richardson, John V., Jr. "Teaching General Reference Work: The Complete Paradigm and Competing Schools of Thought, 1890–1990." *Library Quarterly* 62 (January 1992): 55–89.

— — —, and Rex B. Reyes. "Government Information Expert Systems: A Quantitative Evaluation." *College & Research Libraries* 56 (May 1995): 238.

Ross, Catherine Sheldrick, and Patricia Dewdney. "Negative Closure: Strategies and Counter-Strategies in the Reference Transaction." *Reference and User Services Quarterly* 38 (Winter 1998): 151–163.

Rothstein, Samuel. "Reference Service: The New Dimension in Librarianship." *College & Research Libraries* 22 (January 1961): 11–18.

— — —. "The Measurement and Evaluation of Reference Service." *Library Trends* 12 (January 1964): 456–472.

Saxton, Matthew L. "Reference Service Evaluation and Meta-analysis: Findings and Methodological Issues." *Library Quarterly* 67 (July 1997): 267–289.

Shera, Jesse. "Automation and the Reference Librarian." *RQ* 3 (July 1964): 3–7.

Stone, Elizabeth O. "Methods of Evaluating Reference Service." *Library Journal* 67 (1 April 1942): 296–298.

Taylor, Robert S. "The Process of Asking Questions." *American Documentation* 13 (October 1962): 392.

—— ——. "Question Negotiation and Information Seeking in Libraries." *College & Research Libraries* 29 (May 1968): 178–194.

Van House, Nancy, and Thomas Childers. "Unobtrusive Evaluation of a Reference Referral Network: The California Experience." *Library and Information Science Research* 6 (July–September 1984): 305–319.

Weech, Terry, and Herbert Goldhor. "Obtrusive versus Unobtrusive Evaluation of Reference Service in Five Illinois Libraries." *Library Quarterly* 52 (October 1982): 305–324.

White, Marilyn D. "Evaluation of the Reference Interview." *RQ* 24 (Fall 1985): 76–84.

Books and Reports

Bernstein, Ira. *Applied Multivariate Analysis.* New York: Springer-Verlag, 1988.

Bryk, Anthony S., and Stephen W. Raudenbush. *Hierarchical Linear Models: Applications and Data Analysis Methods.* Newbury Park, CA: Sage Publications, 1992.

Bunge, Charles A. *Professional Education and Reference Efficiency.* Springfield, IL: Illinois State Library, 1967.

Cheney, Frances Neel. *Fundamental Reference Sources.* Chicago: American Library Association, 1971.

Cooley, William W., and Paul R. Lohnes. *Multivariate Data Analysis.* New York: John Wiley & Sons, 1971.

Crowley, Terence, and Thomas Childers. *Information Service in Public Libraries: Two Studies.* Metuchen, NJ: Scarecrow Press, 1971.

Dana, John Cotton. *A Library Primer,* 5th ed. Chicago: Library Bureau, 1910.

Fitzgerald, Jerry, Ardra Fitzgerald, and Warren D. Stallings. *Fundamentals of Systems Analysis.* New York: Wiley, 1987.

Goldhor, Herbert. *A Plan for the Development of Public Library Service in the Minneapolis–Saint Paul Metropolitan Area.* Saint Paul, MN: State of Minnesota Department of Education, Library Division, 1967.

Grimm, Laurence G., and Paul R. Yarnold, eds. *Reading and Understanding Multivariate Statistics.* Washington, D.C.: American Psychological Association, 1995.

Hawley, George S. *Referral Process in Libraries: Characterization and an Exploration of Related Factors.* Metuchen, NJ: Scarecrow Press, 1987.

Hutchins, Margaret. *Introduction to Reference Work.* Chicago: American Library Association, 1944.

Jahoda, Gerald, and Judith S. Braunagel. *The Librarian and Reference Queries: A Systematic Approach.* New York: Academic Press, 1980.

Jennerich, Elaine Z., and Edward J. Jennerich. *The Reference Interview as a Creative Art.* Littleton, CO: Libraries Unlimited, 1987.

Kroeger, Alice Bertha. *Guide to the Study and Use of Reference Books.* Chicago: American Library Association, 1902.

—— ——. *Guide to the Study and Use of Reference Books,* 2nd ed. Chicago: American Library Association, 1908.

Learned, William S. *The American Public Library and the Diffusion of Knowledge.* New York: Harcourt, Brace, & Co., 1924.

McClure, Charles R., and Peter Hernon. *Improving the Quality of Reference Service for Government Publications.* Chicago: American Library Association, 1983.

Mudge, Isadore Gilbert. *Guide to Reference Books,* 6th ed. Chicago: American Library Association, 1936.

Pedhazur, Elazar J. *Multiple Regression in Behavioral Research: Explanation and Prediction.* Fort Worth, TX: Harcourt Brace Jovanovich, 1982.

Public Library Association. *Minimum Standards for Public Library Systems,* 1966. Chicago: American Library Association, 1967.

Radford, Marie L. *The Reference Encounter: Interpersonal Communication in the Academic Library.* Chicago: American Library Association, 1999.

Richardson, John V., Jr. *Knowledge-Based Systems for General Reference Work: Applications, Problems, and Progress.* San Diego: Academic Press, 1995.

Robertson, James, and Suzanne Robertson. *Complete Systems Analysis.* New York: Dorset House Publishing, 1994.

Ranganathan, Shiyali Ramamrita. *Reference Service.* London: Asia Publishing House, 1940.

Shores, Louis. *Basic Reference Books.* Chicago: American Library Association, 1937.

— — —. *Basic Reference Sources.* Chicago: American Library Association, 1954.

Van de Geer, John P. *Introduction to Multivariate Analysis for the Social Sciences.* San Francisco: W.H. Freeman, 1971.

White, Howard D. *Brief Tests of Collection Strength: A Methodology for All Types of Libraries.* Glenview, IL: Greenwood Press, 1995.

Whitlatch, Jo Bell. *The Role of the Academic Reference Librarian.* New York: Greenwood Press, 1990.

Wyer, James I. *Reference Work: A Textbook for Students of Library Work and Librarians.* Chicago: American Library Association, 1930.

Dissertations and Theses

Breed, Paul F. "An Analysis of Reference Procedures in a Large University Library." Ph.D. dissertation, University of Chicago, 1955.

Cole, Dorothy E. "An Analysis of Adult Reference Work in Libraries." M.A. thesis, University of Chicago, September 1943.

Dewdney, Patricia. "The Effects of Training Reference Libraries in Interview Skills: A Field Experiment." Ph.D. dissertation, University of Western Ontario, August 1986.

Gothberg, Helen M. "User Satisfaction with a Librarian's Immediate and Nonimmediate Verbal–Nonverbal Communication." Ph.D. dissertation, University of Denver, August 1974.

Rich, Elaine A. "Building and Exploiting User Models." Ph.D. dissertation, Carnegie Mellon University, April 1979.

Saxton, Matthew L. "Evaluation of Reference Service in Public Libraries Using a Hierarchical Linear Model: Applying Multiple Regression Analysis to a Multi-level Research Design." Ph.D. dissertation, University of California, Los Angeles, June 2000.

Van Hoesen, Florence. "An Analysis of Adult Reference Work in Public Libraries as an Approach to the Content of a Reference Course." Ph.D. dissertation, University of Chicago, December 1948.

Whitlatch, Jo Bell. "Client/Service Provider Perceptions of Reference Service Outcomes in Academic Libraries: Effects of Feedback and Uncertainty." Ph.D. dissertation, University of California, Berkeley, 1987.

Index

By Linda Webster, MIS, ASI member
Entries include personal names; names of institutions and associations; titles of works; and subject concepts. Also included are concepts from the Appendixes. Entries are arranged in word-by-word alphabetical order. Entries beginning with "Mc" are alphabetized as "Mc." Endnotes are designated by a lowercase "n" following the page reference.

Library and Information Science

(Continued from page ii)

Timothy C. Craven
String Indexing

Lois Swan Jones and Sarah Scott Gibson
Art Libraries and Information Services

Nancy Jones Pruett
Scientific and Technical Libraries: Functions and Management
Volume 1 and Volume 2

Peter Judge and Brenda Gerrie
Small Bibliographic Databases

Dorothy B. Lilley and Ronald W. Trice
A History of Information Sciences 1945–1985

Elaine Svenonius
The Conceptual Foundations of Descriptive Cataloging

Robert M. Losee, Jr.
The Science of Information: Measurement and Applications

Irene P. Godden
Library Technical Services: Operations and Management, Second
Edition

Donald H. Kraft and Bert R. Boyce
Operations Research for Libraries and Information Agencies: Techniques for the Evaluation of Management Decision Alternatives

James Cabeceiras
The Multimedia Library: Materials Selection and Use, Second
Edition

Charles T. Meadow
Text Information Retrieval Systems, First Edition